The Spiritual Wisdom of Rav Kook

THE SPIRITUAL WISDOM OF
RAV KOOK

A NEW COLLECTION OF WRITINGS

Translated and Introduced by

RABBI ARI ZE'EV SCHWARTZ

URIM PUBLICATIONS

Jerusalem · New York

The Spiritual Wisdom of Rav Kook
A New Collection of Writings
Translated and Introduced by
Rabbi Ari Ze'ev Schwartz
Copyright © 2025/5785 Ari Ze'ev Schwartz

Typeset by Juliet Tresgallo

Printed in Israel
First Edition
ISBN 978-965-524-376-5

Urim Publications
P.O. Box 52287
Jerusalem 9152102, Israel
www.UrimPublications.com

Library of Congress Cataloging-in-Publication Data
is available from the Library of Congress.

Excerpts from Rav Moshe Tzvi Neria, *Sichot HaRaaya, Likutei HaRaaya, BeSadei
HaRaaya, Shmuot HaRaaya, Moadai HaRaaya* (Machon HaTorah VeHaAretz), are used by
permission of Beit Neria. Excerpts from Chayim Lifshitz, *Shivchei HaRaaya (Beit El: Shilo
Bikatz, 2010),* and *An Angel Among Men: Impressions from the Life of Rav Avraham Yitzchak
Hakohen Kook*, translated by Moshe D. Lichtman (Jerusalem: Urim, 2003)
are used by permission of the author.

Cover Design: Jacob Schwartz

If you have any questions, please email
Rabbi Ari Ze'ev Schwartz: ari1zeev@gmail.com

Praise for *The Spiritual Wisdom of Rav Kook*

"Our broken world is aching for the healing light of Rav Kook, the 'Ba'al Ha Oros.' Rav Ari Ze'ev's masterful compilation is an invitation into the mind and heart of this most exalted visionary."

— RAV MOSHE WEINBERGER, Founding Rabbi of Congregation Aish Kodesh and Author of "The Song of Teshuva: A Commentary on Rav Kook's Oros HaTeshuvah"

"The Spiritual Wisdom of Rav Kook is an excellent introduction for people seeking to discover the joyous and life-affirming Torah of Rav Kook."

— RABBI DAVID AARON, Author of *The Secret Life of God* and *Endless Light*, Rosh Yeshiva of Orayta

"Rabbi Schwartz has succeeded in collecting clear and understandable passages, on a wide variety of topics, which makes it possible to understand Rav Kook's Torah. The introductions, summaries and stories add a touch of personal connection and existential meaning to the words. Rabbi Schwartz's love for Rav Kook and his Torah is evident on every page of the book, and all who read this book will be affected by it."

— RABBI YEHUDA BRANDES, President of Herzog College

"What would you do to receive encouragement from a soul like Rav Kook, whose every word is filled with gems of love, hope and direction? In the book before you, Rav Ari Ze'ev Schwartz has gifted our generation with just that."

— RAV SHLOMO KATZ, Author, singer, and rabbi of Congregation Shirat David

"Few have done more to make Rav Kook's teachings accessible to a broader audience than Ari Ze'ev Schwartz, and few generations need his teachings more than our own. This book is of great importance for any Jew seeking to bring depth, nuance, and *kedusha* to their lives."

— RABBI ZACHARY TRUBOFF, Author of *Torah Goes Forth From Zion: Essays on the Thought of Rav Kook and Rav Shagar*

"Rav Kook's Torah forms the foundation of the religious Zionist movement's ideology, providing the vision and clarity to understand the distinctive generation we are living in: one which is undoubtedly approaching the final redemption. For many years, Rav Kook's wisdom remained inaccessible to the broader English-speaking community. Through Rav Ari Ze'ev Schwartz's erudition and *Kedusha*, he has successfully bridged this gap, making Rav Kook's Torah accessible to all."

— RABBI SHAUL FELDMAN, Director of Bnei Akiva of the US and Canada

"For many of us who feel we are walking in a dark forest, Rav Kook is the clear flashlight that can guide our journey. In this book, Rav Ari Ze'ev finds a way to uncover the light within Rav Kook's spiritual writings."

— RAV YAIR HALEVI, Rosh Yeshiva YTVA-Chovot HaTalmidim

"Rav Kook's teachings seem to mature with time and Rav Ari Ze'ev has arisen as a master distiller of his unique wisdom for our times. On the one hand he offers the reader an opportunity to dig deep into the recesses of personal spirituality in the first half of the book and on the other hand, the second half of the book taps into our broader collective. Ultimately the wisdom of Rav Kook allows one to strive towards unity within and between these layers of Torah consciousness and I commend my dear friend for not just translating selected writings, but mediating their profound depth so that each of us can connect in deeper ways."

— RABBI DR. BENJI LEVY, Co-founder of Israel Impact Partners
and Keshev, past Dean of Moriah College

"Rav Kook was a master of Torah, life, and the inner world of the Jew. His teachings are transformational and healing. Rav Ari Ze'ev is a master of making those teachings accessible and relevant to the modern Jew, seeking a deeper connection to themselves, their fellow humans, the Torah, and Hashem."

— RABBI DOV BER COHEN, Author of *Mastering Life: A Unique Guidebook to Jewish Enlightenment*

"A sensitive soul and an experienced teacher, Rabbi Ari Ze'ev Schwartz has deftly curated and translated an incredible selection of texts from Rav Kook's sprawling corpus. Rav Kook's texts offer a wealth of revolutionary insights about what it means to live a full life – both human and Jewish – but only if you can find them, and read them when you do. In this second volume of selected, translated texts, Schwartz makes the light of Rav Kook's writings on a host of new topics accessible as never before."

— RABBI LEVI MORROW, Senior Rabbi at Yeshiva Orayta,
Author and Hartman Research Fellow and Content Coordinator

"Rabbi Ari Ze'ev Schwartz's book about Rabbi Kook is a truly deep and profound exploration of the life and teachings of an extraordinary figure in Jewish history. Through meticulous research and thoughtful analysis, Rabbi Schwartz provides a comprehensive view of Rabbi Kook's intellectual and spiritual journey, presenting a nuanced understanding of his profound contributions to Jewish thought. This book is a must-read for anyone seeking to gain a deeper understanding of Rabbi Kook's teachings and their relevance in our modern world."

— GEDALE FENSTER, Internationally Renowned Motivational Speaker

"Rabbi Ari Ze'ev Schwartz has produced a remarkable collection of translated passages from the exhilarating writings of Rav Kook. Many of the sources that are cited would be nearly impossible to access and discern without his guiding hand. This is an important contribution to Jewish learning."

— RABBI AARON GOLDSCHEIDER, Author, Senior Rabbi at OU and Gruss Kollel, and Editor of Torah Tidbits

"For many years now, Rabbi Ari Ze'ev Schwartz has been strolling through the vast gardens of Rav Kook's writings, carefully selecting, translating, and arranging exquisite bouquets of the *tzaddik's* teachings. May this latest collection of thought-roses find favor in the eyes of the Almighty and His righteous nation."

— RAV DOVID'L WEINBERG, Senior Rabbi at Yeshiva Orayta and Author of *Reflections on Oros HaTorah*

"Rabbi Schwartz's masterful translation teaches the reader about individual and collective spirituality and the necessity of combining the two to reach our true spiritual selves. Whether you seek guidance, inspiration, or simply wish to deepen your connection to Jewish wisdom, this book is an invaluable resource that will surely enrich your spiritual journey."

— RABBI JOSHUA GERSTEIN, Author of *Mussar Avicha: Rabbi Abraham Isaac Kook On Morals, Ethics, and Character Development*

"Rabbi Ari Ze'ev Schwartz's incredible organization and translation of Rav Kook's writings has allowed me to share these precious teachings with our students across a range of topics. The impact of adding Rav Kook's voice to a discussion has been nothing short of transformative for many students, and resonates in a unique way with young Jews from diverse backgrounds."

— RABBI YONATAN UDREN, RRG Beit Midrash Co-Director

To my son Levi Shmuel

May Rav Kook's wisdom connect you
to your soul and awaken a deep love for all people

Contents

Abbreviations

AT – *Arpelei Tohar*

BSH – *BeSadei HaRaaya*

C – *Chedarav*

CT – *Chazon HaTzimchonut*

EA – *Ein Aya*

EC – *Eretz Chemda*

EY – *Eder HaYakar*

HA – *Heichal HaAhava*

IR – *Igrot HaRaaya*

KYK – *Kevatzim Yad Kadsho*

LN – *LeNevuchei HaDor*

LHR – *Likutei HaRaaya*

MA – *Musar Avicha*

MaR – *Maamarei HaRaaya*

MiR – *Middot HaRaaya*

MoR – *Moadei HaRaaya*

MS – *Midbar Shur*

ND – *Nevuchei Hador*

O – *Orot*

OE – *Orot HaEmunah*

OK – *Orot HaKodesh*

OR – *Olat HaRaaya*

OT – *Orot Hatorah*

OTf – *Orot HaTefillah*

OtR – *Otzorot HaRaaya*

OTs – *Orot HaTeshuva*

PR – *Pinkasei HaRaaya*

SHR – *Sichot HaRaaya*

SK – *Shmoneh Kevatzim*

SR – *Shivchei HaRaaya*

Introduction

Rav Kook's Desire to Write Books of Spiritual Wisdom

One of the unique qualities about Rav Kook was that he was continuously writing down his spiritual insights and wisdom. Whenever he had a spare moment after prayers, between a meeting, or late at night, he would open up his notebook and begin writing down his thoughts. These notebooks were often focused on themes about the meaning of life; how to deal with suffering; how to be a more loving person; what is the best way to connect to one's soul; how to study Torah and pray in a deeper way; and endless other spiritual topics.

In Shivchei HaRaaya, Dr. Yeshayahu Meir Lerman tells the following story:

> When Rav Kook was living in London, I would often come and visit him in his home. Rav Kook would sit wrapped in his small Tefillin, a gift from his father-in-law, the Aderet. Sometimes a flash of insight would take a hold of Rav Kook. He had a note book of empty pages. Each time a thought would pour into specific words, he would write it down into his notebook. (SR, p. 172)

For Rav Kook, it was not enough to have deep insights about life. Instead, he believed it was important that he write them down so that they could benefit the world. This belief was so strong in Rav

Kook that sometimes it caused him pain when an insight of wisdom would come to him yet he didn't stop and take the time to write it down. In Chadarav, Rav Kook writes:

> How many of my thoughts have been strangled over time because I didn't write anything down? To be sure, these thoughts definitely exist somewhere in the depths of the soul; they have not been totally lost from reality. Yet water needs to be continuously drawn and used for some benefit. Thoughts need to be watered and actualized. "Write down the vision and explain it on tablets" (Chavakuk 2:2). (C, p. 65)

Rav Kook believed that one of the main callings in his life was to write books of spiritual wisdom that would resonate with many types of people and help them grow personally, morally, Jewishly, and reach a deeper connection to God. In *Shmoneh Kevatzim* he writes:

> It is not by chance that the God of all souls planted within me a continuous desire for everything hidden, moral, and spiritual... All of this God planted within me in order to illuminate the world. All of this is so I can create popular writings, which resonate with each individual, which are full of the light of the secrets of Torah. (SK 3:259)

Even at the end of his life while he was sick in bed with cancer, Rav Kook had still not given up his goal of writing down his inner thoughts and emotions. In *Shivchei HaRaaya*, Rav Kook's brother, Rabbi Shmuel Kook, told the following story about an interaction he had when he saw Rav Kook crying on his deathbed during the last days of his life.

> Rabbi Shmuel Kook asked Rav Kook, "Why are you crying? Is it because of the terrible pain you are experiencing?" Rav Kook answered, "I am not crying due to the pain I am feeling. Rather, I am crying because of all the thoughts and insights roaming around in my mind, and I don't have the ability to write them down." (SR, p. 386)

Please Help Publish my Writings as a Special Collection

Yet despite Rav Kook's sincere desire to write down his spiritual insights and wisdom for the world, he found it difficult to articulate his thoughts in the usual structured form of essays. Instead, Rav Kook felt this inner longing to express himself in a more free-spirited and non-restrictive way. In *Chadarav* he writes:

> My thoughts are more expansive than many oceans. I am not able to express them in a plain and structured language. It is not for my benefit that I must be a poet, a free poet. I simply am not able to be connected to the structured rules of writing and rhymes. I run away from simple structured writing due to its heaviness and limitations. (C, p. 63)

This was a real tension and struggle inside of Rav Kook.[1] On the one hand, he sincerely desired to write books of spiritual wisdom that would help the world. On the other hand, he did not want to be fake and write in a way that was untrue to his soul and unique personality. After many offers and suggestions from his students and friends, this was one of Rav Kook's main solutions: he would write down in his notebooks all the spiritual insights that he had in an authentic way, in whatever form they came out. And then, he would ask his students to help organize, edit, and transform these notebooks into collections of spiritual writings. In *Igrot HaRaaya*, Rav Kook writes to a student:

> I am pleased with your suggestion to publish my writings as a special collection. Indeed, how wonderful would it be if someone would find the strength to undertake this project. That is to

---

1.   See Yaron, "Mishnato Shel HaRav Kook," pp. 22–31 (WZO, 1974), Bin-Nun, "The Double Source of Human Inspiration and Authority in the Philosophy of Rav Kook," pp. 18–58 (Kibbutz Hameuchad, 2014).

say, to publish and prepare my writings with the help of God; a collection of everything that has been printed up until now as well as a large portion of my notes and other writings. This project would include additional notes, editing, and perhaps even small explanations and introductions.

... But will this dream ever come about? Only God knows. It is my prayer that God will help my wish come true whereby this righteous deed will be done by righteous people. (IR 2, p. 264)

Who was Rav Kook?

Rav Kook was born Avraham Yitzchak Hakohen Kook on September 7, 1865 (16 Elul 5625), in Griva, Russia, and passed away on September 1, 1935 (3 Elul 5695) in Jerusalem, Israel. At the age of eighteen, Rav Kook began studying at the prestigious Lithuanian Volozhin Yeshiva. Rav Kook's learning schedule was very intense; he would learn eighteen hours each day, covering sixty pages of Talmud in depth.[2] Rav Kook became close to the Rosh Yeshiva, Rabbi Naftali Tzvi Yehuda Berlin (the Netziv), who once said of Rav Kook, "It was worthwhile establishing the Volozhin Yeshiva just to produce a student like him."[3]

In 1885, at the age of twenty, Rav Kook married Batsheva. Her father was Rabbi Eliyahu David Rabinowitz-Teomim (the Aderet), the head rabbi of Ponevezh, and later the chief rabbi of Jerusalem. Tragically, in 1889, not long after Rav Kook became the rabbi of Zeimel, his wife Batsheva contracted a fatal disease and passed away at age twenty-two, leaving him with a one-and-a-half-year-old daughter named Freida Chanah.[4] Some say that the tragic death of his young wife caused Rav Kook to search for answers in kabbalah and Jewish

---

2.   Raz, *An Angel Among Men*, p. 26.
3.   Ibid. p. 25.
4.   Ibid. p. 27.

mysticism;[5] he soon developed a close relationship with the great kabbalist Rav Shlomo Elyashiv, author of *Leshem Shevo v'Achlamah*. Rav Kook would travel to his kabbalistic master's home from time to time to study the secrets of the Torah.[6]

Soon after this, Rav Kook married Raiza-Rivka Rabinowitz, the niece of the Aderet. They had three children together: Tzvi Yehuda, Batya-Miriam, and Esther Yael. At the age of thirty, Rav Kook moved with his family to Boisk, where he was appointed rabbi of the city. Rav Kook's reputation spread throughout European Jewry during his service as the rabbi of Zeimel and Boisk. It wasn't long until prominent Yeshivot, such as the Telz Yeshiva, attempted to convince Rav Kook to teach at their institutions.[7]

Rav Kook surprised many admirers when, in 1904, at the age of thirty-nine, he accepted an offer to move to Israel and become the rabbi of Yaffo. Later on, in 1919 he was appointed the Ashkanazi Chief Rabbi of Jerusalem, and soon after, as the first Ashkanazi Chief Rabbi of Palestine in 1921. Rav Kook was one of the first rabbis to attempt to unify the religious and secular Jews in Israel. He was responsible for many groundbreaking innovations such as the founding of The Chief Rabbinate of the State of Israel. Rav Kook was considered a *Tzadik*/Righteous Person, a *Talmid Chacham*/Torah Scholar, a Kabbalist, a Halachik authority, a Zionist, a poet, and is considered the father of the religious Zionist movement.

On September 1, 1935 (3 Elul 5695), after a short but intense struggle with cancer, Rav Kook passed away at the age of seventy. The Jewish people fell into national mourning. The newspaper heading read: "The Jews of the land of Israel have been orphaned: Rav Avraham Yitzchak Hakohen Kook is no longer."[8]

---

5.   Rosenak, "Rabbi Kook," Chapter: "The Death of His Lover and Attempt at Rehabilitation," Jerusalem: Zalman Shazar Center, 2006.
6.   Raz, *An Angel Among Men*, p. 26.
7.   Ibid. p. 28.
8.   Ibid. p. 53.

Words of Rav Kook versus Words about Rav Kook

The book you have in your hands is not a biographical book about Rav Kook's life. Thank God, many authors have succeeded in writing such a book.[9] I personally feel drawn to "words of Rav Kook" and not only "words about Rav Kook." "Words about Rav Kook" include information drawn from biographies, stories and anecdotes about the way he lived his life. In contrast, "words of Rav Kook" include insights and wisdom as expressed through his own writings, commentaries, journals, and letters, which gives us direct guidance about how we should live the ideal life.

What does Rav Kook's own writings and words have to teach me about achieving personal happiness, spiritual meaning and connection to God? How can Rav Kook's own books and words guide me to develop more love, patience and genuine concern for other people? This book invites the reader to encounter the spiritual wisdom of Rav Kook, to learn from Rav Kook's own books, journals, letters, and commentaries, words about how to live a meaningful, ethical and more God-centered life. In this sense, it is possible to say that this book contains not only "words about Rav Kook" but mainly "words of Rav Kook" himself. Rav Kook's own words of spiritual wisdom and guidance for your life is at the heart of this book. To be sure, I have included a small but nonetheless important section at the end of the book that includes "words about Rav Kook," called "Stories

---

9. For biographical literature on Rav Kook, see Rav Moshe Tzvi Neria's all-encompassing 5 set collection of books on Rav Kook's life including *Likutei HaRaaya, Sichot HaRaaya, Chayyei HaRaaya, Moadei HaRaaya and Be'Sadei HaRaaya* (Machon HaTorah VeHaaretz), Lifshitz, *Shivchei Hare'iyah (Beit El: Shilo Bikatz, 2010)* Mirsky, *Rav Kook: Mystic in a Time of Revolution* (New Haven: Yale University Press, 2014), Raz, *An Angel Among Men: Impressions from the Life of Rav Avraham Yitzchak Hakohen Kook,* trans. Moshe D. Lichtman (Jerusalem: Urim, 2003), Schwartz, *"The Spiritual Revolution of Rav Kook: The Writings of a Jewish Mystic"* (Gefen Publishing 2018) pp. 239–265.

about Rav Kook." As you will see, "words about Rav Kook" are powerful when combined with "words of Rav Kook." If you choose to journey through this book, you will encounter Rav Kook's spiritual insights, lessons, and guidance for your life.

So Much of Rav Kook's Wisdom Has Never Been Shared

I have been teaching the writings of Rav Kook in Yeshivot and Midrashot for over thirteen years. Every year I get at least one student who asks me the following question in the middle of a class: "So Rabbi, who would you say is the greatest expert of Rav Kook in the world?"

To this question I usually answer by listing a number of rabbis and professors who have written great books about Rav Kook. Nonetheless, I never really feel satisfied with this answer. The truth is that Rav Kook's collection of writings is so enormous and multi-faceted; they include many topics that demand so many different types of expertise. Therefore, while it is true that there are some people who are immersed in a lot of Rav Kook's writings, it is difficult to be an expert in all parts of Rav Kook. Instead, it would be more accurate to say that there are certain people who are experts in Rav Kook's writings on Zionism and the Jewish people; there are other people who are experts in Rav Kook's writings on kabbalah, mysticism, and philosophy. There are some people who are experts in Rav Kook's writings on psychology and self-growth; while there are still other people who are experts in Rav Kook's writings on Gemara and Halacha.

When I published *The Spiritual Revolution of Rav Kook: The Writings of a Jewish Mystic* back in 2018 my goal was to select and translate pieces that encompass the main topics of Rav Kook's writings. Six years have passed by and I have discovered more of Rav Kook's spiritual wisdom that I did not know about and have still mostly never been translated, released and shared with the world. Despite spending six years working on *The Spiritual Revolution of Rav Kook*, I myself was shocked by how many pieces from the *Kevatzim*/Spiritual Notebooks, *Igrot*/ Letters and *Ein Aya*/Talmudic Commentaries I had not yet come across or encountered in a deep way.

There are pieces that I came across that discuss the importance of solitude and time alone; the need to listen to both one's intellect and emotions; the secret messages contained in dreams, and how to deal with the fear of death. There are other pieces that I found that explain the necessity of unconditional love, the power of *mitzvot* and faith in God, the quest for peace and harmony, and much more. At times I felt like I had uncovered a treasure chest of spiritual wisdom that I felt obligated to share with my students, friends, and the greater world. Even when I showed these pieces to friends of mine who were rabbis and academics, people who had been studying Rav Kook's writings for many years, they too were amazed that they had not come across these specific writings and were stunned by the spiritual wisdom of Rav Kook.

As a response to my own personal exploration of these writings of Rav Kook, over the last six years I have been slowly translating new pieces of Rav Kook one-by-one and using them as material to teach my students in different Yeshivot and Midrashot. These pieces – the pieces that have transformed my life and the life of my students – make up the core of this book *The Spiritual Wisdom of Rav Kook: A New Collection of Writings*.

Too Many Important Pieces of Rav Kook to Translate

When it comes to selecting and translating Rav Kook's writings the main question isn't "Where can I find an important piece worth translating?" but rather, "Which one of the thousands of important pieces should I translate?" In other words, when it comes to

Rav Kook's writings, one is overwhelmed by the endless number of meaningful and insightful pieces of Rav Kook that must be shared with the world.

My constant headache as a translator is "Which piece should I include in this book and which should I leave out?" In fact, I have a large document on my computer called "Translations of Rav Kook not for the book." These pieces were initially meant to be in the book but did not make the final cut when I discovered even more powerful and relevant pieces I needed to put inside the book.

To use a metaphor, just as it is impossible to communicate the true genius and power of Mozart's music by sharing one symphony, so too it is impossible to share the incredible spiritual wisdom and light of Rav Kook by writing one book of translations. It is my hope that this book will further introduce the readers to the enormous spiritual treasure box of Rav Kook's writings. It is my own personal experience that when a person dedicates themselves to studying Rav Kook's writings on a daily basis, one will uncover endless wisdom, light and insight to live one's life by. As it is written in Pirkei Avot: "Ben Bag Bag said: Turn it over again and again, for everything is inside of it. Look into it and become gray and old inside of it. Do not move away from it, for you have no better portion than it" (Avot 5:22).

The Goal of Spiritual Wisdom is to Affect You

This must be made clear from the outset: the goal of studying Rav Kook's spiritual wisdom is not simply to have more intellectual ideas in one's head, nor is it to have more knowledge about Rav Kook's opinions on various topics. What does it mean to study a book of spiritual wisdom? In the beginning of *Orot HaKodesh*, Rav Kook writes:

Spiritual wisdom is greater than any other type of knowledge. It affects a person's inner desires and character traits and brings them closer to the spiritual heights of its content. This is not true for other types of worldly knowledge. Even though worldly knowledge is able to describe beautiful and lofty ideas, nonetheless it does not have the ability to effect change on the inner essence of the person. (OK 1, p.1)

In other words, according to Rav Kook, spiritual wisdom has a very unique and powerful quality to it. Whereas certain types of knowledge attempt to describe reality as it is, spiritual wisdom desires to do something more: to create a real change in the life of the reader. It was clear to Rav Kook that he did not want to teach his students simply more knowledge, but rather spiritual wisdom and insights that would help change and shape their life.

I feel a push from within to talk about *Teshuva*/Spiritual Transformation… I must help our generation understand its depth and guide us to actualize it in our individual and collective lives. (OTs, Introduction)

Therefore, when a person sits down to study the writings of Rav Kook one must not simply read it as more knowledge, more interesting philosophy, or even more inspiring mystical ideas. Instead, the goal is to be transformed and affected by its words. As Rav Kook writes: "Spiritual wisdom is greater than any other type of knowledge. It affects a person's inner desires and character traits." The main posture one should have when studying Rav Kook's spiritual wisdom is: "How does this insight of Rav Kook relate to my inner life and personal struggles?" "How does this lesson shed light into developing a more loving and caring relationship with others?"

Do Not Read the Book Too Fast

In *Shmoneh Kevaztim*, Rav Kook explains the negative effects of learning too many ideas in one go. "Sometimes a person feels exhausted due to the continuous flow of thoughts and ideas. One has not given oneself sufficient time between each spiritual revelation in order to reflect and process." (SK 3:295, OK 1, p. 75)

Instead, Rav Kook encourages a person to take breaks between studying each idea and give one's mind time to reflect and process what one has just learned.

> Such a break helps one better digest the new insight; to analyze it with one's intellect; and to eventually absorb it into one's inner desires and personality. Without such a break, each individual light becomes blurred and diluted… Having stops and breaks enables a person's life, character traits, desires and social interaction to be aligned with their higher insight of goodness and truth. (Ibid.)

In other words, it is important when studying spiritual wisdom to train oneself not to read too much in one go. To use a metaphor, if a person eats too much food in a short period of time one will feel sick. (This is true even if the food is healthy.) Instead, one must eat small amounts at a time, chewing and digesting the food before taking another serving. In a similar way, when it comes to spiritual wisdom, the goal is not simply to consume more and more concepts. Instead, one should try to apply each piece of wisdom to one's life and slowly "digest it" into one's character and life.

Therefore, when studying Rav Kook's words, a person must have the spiritual maturity not to read his writings too fast. One must allow each piece and each chapter to be read in a slow and calm tempo; to digest each piece patiently. Yes, this cannot be emphasized enough: when it comes to studying spiritual wisdom, in order to truly allow the wisdom to affect one's life, one must deliberately read the words slowly and let each sentence affect one's soul.[10]

Individual Spirituality versus Collective Spirituality

There are some people who focus their life on individual spirituality – the quest for happiness, self-growth, and a personal connection to God. For such people, the questions that bother them are: "How can I find the secret to happiness and meaning for my life?" "What is the best path to develop a deeper and more honest relationship to God?" On the other hand, there are people who dedicate their life to collective spirituality – toward bettering the community and creating a society rooted in love and respect between different types of groups. For such people, the questions that bother them are: "What is the secret to developing loving and respectful relationships?" "How can I contribute to the needs and concerns of my community and people?"

In a similar way, amongst the students and followers of Rav Kook's Torah there often feels like a split between these two spiritual paths. For many years, the main books published about Rav Kook in Hebrew were focused mainly on the collective spirituality within Rav Kook's writings. For example, there are countless books that talk about what Rav Kook says about the importance of dedicating oneself to the Jewish people, of making Aliya to Israel, and being a part of something greater than oneself. On the other hand, in the

---

10. In the introduction to Franz Rosenzweig's book on Yehuda HaLevi's poems he writes that the reason he put introductions to each chapter was to slow down the reader and make sure that they don't read too many poems in one go, since each poem must be absorbed slowly and patiently. In a similar way, in this book of Rav Kook's writings, I recommend to the reader to allow the breakup of each piece and each chapter to slow one down and allow oneself to take time to pause, contemplate, and absorb what they have just read.

last ten to twenty years there has been a resurgence and renewed interest amongst the Israeli youth who want to focus more on the individual spirituality within Rav Kook's writings. Today there are many books in Hebrew that focus on what Rav Kook says about psychology, the power of the individual soul, meditation, prayer, poetry and creativity.

According to Rav Kook, the ultimate goal of a person should be to dedicate oneself to both of these paths: individual spirituality and collective spirituality.

> And then there sometimes exists a great *Tzadik* who includes both of these values. At times this person doesn't look outside of one's private realm, while at other times, one's eyes looks at everything. "Lift up your eyes and see, to the north and south, to the east and west" (Bereishit 13:14). (SK 1:306)

I have structured the book based on this piece of Rav Kook in *Shmoneh Kevatzim* 1:306 where he splits up a person's life into two main paths of spirituality: individual spirituality and collective spirituality. The first section of this book focuses on Rav Kook's guidance in matters of individual spirituality. There are chapters where Rav Kook will explain the deep need for solitude and time alone each day; he will discuss the importance of finding the balance between silence and speech, as well as the necessity of listening to one's intellect as well as emotions. In other chapters, Rav Kook will talk about how to confront moments of despair and sadness; he will explain the power of living a life of *mitzvot* and faith in God; as well as how to relate to dreams, death, and much more.

The second section of the book expands beyond the individual self and focuses on Rav Kook's guidance in matters of collective spirituality. There are chapters where Rav Kook will talk about the need to focus on the community; how to develop love toward other people; and how to confront good and evil and the struggles of the generation. In other chapters, Rav Kook will explain how to develop a deep connection with the entire Jewish people; the importance of Aliya, the need for unity, and much more.

The Excitement of Studying the Writings of Rav Kook

Sometimes at the beginning of a class I will say to my students: "I want you to know that out of all the people in this classroom, I am probably the most excited to study the writings of Rav Kook." Being immersed in studying, teaching, and translating the words of Rav Kook on a daily basis has changed my life in a very real way. Rav Kook's Torah has transformed the way I relate to God, myself, my family, the Jewish people and the entire world.

As I write these words in my home in Jerusalem on a cold winter night, I feel a real tangible excitement to share with you "The Spiritual Wisdom of Rav Kook: A New Collection of Writings." May this book be a blessing for all who read it. I know that it has been a blessing in my life.

With love and respect,
Rabbi Ari Ze'ev Schwartz
Jerusalem, 2024

Two Paths of Spirituality

There is a type of *Tzadik*/Righteous Person who shouldn't leave the spiritual feelings of one's heart. Such a person doesn't need to look outside of one's private realm.

However, there is another type of *Tzadik* who is involved with all the different aspects of the world. Such a person looks at heaven as well as earth, from the beginning of the world until the end.

And then there sometimes exists a great *Tzadik* who includes both of these values. At times this person doesn't look outside of one's private realm, while at other times, one's eyes look at everything. "Lift up your eyes and see, to the north and south, to the east and west" (Bereishit 13:14). (SK 1:306)

Individual Spirituality

1

Encouragement

"It is a known principle that after dirty water is washed away from the source of fresh living water, then comes the clear and pure water that revives the soul." (KYK, R.LY 7)

RAV KOOK'S WRITINGS ARE FILLED WITH MANY DEEP PHILOSOPHIcal, psychological and kabbalistic ideas. What is the purpose of life? Who is God? What is the nature of the soul? Yet at the end of the day, when a person is going through a tough time in life, when a person is experiencing feelings of despair, what does one need most of all? Encouragement.

In one piece, Rav Kook writes, "Awaken my soul. Awaken to your divine greatness. Do not give up." (SK 8:69) There are times when Rav Kook uses the power of his pen not only to reflect on sophisticated and deep ideas but also to encourage his students and readers not to give up, not to lose hope, and not to fall into despair. In this chapter, Rav Kook will encourage and urge us not to lose hope when we see that things are falling apart in our lives. Yes, sometimes things we have built and cared for have broken to pieces. This is painful, dark, and demoralizing. Nonetheless, Rav Kook wants us to remember that this destruction is making room for something even greater. "When a person feels that a lot has been destroyed in their spiritual world, they should know that the time has arrived to build something new." (SK 6:60)

This chapter is very unique. It is not simply a chapter of Rav Kook's words trying to explain an idea, but also a chapter where Rav Kook turns to you the reader and attempts to pick you up off the ground of despair and encourage you to get up and keep going. In my opinion, if you read this chapter again and again, it will give you more than just words, it will give you strength and hope.

Do Not Give Up

When Your Spiritual World Has Been Destroyed

When a person feels that much has been destroyed in their spiritual world, they should know that the time has arrived to build something new. This building will be something greater, more exalted, steady and beautiful than what used to exist. One should strengthen themselves and have courage in the act of fixing their actions and ways. One should do this in a balanced way, with a courageous heart, a pure desire, and with a heart filled with strength and inner joy. (SK 6:60, OK 3, p. 251)

Precious Jewels from the Depths of Chaos

Sometimes a person experiences a fall due to a weak spirit in their moral character. They should recognize that they need to draw precious jewels from the depths of chaos. They must return and rise up, renew their strength with courage and inner peace. They must return to the light of the world with even greater strength then before. This principle is true for a generation as well as an entire period in history. (SK 8:104, OK 3, p. 252)

Know Your Worth

Awaken my soul. Awaken to your divine greatness. Do not give up. Do not conform to the overconfident and mistaken people who cannot grasp the movements of your spirit and the subtleties of your soul with its pure thoughts. These people cannot appreciate your soul when it yearns for the highest spiritual realms- toward the divine realm, toward honesty, toward truth and purity. Know your worth and rise up. (SK 8:69)

To Know One's Inner Greatness

A person needs to recognize their inner talents and know for oneself if they were created for greatness. One should not be intimidated by the sin of arrogance of recognizing one's high level of intellect and the worth of one's desires. Just the opposite is true. A person should be much more careful about false humility that depresses the soul and dims one's divine light. (SK 1:318, OK 3, p. 216)

Do Not Compare Oneself to Others

A person who has the character of a spiritual perspective does not need to hold back their attitude due to any obstacle in the world. One needs to keep a clear mindset. This is true both physically and ethically. A person's mind can be compared to an open sea with a continuous wind. However, when a person with this clearer mindset does not believe in themselves; when they assume that what holds back most people also holds them back, then they will experience blocks on their journey. (KYK 2, Pinkas 4:10)

Even if One Suffers from Negative Traits

A person whose soul longs for spiritual heights and clear visions should not abandon one's goals even if sometimes one suffers from negative character traits. Regarding this it is said "If a ruler's anger rises against you, do not leave your post" (Kohelet 10:4). "Eventually, the honor will come" (Nedarim 62a). (SK 7:106)

Be Brave

If what you desire is the source of Torah, then elevate and strengthen yourself to encounter this great spiritual level. For it pulsates within your soul. With all your speech and conversations; with all the spiritual and physical burdens that were placed upon you – be brave. Look directly toward the light that reveals itself between the cracks. (SK 8:7, OK 3, p. 122)

Do Not Despair

A letter to Rav Yeshayahu Kohen, April 12, 1931

Shalom and wishing you much blessings. I received your letter and I am very pained to hear that you are experiencing spiritual and physical distress. I want to encourage you not to have any despair. The power of *Teshuva*/Spiritual Growth is extremely holy and powerful. There is no doubt that ultimately God will forgive everything. A *Lev Nishbar*/Broken Heart is very precious. Eventually you will achieve *Teshuva Be'ahava*/Spiritual Growth motivated by love, where all your sins will turn into merits.

Guard yourself with a strong connection to Judaism and be joyful without any sadness. It is only beneficial to cry during moments of *Viduim*/Confessions, *Tehilim,* or when you arrive at various verses of confessions. By doing this one will experience a great salvation. Be strong and careful regarding keeping the holy Shabbat, saying *Berachot* – specifically *Birkat HaMazon* (the blessing after bread). Act with modesty in all situations, in both behavior and thought. When you are more complete and healthy, I will hopefully send you additional advice. In the meantime, be confident and sure of God's kindness, the "One Who desires *Teshuva*" (from the *Siddur*).

Your friend, Avraham Yitzchak HaKohen Kook.
(IR of the year 5691)

Do Not Waste Your Life Away

The Power of One Action or Thought
Sometimes one action can cause such intense damage that many thoughts and feelings cannot fix. And sometimes one great thought can fix countless damaged actions that many actions cannot fix. (SK 6:118)

Peaceful Productivity
Sometimes there is a type of person who cannot be at peace. This person's true peace is productivity. (SK 1:817)

When the Soul Feels Empty
The soul is empty as long as it isn't filled with wisdom. This emptiness is a great pain for the soul, and it is continuously trying to fill itself in order not to feel strangled by empty thoughts. When the

soul cannot fill its emptiness with thoughts of truth, it fills itself with false thoughts. This quiets down its pain temporarily, yet the soul remains empty inside. In order to truly nourish the soul, one must fill it with true wisdom and thoughts of ethical righteousness. (KYK 2, Pinkas 5:72)

The Pain of Not Actualizing One's Potential

One's thoughts must be allowed to rise up according to how much is hidden inside. And if one does not actualize one's thoughts, one suffers great pains that only those who are addicted to materialism can ignore. But one who is a spiritual person, feels the pain of one's soul and how it is actually caught inside the fires of hell as long as it doesn't actualize its potential. (KYK 2, Pinkas 5:55)

Spiritual Strength and Will-Power

One of the character traits of the soul that is needed for spiritual perfection is the trait of *Gevura*/Strength – specifically, the strength of the soul. It is impossible to be truly perfect in the knowledge and fear of God without this trait. In a similar way, it is impossible to reach important spiritual insights without *Gevura*.

Gevura is when a person has agreed to do something inside of themselves, something they need to do for the sake of spiritual perfection. A person must make this decision in a strong and firm way internally. They should not degrade the many details included in this decision. The strength of one's soul should guide this person.

In the moment when a person's soul is contemplating the awe of God and one's obligations regarding the need to be careful about *mitzvot*, one's soul will naturally be inspired to be immersed in Torah. One will desire to know the honor of one's Creator and how to do acts of goodness in God's eyes. However, when a person is involved in abstract thinking without the trait of *Gevura*, one will lose their initial inspiration. This is true even in matters of holiness and its various branches and details.

Therefore, one needs the trait of *Gevura*/Spiritual Strength in order to be in control of one's soul. Whatever matter a person has commited to for its own sake, one should hold on to and not give it up. One should increase in constant joy, filled with a calmness connected to the higher strength of consistency. One should not change what they are doing regardless of how much deep pain and confusion they are experiencing. (MA 3:1)

The Danger of Too Much Worrying

Taking Oneself Too Seriously
Sometimes a person makes mistakes and falls from their spiritual level due to taking oneself too seriously. (KYK 2, Pinkas 5:69)

Worrying that Leads to Even Greater Sins
Even though one's character traits have not been totally perfected, a person of great spirit does not need to abandon one's spiritual path. Eventually, through a higher spiritual insight one will repair even the worst character traits. All the more so, one should not destroy the souls' happiness due to any worry concerning confusing actions.

The main thing is to be careful with anything that is clearly bad and negative, and as a natural consequence one will also be guarded from any doubtful traits. But God forbid that through worrying about things that may perhaps be considered a sin, one will destroy their peaceful and joyful state of spirituality. Even though it is true that by being careful one guards oneself from possible mistakes; nevertheless, it is far more likely that due to the darkness of worrying, a person will make even worse mistakes. A person should always be confident in God that He will guard his feet from stumbling. (KYK 2, Pinkas 5:77)

Focusing on the Good Inside

When it is too difficult to raise up little by little, one must rise up in one go. A person must use the trait of holy pride and look upon oneself in a very positive way (*eyin tova me'od*); to even find the good qualities inside all of one's imperfections.

Indeed, when a person allows their mind to search for good qualities then all of their imperfections transform into something good. After a person finds a lot of good inside of themselves then they must rejoice in this goodness. Each day one must increase in good actions with a pure heart filled with consoling hope. (KYK 2, Pinkas 4:92)

Looking at One's Flaws with a Spirit of Positivity

A person needs to look at one's imperfections with a spirit of positivity in order that one will be continuously filled with a courage to repair oneself. To be sure, this must come after one has already internalized in one's heart and soul a hatred of evil. (KYK 1, Pinkas Rishon L'Yaffo 110)

Beware of Spiritual Growth That Leads to Depression

Sometimes a person needs to distance oneself from thoughts of holiness and *teshuva* (spiritual growth) if it causes one to feel depressed. The essence of joy, which is connected to the depths of holiness, is more important than any other form of holiness and *teshuva*. Therefore, when thoughts of awe of God and teshuva come to a person in a way that causes depression, one must release one's mind from such thoughts until one is able to experience them in a joyful way. This is fitting for the honest of heart and authentic servant of God. (SK 6:25)

Do Not Overwhelm Oneself

A person should not overload oneself with too many external things. This is true even regarding one's character traits. Although a person should strive to reach the ultimate perfection, nonetheless, one should not totally abandon one's natural desires.

Rather, a person should try to gradually improve one's character towards a higher goal. And if at times a person falls, one should not allow one's heart to become weak. Indeed, a weak heart brings with it many other negative things. Instead, at such times, a person should immediately focus on teshuva be'ahava/spiritual growth motivated by love. "One's sins will then be transformed into merits" (Yoma 86b).

Therefore, one must know that there is really nothing to be afraid of at all. In general, one's main desire needs to be focused on the ultimate perfection – a hatred of evil and a love of good. (KYK 1, Pinkas Rishon L'Yaffo 106)

Sadness that Comes from Worrying

Sometimes sadness comes about because one can sense that spiritual downfalls will occur to them in the future. As a result, a person becomes saddened. To be sure, one always has free choice to overcome these future downfalls. Nonetheless, the sadness overtakes them because according to the present situation it seems likely that one will not overcome these future struggles. Therefore, a person needs to overcome this sadness with pure courage. One must draw inner happiness from clear thinking. Through combining inner courage with the power of decision making, one will create a stable path that is guarded from the obstacles of the spirit. (PR 4, p. 258)

The Struggle of the Soul

When a person desires to be purified, one feels an iron wall separating oneself from God. This person thirsts for the divine light, but sees that one is far from God. In fact, one's soul feels pained because one's thirst is not the deepest thirst. Such a person desires to feel the frustration of being thirsty, of being withheld from the greatest value. One's heart feels frustrated due to the fact that one does not actually feel such a thirst. This person walks around like a shadow, accusing oneself of lies and self-deception.

However, if a person was a true warrior, filled with a pure heart and connected to the straight path, one's happiness would not collapse. Instead, this person would do whatever one is able to do: improve one's actions, repair one's path, and purify one's character. In addition, one would increase study, develop one's emotions through acts of devotion – prayer, praise, poetry and songs. Also, such a person would strengthen their interactions with good and honest friends, dwell more regularly in the Holy Land, and dedicate oneself to speaking constantly in the holy language. One would continue doing all these things until the divine light shines upon them and one's spirit returns. (YKY 1, Eighty-One Pinkasot from Yaffo, 72)

Trapped in a Narrow Structure

Who can understand the suffering of a person with an expansive heart, of the soul who yearns for divine expansion, when it is trapped in a narrow structure? This is similar to an eagle that is trapped in a chicken coop. (KYK 1, Pinkas 5:17)

Focus on the Journey

The Ups and Downs of Life

The ups and downs of both an individual person and the entire world are a regular occurrence. Nevertheless, the overall movement is a direction of rising higher and higher. The changing moods, even at the times of the greatest lows, are no different to the waxing and waning of the moon; the high and low tides of the ocean; the act of breathing in and out, of being awake and asleep. Even though all these seem to contradict, nevertheless, it is the combination of these two qualities that creates a balanced life. (SK 1:690, OK 2, p. 521)

Growth Matters and Not Only the Destination

We should not despair if after many years of effort, we find ourselves standing with the very same goals we had at the start. Indeed, sometimes when it comes to moral growth, we find ourselves on the low level that we began at, with the need to fix ourselves with the very same amount of effort. And yet, after all this work we recognize that our effort was not in vain; that through our soul's struggle it attained a great wealth. All the darkness that we experience after the long and numerous journeys comes to show us a clear path to life, so that until old age we will still be standing armed with great spiritual strength, to work and to labor. We will never say that we have finished the task, because arriving at a definite and known destination is not our goal. Instead, what we desire is to grow and continually move higher and higher.

Sometimes the voice of laziness comes to intimidate and weaken us from our efforts; a sudden cold darkness comes upon us; it says that all our efforts in the past didn't produce any fruit. We feel as if we are standing in the same position of poverty and worthlessness that we stood in when we were at the beginning of our efforts. All this comes to teach us that we are not called upon to reach a specific goal in spirituality, but rather, to continuously grow in our efforts and work.

"Happy is the person who is in awe of God, and in God's *mitzvot* he desires greatly" (Tehilim 102:1). "This person desires God's *mitzvot* and not the reward of God's *mitzvot*" (Avoda Zara 19a). When we fully accept all the darkness of the journey, we will comprehend new and old lights. "God is my light and salvation, who will I fear?" (Tehilim 27:1). (SK 8:36)

Teshuva Assumes Human Imperfection

Without the attitude of *teshuva* as something certain and sure, a person would not be able to find any peace and rest. One's spiritual life would not be able to develop in the world.

Within each person exists a moral instinct that demands righteousness, goodness and perfection. And yet, a person is so distant from actualizing this ethical perfection. A person is so weak from being able to direct their actions toward this ideal righteous purity. And so, how is it possible to aspire toward that which is not in one's ability?

For this reason, *teshuva* is something natural to a person – it comes to complete them. A person is bound to make mistakes and be imperfect in realms of righteousness and morality. Nonetheless, this does not damage one's ultimate perfection. At the end of the day, a person's main foundation of completion is the firm and continuous longing and desire for a higher perfection. This desire is the foundation of *teshuva*; it is something that helps one overcome obstacles throughout life and truly completes them. (OTs 5:6)

When Inspiration Passes Away

When a person becomes elevated through a spiritual insight, this brings with it a time period of inspiration. And even when the noticeable appearance of this inspiration has passed away, it continues to affect a person in a hidden way. (PR 4, p. 370)

Transforming One's Past

A person's actions, essential desires, and the greater world, are always interconnected and can never be separated. A person's desires are connected to one's actions. Even past actions are not disconnected from the essence of life and from one's deepest desires. Now, since nothing is completely disconnected, a person has the ability to impact one's past actions. This is the secret of *teshuva*/spiritual growth, which God created before forming the world. In other words, God expanded the soul's spiritual creativity so that one has the ability to impact even one's past actions and existence.

Negative actions continue to impact and cause filth, damage, and destruction, as long as a person has not given them a new perspective. However, once a person has imprinted a positive attitude toward this negative action, it begins to transform into something good and pleasant. The joy of God and its light. (YKY 1, Eighty-One Pinkasot from Yaffo, 34, OTs 6:5)

Focus on Improving the Future

The foundation of *teshuva* needs to always be focused on improving the future. At the beginning, one should not place such a big emphasis on what happened in the past. It has been promised that if a person truly works toward fixing one's actions for the future, then God will help a person repair the past. However, if a person immediately attempts to repair the past, they will discover many obstacles, and their pathway to *teshuva* and closeness to God will be difficult. (KYK 1, Pinkas Rishon L' Yaffo 97)

The Journey from Darkness to Light

When a person feels worthless and empty; that they have no more spiritual strength. They see that that they have fallen and are falling apart. At such moments, they should know that a great light is waiting for them. All of the imperfections and wasted moments of their entire life – both practical and spiritual, positive and negative – are standing before them. All of their sins are testifying against them. They are in shock, filled with regrets amidst immense suffering.

And then, they raise up and return. They go from the depths of the abyss to the highest mountain, from impurity to purity, from darkness to great light. On their journey out, as they ascend upward, they pass by all the generations of darkness. This exhausts them intensely. Nonetheless, they comprehend that "God is compassionate and merciful" (a paraphrase of Shemot 34:6). That "even though they walk through the shadow of darkness, they fear no evil because God is with them" (a paraphrase of Tehilim 23:4). This person cries out to God from the depth of confusion. Their voice is heard. They call out to the light of wisdom and God illuminates them. Wisdom and kindness supports and crowns them.

They swiftly return to a place of security. They become filled with wisdom, joy, and strength. (SK 3:97, OK 3, p. 252)

Pain is a Meaningful Part of Growth

Detaching Oneself from Negativity

A person feels pain when they are first touched by the thought of *teshuva*. This pain comes from the act of being detached from the negative parts of the soul. There is no pathway to healing as long as these negative parts are connected to the soul, which damage and hurt the entire soul. *Teshuva* comes to detach and uproot these negative parts from the essence and root of the soul. In truth, any type of separation causes pain. This can be compared to the pain of uprooting damaged limbs and cutting them out for the sake of healing. These are the most internal types of suffering. On the other hand, it is precisely through such pain that a person is able to become free from the dark slavery of sins, from one's lowly desires and their bitter effects. (OTs 8:1)

Weakness and Fear are Symptoms of Growth

Weakness and fear are symptoms of one who is growing towards greatness. Nonetheless, the trait of greatness raises even above these symptoms. Weakness transforms into strength and fear turns into confidence.

The journey toward greatness does not allow any trait to remain permanent; the flow of the soul moves like a raging river. Yet since the soul desires to be in a permanent state of peace, it discovers inside of itself a continuous unsatisfied frustration. This expresses itself through symptoms of weakness and fear. Nonetheless, at the end of the day, even in the depths of weakness and fear, even when they are controlling a person, strength and confidence still exist inside. (SK 8:97, OK 3, p. 259)

Bitterness Sourced in Ethical Sensitivity

The more one's ethical sensitivity becomes refined, the more a person witnesses their own nakedness. Such a person encounters an increased bitterness within their soul due to their imperfect and undeveloped ethical standards. Sometimes this feeling can become painfully bitter.

Nonetheless, a person with an honest heart will recognize the need to accept this feeling with love. It comes to purify a person and bring them to precious and pure character traits. Regarding this it is said, "Blessed are those whose help comes from the God of Yaakov, whose hope is in Hashem his God" (Tehilim 146:5). "It is pleasant for *Tzadikim* to place their hope in the precious garden of God" (an allusion to Zohar VeYakhel 198). (SK 5:6, OK 3, p. 253)

External Symptoms of a Sin

Every sin causes a specific symptom of distress on the soul. This distress will not go away until a person does *teshuva*/grows spiritually. The deeper a person does *teshuva*, the more this inner distress will transform into self-confidence and courage.

It is possible to recognize a symptom of distress caused by sin. Such distress can be seen in a person's facial expressions, body movements, voice, behavior, hand writing, and in the way one speaks. Most of all, this inner distress can be recognized through the way a person writes, organizes, and teaches ideas. And wherever one can recognize the distress that is where the sin is blocking out the light. Any person with open eyes will be able to recognize the symptom; it all depends on the intensity of the sin as well as one's specific relationship to the sin. (SK 3:88, OTs 8:13)

When Dirty Water Washes Away

It is a known principle that after dirty water is washed away from the source of fresh living water, then comes the clear and pure water that revives the soul. (KYK, Rishon LeYaffo 7)

2

Solitude and Time by Oneself

"The deeper a person is, the more they need to search inside of them-selves... One needs to spend a lot of time alone Be'Hitbodedut – elevating one's thoughts, deepening one's opinions, and freeing one's mind." (SK 8:149)

ACCORDING TO RAV KOOK, EACH PERSON'S SOUL IS FILLED WITH endless depth and wisdom. There is a hidden treasure buried inside of each individual. Nonetheless, due to the loud and fast-paced na-ture of life, a person is often distracted from their soul and finds it difficult to hear one's inner voice of wisdom and guidance.

In response to this, Rav Kook says that a person must spend time doing *Hitbodedut*, which literally means to cause oneself to be alone in solitude. This alone time helps a person get in contact with their soul, reconnect to God, and become realigned to their inner voice of guidance that is so often ignored and forgotten. To be clear, Rav Kook says that the ultimate goal is not to run away from society but rather to recharge oneself and thereby enable oneself to come back to society with more clarity and with a renewed strength.

In this chapter, Rav Kook will describe the importance of spend-ing time alone and give guidance about what one can do during these moments of solitude.

Time Alone

A Deep Person Needs *Hitbodedut*/Time Alone

The deeper a person is, the more one needs to search inside of oneself. This person's understanding of oneself is hidden due to the great depth of their soul. One needs to spend a lot of time alone *Be'hitbodedut* – elevating one's thoughts, deepening one's opinions, and freeing one's mind. By doing this, one's soul will eventually reveal itself. A small ray of light will shine forth from the enormous illumination of one's soul. (SK 8:149, OK 3, p. 270)

Individual and National Introspection

There are moments when a person feels that one's soul has entered into the inner depths. Such a person is deeply focused on one's internal essence. The external world has no effect on them at all. This person is attached to *Hitbodedut HaPenimit*/the inner depths of solitude.

If another person comes and looks upon him from afar, this person will not know what is happening inside his soul. This outside person may judge him very negatively: Why is this person not being social? Why has he distanced himself from people? Why has everything, the world and all of life, become alien to him? However, in the true depths of this person's soul, he feels a great unifying harmony; he feels a deep goodness inside. The inner peace that the entire world is searching for, this person is currently experiencing inside of himself. Such a person is truly dwelling in the highest consciousness of the world.

In fact, it may even be possible that the powerful energy of life contained inside of this person is affecting society without their knowledge. It is having a greater effect on the world than all of the loud demonstrations.

Just as this principle is correct concerning an individual person, so too it is correct concerning an entire nation. When the Jewish people enters inside of itself it feels a great fullness. The nation is able to build its own world and does not need to chase after all the loud noises of the world. Instead, the Jewish people become refreshed; its life pulsates with strength; and it recognizes its own power. The nation transforms the world through transforming itself.

The current time period of building is chaotic. The desires of the nation change from one moment to the next. When the various national proposals are not enough to comprehend the inner happiness of strengthening the national internal spirit, then the nation's thoughts focus only on the outside world. The nation searches for happiness but does not find it.

At the present moment, our task is to strengthen the inner spirit of the Jewish people, to concentrate on using all of its talents – both internal and external. The insights gained from this inner concentration will lead to a feeling of inner peace. "And he will see how good is his resting place" (Bereishit 49:15). (SK 7:3, OK 3, pp. 269–270)

Seclusion for the Sake of Society

A person whose soul is shining light from the inside needs Le'Hitboded Harbeh/to spend a lot of time alone. The constant social interaction with people who are mostly focused on materialistic values dims the shining light of one's soul. As a consequence, one's important contribution to society decreases. Through Hitbodedut/ solitude and large amounts of time away from society, this person's spiritual connection to the world does not necessarily stop; one is still able to bring much goodness to society. One can concentrate on the needs of the generation; to pray for them; to focus on the treasure of goodness contained inside of them; and to plan different ways to help them.

However, when this person does not spend enough time alone, one descends lower and lower. Through constant social interaction, the darkness of society darkens one's own spirit. Therefore, a wise person needs to "make oneself like a necklace that is loose on the neck, which is sometimes seen and sometimes not seen" (Eruvin 54a). (SK 3:319, OK 3, p. 271)

The Temptation to Avoid *Hitbodedut*

The *Yetzer HaRa*/negative inclination tries to tempt and entice a person to grab a hold of whatever is the smallest level. If the *Yetzer HaRa* sees that a person is able to ascend to a great spiritual level, then it tempts a person with a lesser spiritual level in order to prevent them from reaching the higher level. Therefore, sometimes the *Yezter HaRa* will tempt great *Tzadikim*/righteous people to study a lot of Torah in order to prevent them from doing *Hitbodedut*/being alone with their higher thoughts. Indeed, higher thoughts are the most perfect type of Torah, something greater than any Torah that is learned from words.

The truth is that this happens even with regular people. Sometimes the moment will arrive when a person is ready to ascend and align oneself to the illuminating path of *Teshuva*/returning to God. When the *Yetzer HaRa* sees that it cannot distract this person, the *Yezter HaRa* will distract them with the obligation of studying Torah. Therefore, "a wise person must have eyes in their head" (Kohelet 2:14) and contemplate each situation to see which matter will elevate them to a higher level. A person should not be satisfied with a smaller spiritual level. (KYK 2, Pinkas 5:5)

Purifying One's Character

Even though the Torah and *mitzvot* purify a person's character traits, nevertheless, it is impossible to rely on this alone. Instead, one must be immersed in purifying one's character traits, and specifically, developing one's ethical nature. (SK 1:277, OK 3, p. 233)

The Danger of Being Involved with Materialistic People

It is very damaging for deep people who are filled with the strength of God, to be spiritually connected with materialistic people whose entire life is filled with a superficial fear of God, anxiety, negativity, and bitterness. The soul of a deep person suffers great pain when involved with these types of people in conversation, prayer, and any matter of holiness.

A person needs great preparation in strengthening one's spiritual energy and the divine light in one's soul in order to shield oneself. A person must be careful that one's soul does not become damaged due to these damaged souls. Such people contain a superficial fear of God and are not filled with great desires but rather the weakness of gloomy fear. (SK 1:91, OK 4, p. 422)

It Exists Inside of One's Soul

Sometimes it is impossible to pay attention to outside matters due to the great, illuminating, and infinite spiritual energy that flows from the source of one's soul. At first glance, it seems as if one is trapped in a prison that prevents one from perceiving the great expansiveness of existence. However, as time goes on and the heart roots itself on internal foundations, one discovers how the great expansiveness that the soul yearns for exists deep inside of oneself. (KYK 1, Pinkas Yerushalayim 17)

Seclusion versus the Middle Path

It is true, the middle path is the path of life, the path of happiness; and it is appropriate for all people. This middle path is God's advice given through the Torah... Nevertheless, due to the nature of different types of souls, there exists certain individuals who for them, it is more fitting to be immersed in a higher vision, a life of intense seclusion and purity. By doing this, such souls are able to discover a deeper way of living for the entire world; they are able to shed light on the path of the infinite.

These great souls experience inside of their extreme seclusion a deeper form of satisfaction and happiness than most people experience by walking down the middle path that is suitable for them. Such unique souls, who are filled with a great level of spirituality, are also included in the holiness of the Jewish people. And sometimes in the darkness of exile, it is precisely these giant souls who illuminate the darkness for all of us. They straighten our ways from darkness to light. (SK 6:22, OK 3, p. 267)

Helping People Through Staying at Home
When a *Tzadik* walks around in their home immersed in the search for truth – even when their thoughts cannot be put into words – they help many souls. (KYK 2, Pinkas 5:90)

What Should One Do When Alone?

Developing Self-Awareness
When a person of deep reflection is *Mitboded*/spends time alone, one's soul reveals its inner spiritual strength. This person becomes aware of all the imperfections that have occurred to one's soul due to the impact of negative actions and character traits. This person suffers a deep internal pain and searches in one's soul how to repair these imperfections. When one's inner suffering reveals itself with great intensity, when the external situation becomes unstable due to a mistake or physical pain, then one's internal emotions are not filled with great strength. Nevertheless, even at such moments, a person can come to a high level, because spiritual growth due to pain is also a form of growth. (SK 1:256, OTs 8:9)

Writing a Book of Personal Learnings and Insights
It seems that it is only possible for a person to fulfill the obligations of the heart through writing down their own personal learnings and insights into a notebook. These insights may include anything from individual issues as well as collective and communal matters. In general, a person better comprehends something when it is produced from their own spirit. And if a person has already reached this point where they are able to lay out ideas and thoughts in an intellectual way, then it is impossible for them to reach perfection without setting their mind to this task. (MA Intro, 1)

Writing as a Therapeutic Tool

Sometimes the only way for a person to lift oneself up from sadness is through writing down the thoughts of one's heart. Through doing this, one repairs the inner sicknesses caused by materialistic tendencies. "Then I said, 'Here I am, I have come with a scroll that is written for me. I desire to do Your will, my God; Your Torah is in my depths'" (Tehilim 40:8–9). (SK 6:34)

The Need for a New Perspective on Life

Often a person does not feel at peace inside. One is filled with complaints toward themselves. The main cause for this is that a person needs to give birth to an entirely new perspective; one must elevate one's general ethics and consciousness to a higher place than one is currently standing in. Such a person is not able to quench their thirst by adding a few small details of goodness and virtue. Rather, one must strengthen oneself with divine courage and create an entirely new path in one's heart that is much greater and holier. (KYK 1, Pinkas Rishon L'Yaffo 9)

Thinking Things Through at Length

When a person has reached the spiritual stage of having something to contemplate and clarify, it is essential that they think things through at length. Sometimes a person shortens one's thinking. It does not matter if this happens due to being busy with meaningless matters. Or even if this is due to a person being busy with studying Torah and *mitzvot*.

Ultimately, a person who does not finish what is assigned to them – to increase the power of their inner thinking – will lose out for themselves. "The wise person's heart will know the proper time and procedure" (Kohelet 8:5). (KYK 1, Pinkas Rishon L'Yaffo 16)

Finishing Your Thoughts

Any thought that isn't finished properly becomes understood in a distorted way. For the most part, such thoughts cause fear and sadness. Therefore, you will sometimes find that a person who doesn't contemplate a lot will be happier. In contrast, a person who has a talent for thinking and contemplating will experience happiness when they reach the level of finishing their thoughts. However, as long as one's thoughts are not finished, they will feel disturbed and sad. Therefore, it is an obligation for *Talmidei Chachamim*/Wise Scholars to try to clarify their thoughts in order that they will be filled with happiness and divine strength. "The righteous will be happy and rejoice before God; they will be excited and joyful" (Tehilim 68:4). (KYK 1, Pinkas Rishon L'Yaffo 61)

Valuing Ideas that Come to One's Mind

Every thought and idea that comes to the soul, that descends into one's mind, that is filled with the energy of holiness, needs to be valued and embraced. Such thoughts need to be processed in the mind, to be rooted in action, and to be held onto as a possession for life. They also need to be written down in a book and preserved as a holy matter for eternity. "Blessed is a person who does this" (Yeshayahu 56:2). (KYK 1, Pinkas Yerushalayim 5)

Subjective Experiences Matter

The thoughts about reality that come about due to our subjective experience are more important than the objective truth of reality itself. We can never fully grasp the true objective reality, but our own subjective experience we can live and feel. In fact, all of the different experiences that are manifested in reality throughout all the generations come from the subjective attitude of a person. It is important to pay attention to such experiences and attempt to comprehend their implications. (KYK 1, Acharon B'Boisk 1)

3

Silence and Speech

"The greatness of silence... comes about due to an inner explosion from the wellspring of the soul." (SK 5:101)

JUST AS A PERSON NEEDS TO DEVELOP THE ABILITY TO COMMUNI-cate and speak, so too a person needs to develop the ability to be silent. Rav Kook says that there are moments when a person goes through an intense experience and needs to quiet down the out-side noises and enter into the world of silence. At such delicate mo-ments, talking and interacting with others can disrupt the process a person needs to go through inside of their soul. Silence enables a person to filter through one's feelings and thoughts and allow for new insights to come about.

On the other hand, Rav Kook says that there are times when a person has spent enough time in the world of silence and needs to push themselves outwardly into the world of speech and interaction with others. The more elevated a person is, the more one recognizes the tremendous power words and speech have in transforming one's own life as well as the entire world.

This is the question: How can a person find a balance between silence and speech, between the need for inner quietness and the need to communicate? In this chapter, Rav Kook will teach us when we should enter into the world of silence and when we should enter into the world of speech. As King Solomon writes, "There is a time for silence and there is a time for speech" (Kohelet 3:7). Rav Kook will point out the positive effect words can have on our life when used responsibly, but also warn us about the negative effects words can have when used irresponsibly.

Silence

The Greatness of Silence

The greatness of silence and its connection with *Ruach HaKodesh/* the Holy Spirit, comes about due to an inner explosion from the wellspring of the soul. This inner spirit requests expansion to a place without any external pressure. *Hitbodedut HaPenimit/*inner aloneness is a very serious thing; it needs time to expand without any worldly disturbances.

When this happens, the soul creates its value and uniqueness from its own inner strength. The spiritual light, the beauty of life, and its root power become stronger and stronger. Speaking words at such a moment disrupts one's inner building, it takes from the old, from what is already blurry, dark, and limited. Speaking gets in the way of the fresh stream that yearns for newness and freshness. Just as there is *Shetika HaDiburit/*silence in relation to speaking, so too, there is *Doomya Machshavatit/* silence in relation to thoughts. (SK 5:101, OK 3, p. 273)

The Kingdom of Silence

Sometimes the inner light of "a time to be silent" (Kohelet 3:7) appears and the holiness of muteness fills the soul in all its beautiful honor and heaviness. A great destruction comes about in the depths of the soul if a person rebels against this energy of silence and breaks out to speak words. This rebellion against the kingship of silence destroys all the buildings of purity, honesty, depth and higher connection. Everything becomes damaged. Now, if after doing this, a person desires to repair one's damages, one must start building everything from the beginning. "Therefore, the wise person keeps silent at such times" (Amos 5:13).

On the other hand, when a person gives silence its deserved respect at the time of its appearance, then silence rules its kingship, develops its muteness, pierces into the depths, and reaches to the abyss of confusion. From this place, sprouts shoot forth, incredible branches stem from this great and fresh plant. The conversations are then filled with strength. "Praise on their lips" (Yeshayahu 57:19) will then come about.

Then begins "a time to speak" (Kohelet 3:7) in all of its beauty and honor. The spirit of silence becomes like a guardian. Silence influences the flow of speech, which flows like a stream in all its richness and beauty. "I will create praise on their lips. 'Peace, peace, to those far and near,' says God. 'And I will heal them'" (Yeshayahu 57:19). "Their fruit will serve for food and their leaves for healing. To liberate the mouth of the mute" (Sanhedrin 100a). (SK 5:104, OK 3, p. 274)

Silence is an Essenial Demand

Silence is an essential demand that comes from the depths of the soul. This demand comes about as a result of higher reflections that are beyond the world of speech. Such higher reflections are a permanent matter inside of us. When a *Baal HaMachsava HaDomemet*/a master of silent thoughts immerses oneself in one's higher silence, many worlds are created and built; exalted songs rise up in their highest holiness; a higher strength is elevated in its holy perfection beyond all spiritual realms. (SK 1:868, OK 3, p. 274)

Being Patient with One's Hidden Feelings

A person should not be forceful with the hidden feelings that awaken within one's soul. Rather, one should give them time to deepen, to blossom, to increase buds and flowers; and eventually to grow fruit that will be stored in a place hidden from the surface... Fortunate is a person who waits patiently; who listens to the silent voices of the longing soul even before they have expressed themselves in words and letters. (SK 8:5, OK 1, p.129)

Different Spiritual Moods

Sometimes a *Tzadik* needs a great amount of study and prayer, and sometimes a very small amount is enough in order to express the true point of his holy desires. And sometimes a *Tzadik* needs to simply think and feel, since they are higher than any word or speech. (KYK 1, Pinkas 5:141)

Unable to Study

Sometimes I am unable to study and I want to do nothing. This is because I need to focus my attention toward my inner thoughts or my inner expanded emotions. Such moments are even more spiritually elevated than regular study or any other religious action. (C, p. 138)

Choosing Between Different Desires

It is very difficult to choose between different desires within the soul. This is especially true between different spiritual desires. On the one hand, the spiritual desire that inclines toward higher thoughts and goes beyond any limited idea or object. On the other hand, the spiritual desire to be immersed in self-discipline, Torah, character development, Halacha, Agada, and anything limited and measured. (SK 3:190)

The Need to Digest New Ideas

Sometimes a person feels exhausted due to the continuous flow of thoughts and ideas. One has not given oneself sufficient time between each spiritual revelation in order to reflect and process. Such a break helps one better digest the new insight; to analyze it with one's intellect; and to eventually absorb it into one's inner desires and personality. Without such a break, each individual light becomes blurred and diluted.

The Torah also creates breaks. "To give a break of reflection between one section and another, something which is all the more necessary for an ordinary person receiving instructions from another person" (Rashi, VaYikra 1:1). This principle is also true regarding any intellectual insight that comes to one's soul. Having stops and breaks enables a person's life, character traits, desires and social interaction to be aligned with their higher insight of goodness and truth. (SK 3:295, OK 1, p. 75)

Letting Go of Actions

There are certain spiritual moments when the soul feels a yearning toward God; one needs to be filled with words and actions that channel and connect oneself to this holy spirit. However, sometimes the spirit comes in a way that each word and action block its movement. At such moments, the way to deal with this powerful spirit is to let go and allow it to strengthen on its own. (KYK 1, Pinkas 5:71)

Not Forcing Oneself to Learn from a Book

Sometimes one cannot learn because one's thoughts are focusing on something higher, which is an even higher Torah than can be absorbed from anything one studies. At such a moment it is forbidden for a person to force one's soul to study. This would be dragging one's thoughts down from heaven to earth. (KYK 1, Pinkas 5:68)

A Deep Thinker Must Ignore Superficial Thinking

One who has the ability to sense the depth of life, needs to stay firm in one's path and not pay attention to conventional beliefs, since most of them are founded on superficial thinking. And when a person is sincere in one's path, one will recognize its joy, and the divine light will truly shine upon them. (KYK 1, Pinkas 5:58)

Spiritual Worlds Exist Inside of Us

We see all the spiritual worlds inside of us. And since we see them, they are really there. We elevate them when we elevate our own existence, and we lower them when we lower ourselves. And it is impossible for it to be any other way. (KYK 1, Pinkas 5:3)

The Creative Soul

A person who has a creative soul needs to create thoughts and ideas. Such a person cannot restrict himself to simple study. The flame of the soul ascends on its own, and it is impossible to stop its movements. (SK 7:190, OK 1, p. 177)

The Melody of the Soul

In the moment the soul asks for its melody, do not withhold it. (SK 7:184)

Thinking is Deeper Than Writing

Literature and writing place limits on the mind. The author thinks that any idea that cannot be written down is not an important talent. As a result, one removes one's mind and desire from this idea. In a similar way, the reader of a book thinks that one's thoughts need to be restricted to what is written in a book. However, what both the author and the reader do not understand is that the greatest and most beneficial thoughts are the spiritual content that floats in the air of ideas. This is something that cannot be grasped and written down. It is something that can never fit into the limitations of writing.

As long as a person thinks that writing is an absolute necessity to one's spiritual life, it is very difficult to get rid of this essential mistake from one's heart. The highest spiritual life protests against writing. From ancient times a person understood their authentic way of communication. "I will put my law in their minds and write it on their hearts" (Yirmiyahu 31:33). We have only one book that is necessary, something that is the light of life itself. "I wrote and gave My soul" (Shabbat 105a). "In the light of Your face, Hashem our God, You gave us the Torah of life" (from the Siddur). (SK 4:115)

Different Ways of Reacting to a Spiritual Insight

Sometimes a person experiences a feeling of weakness when receiving higher spiritual insights. One should not despair as a result of this weakness. Prophecy was also known for exhausting one's physical and mental strength. And yet, we are still thirsty for prophecy.

A person must strengthen one's mind with clarity and purity. One must do Teshuva Gammura/a complete return to God, which cleanses oneself and produces a logical mind and an understanding heart. This weakness will transform into strength. One's higher spirit that was inspired by the divine spirit will then be able to defend itself against all types of destruction.

A person should not cut down the hopes of one's soul, but instead, strengthen and expand them. Whatever one is able to ponder in one's mind in an organized way, one should ponder. Whatever one is able to articulate with clear words, one should express and speak about. Whatever one is able to express on a page with a pen, one should write down. And whatever one is able to materialize in sensitive and pleasant actions, one should actualize. This person should fill oneself with a strong and joyful spirit, which causes great actions in the world. And whatever one is not able to materialize through any form of expression, one should simply ponder and connect oneself to the divine spark inside of these spiritual insights. (YKY 1, Eighty-One Pinkasot from Yaffo, 42)

Speech

Silence Leads to an Appreciation of Words

Ruach HaKodesh/the Holy Spirit comes to a person through silence. On the other hand, the more intense a person feels the holy spirit inside, the more one recognizes the great significance of speech. A person then understands the great impact of speech and its powerful control over actions. In fact, the more a person appreciates the importance of words in general, and the importance of one's own words specifically, the more significant one's words truly are. Such a person's words have wonderous effects. A spark of the inner element of Israel comes upon such a person. "The voice is the voice of Yaakov" (Bereishit 27:22). "Any prayer that is answered contains the seed of Yaakov" (Yalkut Shimoni, Bereishit 27:115). (SK 8:143, OK 3, p. 276)

The Connection Between Speech and the World

Sometime one feels the connection between one's speech and the world. This is the beginning of the consciousness of redeeming speech from exile. Even when a person only imagines this connection, this is also a good sign. "The righteous will hold strong in their path and those with clean hands will grow stronger" (Iyov 17:9). (SK 6:14, OK 3, p. 285)

The Conversations of Torah Personalities

There is a spiritual principle called "the simple conversations of *Talmidei Chachamim*/Torah Scholars must be studied" (Succot 21b). A conversation is something which grows naturally without any forced effort from the person. This can be compared to a plant in the field that grows in a natural and general way. Therefore, this is the explanation of "the simple conversations of *Talmidei Chachamim* must be studied." When people are continuously immersed in the words of the Torah, their simple conversations also become words of Torah. This happens on its own without any forced effort....

To be sure, it is good to have a small amount of simple conversations. This causes people to have respect for the Torah. This is the meaning of the end of the line "these conversations must be studied." Indeed, the deeper source of these conversations are words of Torah. On the other hand, the external form of the conversation is still considered simple and secular. This helps people respect the Torah. (KYK 1, Pinkas Rishon L'Yaffo 56)

The Continuous Elevation of Your Soul

Pay attention to the continuous spiritual elevation of the universe. Recognize how in a similar way, your soul is continuously growing and rising up. Listen to the inner voice, which is a shield of life for spoken words. It is then that you will comprehend the many spiritual levels you ascend with every thought that you articulate, comprehend, and use to help others. When all the wasted conversations and vanities of life are thrown away, your soul is filled with courage and strength. New spiritual levels become revealed to you through prayer, Torah, conversations, and inner logic. "A song of elevation" will sing its eternal worth. "For the conductor, a song." (SK 8:8, OK 3, p. 278)

Expressing Depth in a Simple Language
Spiritual and philosophical thinkers need to train themselves to articulate ideas in a simple language when speaking and writing. And sometimes precisely through doing this, the greatest insights will be expressed. (SK 3:286)

Words that Are True but Still Cause Damage
One should be careful about speaking words that could cause moral damage to another person's life. In fact, even if the idea is correct in and of itself, it may still damage the listener. This is especially true when the listener is connected to a certain moral world that is in contradiction to the idea they are currently hearing. (SK 6:57, OK 3, p. 282)

Dangerous Beliefs That Contain Truth
There are certain beliefs that naturally confuse a person, decrease ethical responsibility, and damage one's connection to the community. Such beliefs have a tendency to cause people to disrespect society and lead to other similar types of negative qualities. These beliefs, taken on their own may be full of truth; nevertheless, they contain the danger of false ideas due to the negative qualities that they so often lead to. Their main problem is the way they are spoken about and not the belief itself. As a result, it is not possible to teach and discuss such ideas to the masses.

On the other hand, it is possible to explain these ideas in a sophisticated way; and as long as they are simply thought about in one's mind, they will not lead to any damage. In fact, when these beliefs contain great truths, they may be capable of causing a deep transformation. (SK 4:2)

Evaluating One's Own Speech

A person can understand one's own spiritual level depending on the clearness of one's speech. The more alive the illumination within the soul is, the more a person will sense how each of their words shoot out like an arrow, like a stream of fresh water. A person will be able to sense how one's words are flowing from the source of life and are having an effect on the world. To be sure, the quality of speech must be measured by the specific type of elevation of the soul – each person according to their own level. (SK 6:78)

Speaking Meaningless Words Damages You

Meaningless words/*Devarim Be'Teilim* draw their lifeforce from a weak, worn-out, and dead spirit. When a person speaks meaningless words, it raises up an unclean and dirty energy and infects the soul. As a result, the general atmosphere of the world becomes dark and gloomy. Therefore, a person who desires to immerse themselves in matters of holiness, will avoid meaningless words. This is true regarding even a single meaningless word. Through doing this one will merit a hidden light that is filled with life. Such a person's words will be like burning fire, filled with a holy love – a love of God and all the worlds; a love of all humanity and all creatures that is filled with the spirit of life. (SK 5:212)

Releasing Resentment

Sometimes a person needs to scream out loud in order to uproot the suffocating resentment in one's heart. (KYK 2, Pinkas 5:118)

Revealing the Soul

It is impossible to totally reveal the light of one's soul except though prayer and screaming out loud. (KYK 2, Pinkas 1:54)

4

Intellect and Emotions

"It is impossible for a person to live with intellect alone or emotions alone. There must always be a combination." (SK 1:271)

One of the most difficult questions in life is: Should I trust my intellect or my emotions? Should I rely on the logic of my mind or the gut instincts of my feelings? Indeed, there are many situations where a person's mind tells them to do one thing, while their emotions tell them to do something else completely. According to Rav Kook, both the intellect and the emotions contain immense wisdom and guidance for one's life. He therefore does not think it is correct for a person to make a simplistic rule such as: "I should always listen to my intellect, or "I should always trust my gut feelings."

In certain matters such as character development the intellect must be listened to. "Intellectually purifying one's character traits should precede emotional purification." (KYK 2, Pinkas 5:113) In contrast, in others matters such as prayer, the emotions should be trusted. "Sometimes we discover more truth in the emotions than in the intellect. Indeed, sometimes quality prayer contains a treasure of Torah that much intellectual learning cannot provide." (SK 4:107)

In this chapter Rav Kook will explain what are the different spiritual truths contained in the intellect versus the emotions as well as which situations we should listen to the mind versus trust one's gut feelings. In addition, Rav Kook will discuss how certain souls are more connected to their intellect while other souls are more connected to their emotions. In general, Rav Kook will encourage us to enter into a holistic approach to spirituality whereby we embrace all the different parts of our soul.

Intellect

The Logical Mind

The source of all impurity and evil in the world is because we do not use the logical mind /Sechel HaYashar. And the secret to present and eternal redemption is training people to use the logical mind/Sechel HaYashar. (PR 2, p. 200)

Uncovering Layers of the Unconscious

Every thought has many layers and levels – this one above that one. However, only one layer reveals itself to the conscious mind. This is how we know the things we think. However, a thought contains many hidden layers within the subconscious. All of our essence is contained in it; it is influenced by the subconscious and causes influence upon it.

The closer we come to the illumination of the intellect, toward the purity of the soul, the more each thought reveals additional layers. These layers are higher and more hidden; greater in worth; and heavier in their influence.

Fortunate is the person who walks in the path of purity; sanctifies their ways, and straightens out their practical and spiritual life. Such a person will elevate themselves to such a level where each conscious thought will reveal many layers due to the richness of the thought. A person's thoughts will illuminate all the storehouses of their soul in its precious light. "The divine secret comes to those who are in awe of God" (Tehilim 25:14). (KYK 1, Pinkas Yerushalayim 8)

The Importance of In-Depth Thinking

Without thinking something through at length and in-depth, no spiritual idea can be truly understood. (KYK 2, Pinkas 5:10)

Discovering Truth

Developing a spiritual perspective must automatically start with a mixture of false beliefs. A person who expects to begin with perfect thoughts will not attain anything. However, one who instead seeks to investigate truth, even though one has not reached it at the beginning of one's investigation, this person is rooted in the realm of truth. (KYK 2, Pinkas 5:60)

Intellectual Freedom

The light of God only reveals itself through intellectual freedom. (KYK 2, Pinkas 5:18)

The Never-Ending Search for Truth

If a person thinks that one is able to understand all truths, this will cause them to feel depressed by one's limited level of comprehension. Such a person will feel frustrated that one cannot ever reach this absolute goal. Yet depression is in contradiction to the nature of perfection. A person must instead recognize that it is certainly impossible to reach absolute truth; but what is possible is to arrive at the greatest understanding according to one's limited nature. Indeed, a person's true perfection comes about through the very act of seeking. This enables a person to be in a state of constant emotional well-being. (KYK 2, Boisk 2:8)

There is Intellectual Nourishment in Everything

A person must recognize that even in lowly matters and their various details exists a tremendous amount of intellectual nourishment. Of course, this principle also applies to higher matters. (PR 4, p. 370)

Intellectual Reflection Comes After Inspiration

Regarding matters of the spirit, insights reveal themselves suddenly without any systematic order or reason. Only afterwards comes the intellect, which attempts to contemplate and organize the various branches of knowledge, trying to uncover its possible motivations and context. "A sage is greater than a prophet" (Bava Batra 12a). Intellect is the final stage of prophecy. "The archers fight first, while the warriors win the battle" (Nazir 66b). (SK 3:328, OK 1, p. 75)

Intellectual Change Before Emotional Growth
Intellectually purifying one's character traits should precede emotional purification. Since if one does not know what is good and what is bad, how can one train and eventually internalize in a natural way good emotion and to distance negative emotion? (KYK 2, Pinkas 5:113)

The Limits of Intellect

The Limits of Intellect
The most perfected type of faith illuminates all darkness of existence; it does not have any fear of human intellect or logic. This faith comprehends that the intellect is the most limited possession of human beings. The intellect should be used for things that are suitable for it. However, it does not have the right to darken any lights that are outside of its realm, such as emotions and faith in general. (YKY 1, Eighty-One Pinkasot from Yaffo, 8)

Liberating Oneself from Human Intellect
Sometimes a person needs to do a *Siguf Sichli*/intellectual form of self-denial. One must liberate one's thinking from the slavery of human intellect. Indeed, sometimes the foolishness of intellect is greater than its wisdom, whereby the intellect has a tendency to enslave a person. This is the source of darkness that too much in-depth reflection becomes darkened by its own shadows.

When a person tries to overcome this darkness, a wave of spiritual suffering comes upon them. What is needed is a higher form of strength, whereby a person overcomes their own spiritual inclination and breaks past the walls that separate them from their Father in heaven. This is a higher form of truth and peace that comes from their ultimate source (a reference to Zechariah 8:19). (SK 3:320)

The Web of Over-Sophistication
It takes great wisdom to comprehend the depths of one's pure and natural soul, which has not yet been caught in the web of over-sophistication. (KYK 1, Reshimot M'London 11)

Beyond the Intellect
The desire to imagine that which is beyond the intellect strengthens one's soul. However, if a person desires to imagine – using their intellect – that which is beyond the intellect, this will lead to a broken heart and a weakened spirit. (PR 4, p. 370)

Accepting That One Cannot Understand
When a person studies higher matters, one must recognize that certain ideas will not be understandable at all. To be sure, some ideas will be half-understood, a third-understood, a quarter-understood or even less than this. One should recognize that a lack of understanding causes pain and suffering – sometimes in a tremendous way. Nonetheless, a person must overcome this pain and not abandon this higher study. Eventually, one will see the ultimate goodness hidden inside. (PR 4, p. 370)

The Power of Imagination
The imagination has certain levels of insight that the intellect lacks. The imagination helps us perceive the world in a spiritual way. As a result, it develops our spiritual essence. To be sure, when the imagination increases too much it blurs the borders of the practical world.

On the one hand, scientific experiments taken from around the world have helped to enrich practical knowledge and even certain types of spirituality based on scientific logic. On the other hand, scientific experiments have also weakened and lowered the world of imagination and the greatness of life contained inside of it.

As a result, people in today's generation are weaker in their imagination then people were in the ancient past. This is especially true of the great visionaries of the past whose imagination was very strong and who acquired the necessary skills from their practical mind. We would therefore be correct even today, after all of the great intellectual development of modernity to say: "If the earlier generations are like angels, then we are like human beings, and if the earlier generations are like human beings, then we are like donkeys" (Shabbat 112b). (SK 3:73, OK 1, p. 225)

Prayer Works Even If the Mind Cannot Understand It

Faith knows how to pray; it asks God for everything that a person lacks. Faith comprehends the great worth of prayer and its immense power to uncover all the honest and good desires within one's heart. Faith does not need to explain to the human intellect how prayer works and how exactly it influences.

Faith in the heart, that pure and simple desire, knows that there is a God, that there is a Father in heaven. The complete perfection and holiness of absolute divinity stands firms in one's mind and in the depths of one's life. Only this simple and pure faith can bring about prayer and achieve all its goals. (YKY 1, Eighty-One Pinkasot from Yaffo, 9)

Emotions

There is More Truth in Emotions

Sometimes we discover more truth in the emotions than in the intellect. Indeed, sometimes quality prayer contains a treasure of Torah that much intellectual learning cannot provide. (SK 4:107)

Drowning in the Swamp of Darkness

The purest thinkers come to their greatness through expanding their thoughts. However, they too need to lift up their emotions. When they are drowning in the swamp of darkness they need to call out with enormous strength to awaken their soul – "to go from darkness to light" (the Pesach Hagada). "Then their hearts cried out to God" (Eicha 2:18). (SK 1:43)

The Unique Way Emotions Listen

Inside the essence of the soul are hidden all the greatest and deepest desires. However, one needs to actualize them. Speech is the best tool for this; it impacts one's thoughts and perception. Prayer, is therefore very important. It enables the most exalted emotions to come out. Prayer is in a form that is aligned to the feelings of the heart, whose way of listening is different from the way of listening of the mind. (SK 1:33)

Emotional Prayers versus Intellectual Prayers

Rabbi Chanina Ben Dosa went to study from Rabbi Yochanan Ben Zakai. During that time, Rabbi Yochanan Ben Zakai's son became sick. Rabbi Yochanan Ben Zakai said to his student: "Chanina, pray for mercy for my son and he will be healed. Chanina placed his head between his knees and prayed for mercy and Rabbi Yochanan Ben Zakai's son was healed. Rabbi Yochanan Ben Zakai said to his student: "If I would have put my head between my knees all day long, God would not have answered my prayers." Rabbi Yochanan Ben Zakai's wife said "But is Chanina really greater than you!?" Rabbi Yochanan Ben Zakai said "No. However, he is similar to a servant before a king while I am similar to an officer before the king." (Berachot 34b).

There is a type of person who journeys toward God through an intellectual spiritual path of service. On the other hand, there is another type of person whose spiritual path of service is more dependent on the goodness of emotions. Both paths are included in a good heart: the good and true intellect that guides the forces of the soul as well as the good emotions that guides a person. One who focuses on the spiritual service of intellect, their main goal is true and pure enlightenment. As a result, their prayers do not add perfection to their spiritual path.

On the other hand, a person who chooses the pathway of emotions, their service will be elevated through the act of prayer and its fulfilment. For this reason, this second person's prayers are more accepted. "God's eyes are focused on the ones who fear Him" (Tehilim 33:18). Even though the service of intellect is higher than emotions, nonetheless the prayer of one who places their main focus on purifying their emotions will be more effective... Therefore, a person who serves God through the service of emotions "is similar to a servant before a king." While a person who serves God through the service of the intellect is "similar to an officer before the king." (EA Berachot 1, p. 166)

One Idea Affects Different People in Different Ways

All the foundations of faith depend on the combination of thoughts; how one element of one's mind affects another. In general, so much has to do with the differences between people's personality, and even more so, their generational differences.

On the one hand, sometimes we will find that the logic of a specific idea is able to build an entire spiritual world of ethics and holy feelings for one type of person. On the other hand, this very same idea will have no effect on building the spiritual world of another person. In fact, even this idea we are speaking about, for one person it will damage them, whereas for another person it will transform them. (SK 1:11)

Appears and then Disappears

A person can attain an intellectual insight at all times, but an emotional insight appears only for a moment and then disappears. (KYK 1, Reshimot M'London 13)

Combining Intellect and Emotions

The Unification of Intellect and Emotions

It is impossible for a person to live with only intellect or only emotions. There must always be a combination. Sometimes a person desires to be a master of intellect and break past one's own emotional capabilities. This damages one's emotional sensitivities and causes great flaws and imperfections. On the other hand, it is clear that if a person only focuses on emotions, this will cause one to fall into the depths of foolishness. Doing this will bring much weakness and mistake. Only through the characteristic of balance, which unifies the intellect and emotions, will a person reach ultimate freedom. To be sure, one must also awaken the characteristic of practical actions as well as a social ethical sensitivity. (SK 1:271)

Intellectual Spirituality versus Emotional Spirituality

There are some *Tzadikim* whose spiritual growth comes about through the path of intellect. They are filled with wisdom and logic, and cannot bear the simplistic spirituality of pure emotions, which do not have clear intellectual foundations. And there are *Tzadikim* who are the opposite, whose entire personality is focused on spiritual growth through simple and pure emotions, and cannot bear any form of intellectual investigation. Each one of these *Tzadikim* have many followers who fit their type of personality, and these followers need to go down their matching paths of spirituality.

People who are immersed in a spirituality of the intellect are able to recognize the value of the spirituality of emotions, even though they understand that for their unique personalities it is not sufficient. This is because the mind is more expansive than the emotions. Nevertheless, they will not insult emotions. However, people who are only connected to emotions do not recognize the value of spiritual growth that comes through intellect. It seems to them that this path of intellect is full of hazards and damages. These emotional people will warn others with a passionate heart and great intensity that no person should come close to these intellectual paths. And the truth is, such words are correct when applied to those whose simple and pure emotions are sufficient for them in their spiritual growth. (KYK 2, Pinkas 5:146)

The Different Ways of Intellect and Emotions

Emotions are faster than the intellect. The emotions comprehend the depth of the word "God" even before it has solved all the hidden mysteries contained inside this concept. In stark contrast, the intellect needs to go through stages of hard work and development. Without in-depth study, the intellect will not understand anything.

Sometimes one tries to swap the emotions and the intellect. A person desires to use their intellect without going through hard work and development. One tries to use the intellect in the same way the emotions work – of simply being able to comprehend an idea immediately. As a consequence, one's world becomes darkened, and much confusion will develop in one's spiritual world. A person will become continually tangled. This will become a stumbling block for one's spiritual path. "One with a wise heart knows the proper time and way" (Kohelet 8:5). At times one needs to fully enter into the kingdom of emotions in order to experience its pleasures. At other times one needs to enter into the world of intellect in order to work and develop. Only then will divine knowledge enter one's heart in the best possible way. (SK 1:145)

5

Faith

"Sometimes a person desires to be simple in their relationship to serving God. However, since they have the ability to comprehend things on a deeper level, their mind does not give them rest." (KYK 1, Pinkas Rishon L' Yaffo 48)

RAV KOOK BELIEVED THAT TOO OFTEN A PERSON TRIES TO KEEP THE same type of simple faith that they had when they were a child even when they have grown up into a sophisticated adult. Regarding all matters of life their mind has developed and matured, only in matters of faith they have stayed undeveloped. In a lot of Rav Kook's writings, he discusses how this refusal to "grow up" in matters of faith causes immense damage to a person's life and has the potential to cause them to lose faith altogether. Just as a person must learn to grow older and mature in the way they think about life, so too a person must mature and develop their faith.

On the other hand, there are other parts of Rav Kook's writings where he says that there is something incredibly important and eternally valuable about the simple and pure faith one has as a child. *Emunah Peshuta*/simple faith is the dimension of a person that is able to be totally dedicated to God, a person or a cause in an unconditional way. Precisely because it is not built on the reflective and logical part of the mind, simple faith cannot be broken apart due to some sophisticated argument; it is therefore able to stay loyal and trustworthy in the long term. For Rav Kook, even as a person matures and develops into an adult, one must strive to maintain and guard a dimension of simple faith in God.

In this chapter, Rav Kook will guide us toward finding the balance between developing a more sophisticated understanding of faith as well as respecting and maintaining a pure and simple connection to faith.

What is Faith?

Faith is Not a Thought or Emotion

Faith is not a thought or emotion. Rather, faith is the most essential revelation of the essence of the soul. Therefore, one needs to guide faith in its own unique way. When a person does not damage the natural ways of faith, one does not need any outside help to support it. Instead, faith is able to find everything on its own.

However, when the light of faith is weak, then the intellect and emotions come to clear a pathway for it. Yet even in such situations, faith still needs to understand its unique worth in order that the intellect and emotions do not enslave it. When the place of faith is strong and firm, then the intellect and emotions will succeed in clearing a pathway for faith; the mind and emotions will succeed in offering intellectual and ethical tools to remove any obstacles on the pathway of faith. (SK 1:219, MaR, p. 70)

Only Through Faith Do We Encounter God

One must know that it is not possible to encounter God through any form of intellect; not through any form of emotion; and it goes without saying, not through any form of physical sense. Rather, it is only possible to encounter God through faith itself.

Prayer is faith. Fear and love of God are also expressions of faith.

However, that which people call "the sense of faith," "a feeling of faith," and certainly if we say "the science of faith," and "the intellect of faith," these are all just borrowed names. In truth, the essence of faith is neither one of them. Rather, faith is something beyond; something that does not have the imperfections of these words. Faith is something that includes the essential qualities of all these terms, yet in a higher, more holistic and unified way. (SK 1:220, MaR, p. 70)

Three Types of Faith

There is a type of faith that comes about as a result of the world, a natural vision of faith. Then there is a type of faith that comes about as a result of Torah and faith in traditional miracles. And finally, there is a type of faith that comes about from the inner depths of the soul, from an inner sense of faith. These are three great lights.

Each type has its own special conditions and tasks they seek. Sometimes they combine together their different strengths. However, at other times one spirit comes in full force and attempts to conquer the entire heart and all ways of life. During such a situation, a person needs to know how to behave toward the other spirits. At such a moment, the other spirits are in a state of spiritual slumber. When the right time comes, they will ascend to a higher source, to change places and add extra blessings – a renewal of the spirit. (SK 7:108, MaR, p. 70)

The Ability to Comprehend

Sometimes a person desires to be simple in their relationship to serving God. However, since they have the ability to comprehend things on a deeper level, their mind does not give them rest. This is in order that one will put in the effort to uncover pearls that will bring a great benefit to the world. This is a spiritual form of *Yesurim Shel Ahava*/sufferings of love. (KYK 1, Pinkas Rishon L' Yaffo 48)

Continuous Work of Purification

A person's internal perception of God needs a lot of purification. In general, the act of purification is the continuous work of a person. And the more a person ascends from level to level the more it betters oneself and the entire world. (KYK 1, Pinkas Rishon L'Yaffo 103)

The Danger of False Religious Beliefs

Sometimes false beliefs about the fear of heaven can be more damaging than any other false belief in the world. (KYK 2, Pinkas 5:98, MiR, *Yirah* 11)

What Does It Mean to Have Great Faith?

Great faith is not dependent on the number of things one believes. A fool believes every matter. Instead, the foundation of faith is developing a deep sensitivity to faith and the expansion of this feeling upon everything. One becomes aware that the foundation of everything is divine. (SK 6:62)

Thinking About God versus Living God

The need to think about God is a low level of spirituality that humanity needs like a medicine. Atheism is a negative preparation required in order to rise up to a spiritual level where there will be no need to think about God.[11] Instead, life itself will be the light of God. (KYK 2, Pinkas 5:104)

Knowing About God

When one knows about God, even though one does not know about anything, one knows about everything. And when one knows about everything but does not know about God, then one knows about nothing. (SK 1:798)

You Cannot Define the Soul of Judaism

While it may be possible to define Judaism based on its external elements; nevertheless, those who try to define Judaism's soul and its spiritual content are mistaken. The soul of Judaism includes everything; all revealed and hidden spiritual desires are included inside of Judaism just as everything is included in the infinite Divine. (SK 1:273)

---

11. One of the central themes of Rav Kook's writings is to encourage his students not to feel threatened by the questions and doubts of atheists and secular people. Often there is truth in their arguments even if they haven't reached the ultimate understanding. In many pieces, Rav Kook says that if a person trains themselves to listen to the sincere questions and criticisms people have of religion, one's own faith in God may in fact become enhanced and developed into something even more profound. See Orot, Zeronim 5. In this book, Rav Kook returns to this theme a number of times. See p. 80, p. 140, pp. 207–208.

Purifying Negative Attitudes of God

People who discover inside of their hearts a desire for closeness to God are being called upon to take pleasure in God and expand the divine light in the world. They must purify attitudes and feelings regarding the understanding of the divine. Through the inherent spiritual connection between all souls, such people purify and elevate the entire world as a result of their own purification and elevation.

Do not let any obstacle come between you and this courageous thought – not those of small faith who come with blindness that grows even greater due to the materialistic body and its illusory lusts. Such people are so consumed by these material lusts that they think this is the essence of reality and life.

However, *Tzadikim*/Righteous People who stand in the presence of God always lift themselves up beyond the conventional thinking of society. Such *Tzadikim* stand above all groups and sects. Their hearts are not trapped in any specific group. Even groups that they are connected to as a result of their ancestral and historical connection do not close them off from the most expansive spiritual life, the light of God, which branches out beyond all limitations. These *Tzadikim* love all types of people and the compassion of God fills their heart. (YKY 1, Eighty-One Pinkasot from Yaffo, 18)

Faith Motivated by Fear

Fear of Sin

A person needs to fear sin, specifically in relation to themselves. One should be afraid of sinning, whether in something heavy or in something light. Included in this principle is anyone within a person's surroundings that they have the ability to prevent from sinning. This too is a part of one's responsibility.

However, all the sins of the world that are outside of a person's surroundings, one should always know that "just as the praise of

God comes out of the *Tzadikm*, it also comes from wicked people. Indeed, just as praise comes out of Gan Eden, it also come out
of hell" (a paraphrase of Shemot Rabbah 7, 4). (SK 3:115, MiR,
"Yirah" 16)

When the Soul is Sick

Teaching people to serve God based on a fear of punishment is
only necessary in a situation where the intellect knows that something is correct, yet the soul is presently sick. In a healthy situation
however, there is no need to teach a fear of punishment. In fact, in
situations where there is no need for the defensive mechanism of
teaching a fear of punishment, using it will only damage a person.

To be sure, when it comes to *Mitzvot Shimiot/mitzvot* that are
difficult to comprehend, teaching a fear of punishment may sometimes be necessary. Nonetheless, we must continuously use our
minds to research and teach the explanations of *mitzvot* – both
their general principles and specific details – in order that *Mitzvot Shimiot/mitzvot* that are difficult to comprehend will eventually
become understandable just like *Mitzvot Sichliot/mitzvot* that are
easier to understand. As a consequence of doing this, the path of
intellectual love will expand over the entire Torah. We will then no
longer need to emphasize the teachings of the fear of punishment,
which are nothing but an external motivation. Instead, we will be
able to focus on love and divine awe. (KYK 1, Rishon Le'Yaffo 70)

Excessive Fear

Excessive fear is the worst type of sickness. A person needs to liberate themselves from this type of fear just as much as one must liberate oneself from sadness, arrogance, anger and emptiness. Atheism
has come to the world to dilute the excessive fear that immature
faith causes. When atheism accomplishes its task then it actually
increases the strength of faith. (KYK 2, Pinkas 4:91)

Fear that is Actually Inner Strength

Anxiety is a bad form of fear, and its influence destroys the wealth of wisdom contained in authentic fear of heaven. Therefore, one must be educated based on a philosophy of inner strength and courage. Only then will a person be able to receive a type of fear that is actually inner strength. (KYK 2, Pinkas 5:101)

Removing Weakness Within One's Soul

A person needs to overcome elements of weakness within their soul. Even if such weakness comes from a dimension of holiness and fear of heaven, nonetheless it is still a negative trait and damages all the talents and virtues of holiness. A person needs to purify their fear of heaven and fear of sin so that there will be no left-over elements of weakness. "God gives strength to His people" (Tehilim 29:11). (SK 8:92)

The Land of Israel is More Suited to Love

The land of Israel has a unique potential to create a love of God. Therefore, the right guidance for the Jewish people living in its land needs to be through ways of love, and not through fear of divine punishment, which anyway shouldn't be used regularly.

Now, since the power of loving God… is more available in the land of Israel, teaching religion through a fear of divine punishment will not be successful. In fact, it will only awaken feelings of opposition from many different viewpoints. Instead, the main path that is fitting to elevate the Jewish people in the land of Israel is the expansion of morality, which is sourced in a love of God, His people and His land. (KYK 1, Rishon Le'Yaffo 61)

True Self-Respect

Sometimes a person with a very high and spiritual soul becomes immersed in small matters – even matters that are connected with the fear of heaven. Yet as a result of being involved in such small matters, it causes them to descend from their spiritual level. Such a person feels bothered and pained by negative character traits. This will continue until they return to their spiritual level of greatness. In fact, precisely when they do this, they are filled with humility. Such a person recognizes the great worth of true self-respect. By doing this, they are able to abandon all illusionary honor. (YKY 1, Eighty-One Pinkasot from Yaffo, 30)

Fear of Punishment is like a Seed that Needs to Grow

There is both a quantitative and qualitative difference between serving God due to a fear of punishment and serving God due to a higher awe and love of God. When it comes to a quantitative difference, one only needs to complete it and fill in what is missing. However, when it comes to the qualitative difference, a person needs to not only fill in the missing parts, but to actually grow, purify and build new buildings inside of one's internal perception.

In this sense, the sprouts of a fear of punishment are similar to garden seeds that cannot be eaten. Such seeds are planted in a small and narrow garden bed, where they are unable to reach their full potential. However, when these seeds finish their first stage of growth and are able to be given to cattle, they are uprooted and planted in a large and spacious garden. In such a place, these seeds will be able to reach their full potential of being healthy food for the enjoyment of human beings. (KYK 1, Pinkas Rishon L'Yaffo 39)

Not Insulting the Lesser Virtue

It is true that a person needs to strive toward reaching higher levels of virtue. However, when a virtue is good, one should not insult the lesser virtue that is nonetheless still good. Instead, a person should place their main focus on reaching the highest virtue that one can achieve. While at the same time, the lesser virtue will also remain a part of them....

However, when one assumes that in order to hold on to a greater virtue, a person must let go of the smaller and lower virtue, then it is very possible that it will damage the higher virtue as well. Such a person will be torn and stuck between these two different virtues.

This principle often takes place in spiritual self-development. For example, when trying to acquire the smaller level of serving God due to a fear of punishment versus serving God due to the higher level of awe and love of God. (KYK 1, Pinkas Rishon L'Yaffo 37)

The Importance of Simple Faith

Simple Faith
The highest spiritual virtues, whether in thought, emotion, or action, need to be connected to *Emunah Peshuta*/simple faith. This type of faith already exists in the heart of the youth. In its inner essence, this faith is greater than anything that can be learned and studied. (MiR, "Emunah" 23)

Simplicity
The essence of spirituality, at its highest and most transformative level, is reached through simple faith. This simplicity must be connected to the depths of one's soul, with a true inner passion, and through dedicating oneself to many practical deeds of *Chassidut* (going above the letter of the law) as well as following even the smallest details of *mitzvot*.

To be sure, the enlightened intellect is certainly the crownpiece of all of these traits. Nonetheless, it is not the main element of inner perfection and transformation. Instead, the main thing that elevates a person's willpower is through connecting oneself to divine simplicity. This simplicity is also connected to *Kannaut Hashem*/a zealousness for God.

This inner spiritual connection transforms a person into a *BaAl Mofet*/master of wonders, who is able to do wonderous things with their prayers. Such a person has the ability to channel the power of life from the Source of life through directing their desires and thoughts. Such a person is like a "servant before a king" (Berachot 34b), "a faithful servant" (from the Shabbat *Shacharit Amida* prayer). "And God carries out the words of His servant" (Yeshayahu 44:26). (YKY 1, Eighty-One Pinkasot from Yaffo, 35)

Respecting Simplicity

A person should always respect the dimension of simplicity inside of oneself. This is a dimension where the sophisticated intellect has not yet entered into, and where the simplicity of the soul can follow its natural movements. Indeed, it is precisely the dimension of simplicity where the divine light penetrates without any intellectual limit and restriction. At the same time, simplicity can always become more purified with the addition of the light of Torah and wisdom.

In addition, a person should respect the natural simplicity within the world in general, as well as the simple feelings of the masses. A person should learn to receive from the masses many good and righteous traits. In fact, as a result of this brotherly connection, this inner purity will spread within the structure of the masses. There will be an increased blessing in the world. (SK 5:226)

The Higher the Truth, the Simpler It Is

The higher the truth, the simpler it is, and the more essential it is for everyone. The closed-mindedness of a person is responsible for trying to analyze truth, break it up into separate pieces, and make it smaller. One is afraid of the greatness of truth. A person assumes that by making truth smaller, it will become more popular and relevant to everyone.

However, precisely by doing this, one causes truth to become a burden, and blocks people from what they need most of all. The ultimate truth, the divine truth, is something that all people demand. There is a desire for all of the truth, in its higher light, with its fullest form. For this reason, truth is relevant to all – all people, all creations, and all beings.

While science stands at the center, after all its great effort in trying to explain truth, of trying to make it smaller and relevant to the masses – it now needs to return to its greatness and purity. (SK 5:15, OK 1, p. 4)

How Do We Know?

Concerning the greatest spiritual truths, it is impossible to ask "How do we know that they are true?" When we discover inside the soul a higher spirit, a perfectly ordered treasure of wisdom, this is the greatest type of proof. All knowledge that comes about through research and study are nothing but a tool to reach this higher wisdom, that which the soul already knows in its inner depths. The greatest tools to reach this higher wisdom is developing a connection to the divine as well as the inner logic of mysticism. (SK 2:26, OK 1, p. 209)

Simple and Sophisticated People Influence Each Other

Natural spirituality, in its strongest purity, is buried in the depths of the natural and simple heart. The more that simplicity is guarded and not allowed to be abstracted for research and the toil of academia, the more it imprints itself into the depths of a person's essence. At the same time, this causes a lack of development.

When the sophisticated people connect themselves with natural people, they receive strength from each other. The students give the purest and most natural strength, and the sophisticated people give the illumination of learning. Together, with the light of wisdom, the students get back their pure and natural strength. However, now, it contains the added blessing that the sophisticated people have poured onto them from their spirit. This principle is true in all the dimensions of receiving and giving. (SK 5:224)

Positive Images of God

Negative theology of God is closer to the truth since our perception of God is always lacking.[12] Nonetheless, negative theology also distances a person from the living perception of the exalted and holy living God. Therefore, we are in need of positive images, which are drawn from the source of God's true reality. Such images are rooted in the knowledge that God alone created our soul and our thoughts are from Him. (KYK 1, Pinkas Rishon L'Yaffo 82)

Faith is Greater than Intellect

Inner faith is so much greater than the intellect that whoever doesn't have a truly free mind will assume that faith is the opposite of intellect. (MiR, "Emunah" 33)

Faith Means Anything is Possible

With the greatness of faith, a person can comprehend everything. Indeed, when it comes to the higher realms, which are above all names and logic, there are no obstacles and all matters are possible. In such a dimension, the secret of faith exists. "God is greater than all other gods" (a paraphrase of Tehilim 95:3). In such a place, a higher freedom and liberty exists that transcends any positive type of affirmation. In fact, any form of limitation comes about only in a place where narrow intellect and limited faith exists. However, in the place of a higher wisdom, one is able to delight in the freest type of faith. Heavens above all clouds, "rejoicing always in God's

---

12. When Rav Kook says "Negative Theology," he is referring to a theological attitude that says one should approach the knowledge of God by negating any positive/human/emotional statements about God. This approach encourages a person to be humble and accept that God is beyond all language and concept. In contrast, "Positive Theology" refers to a theological attitude that says one can approach the knowledge of God through describing and affirming positive/human/emotional statements about God's perfection. This approach encourages a personal connection with a living God.

presence, rejoicing in God's whole world and delighting in human-kind" (Mishlei 8:30–31). (SK 6:50)

The Foundation of Trust and Happiness

The foundation of trust and happiness comes from the consciousness that one should only desire what God desires – this includes matters for oneself. The more a person makes this consciousness clear in one's heart and aligns one's life to this higher mindset, the more one will be filled with happiness and courage. (KYK 1, Pinkas Rishon L'Yaffo 34)

The Source of Sadness

All sadness in the world comes about because a person does not truly desire what God desires. (KYK 1, Pinkas Rishon L'Yaffo 101)

Life Without Faith in God

A philosophy of life without faith in God lacks all the light of life. A person's inner soulful longing dries up on its own due to a naked-ness and lack of nourishment. The animalistic trait awakens and strengthens with rage. It eventually grows even stronger as a result of evil and polluted world beliefs. (YKY 1, Eighty-One Pinkasot from Yaffo, 16)

6

The *Tzadik* Within

"A person knows inside of one's soul if one is a Tzadik Gammur/great righteous person." (YKY 1, Eighty-One Pinkasot from Yaffo, 41)

The term *Tzadik* is usually translated as a Righteous Person or Saint. A *Tzadik* is someone who has reached the peak of spiritual and ethical enlightenment. However, in many of Rav Kook's writings, the term *Tzadik* does not refer to a person who has reached absolute perfection, but rather one who has a deep passion for growth. As is written in Mishlei, "A Tzadik falls seven times and rises up" (24:16). At times a Tzadik will experience moments of anger, frustration, and sadness. Nonetheless, at the end of the day, this is rooted in their desire for a higher perfection that they never stop pursuing.

Sometimes a *Tzadik* will become confused and experience great anger toward the world. This is a result of their immense desire for higher perfection. (SK 3:170)

In this chapter, Rav Kook will redefine what it means to be a *Tzadik* as well as encourage his readers to identify with and embody this spiritual and ethical path of living. There is indeed a *"Tzadik* Within" each individual waiting to be uncovered. For Rav Kook, the word *"Tzadik"* should not be seen as some lofty and unreachable title, but rather used as an archetype and ideal way of living that each individual can and should aspire toward.

The *"Tzadik* Within" is a measuring stick with which to evaluate oneself, straighten out the crooked, and challenge a person to live up to their divine potential. In Rav Kook's eyes, having a description of how the *"Tzadik* Within" thinks, feels, and acts in moments of ups and downs, successes and struggles, is an extremely important tool for spiritual and ethical transformation.[13]

Connecting Oneself to a *Tzadik*

The Importance of Telling Stories of *Tzadikim*

There is great value in telling the stories of the *Tzadikim* of the Jewish people. It is important to increase the impact of this incredible vision, of the life of spiritual people who elevate themselves above the superficial desires of life. Such people live totally inside of the consciousness of holiness and purity, righteousness and honesty. Their light shines and penetrates into each moment little by little, depending on the person's ability to receive it and the conditions of the current situation. (EY, p.22)

The Difficulty of Describing the Image of a *Tzadik*

It is certainly a difficult task to describe the inner image of a great soul. This is because we can only describe it based on the external details that we have – the behavior, customs, conversations, writings, and moments of the spirit. These are only small and individual details from the great light of this elevated soul.

... Nevertheless, despite the lack of details, we are not absolved of trying to describe their spiritual light filled with illumination and precious glow. The soul that appeared in the world for a certain number of years was like a beautiful stone for many people's hearts. (EY, p. 24)

The Combination of Natural Gifts and Hard Work

Geunot/Spiritual and Intellectual Greatness comes about through the continuous combination of receiving a gift and working hard.

---

13. For a more extensive discussion of how Rav Kook uses the term "*Tzadik*" in his writings, see Dov Schwartz's book *The religious genius in Rabbi Kook's thought: National "Saint"?* p. 29. "It is noteworthy that Rabbi Kook himself did not present the *Tzadik* as a homogeneous figure. At times he distinguished between different types of *Tzadikim*, and left the reader to decide to which category he himself belonged. The discussions about the perfect and ideal person are an example for the need of interactive reading to interpret Rav Kook's words."

This is true whether we are referring to the spiritual greatness of the mind or the spiritual greatness of ethics. Both of these come about only when a person combines the following two things. On the one hand, the gifts they received from God of having a special soul that includes various good traits and certain natural genes. On the other hand, the orientation of consistent dedication as well as accepting upon oneself this workload from a motivation of love. This workload includes developing one's talents and actualizing one's hidden potential.

To be sure, we sometimes find *Geonim*/spiritually and intellectually great people who achieved what they achieved entirely through hard work and incredible dedication and discipline. Any person with a discerning eye will recognize the difference between natural greatness and developed greatness. This can be compared to the difference between nature and human creation.

Yet the truth is that even the wonderous ability to be disciplined and love hard work in order to reach lofty goals is also a natural trait of greatness – especially when it is disproportionately strong. Therefore, at the end of the day, the true source of *Geonut*/spiritual and intellectual greatness is a natural treasure within creation that a person either chooses to strengthen or weaken. (EY, p.23)

Two Benefits to Studying Stories About Great People

There are two main benefits to studying the life of a *Geon*/spiritually great person: a practical benefit and a spiritual benefit. The practical benefit is connected to the principle: "Jealousy of wise people increases wisdom" (Bava Batra 21a). When the reader sees the spiritual glory and inner beauty that this person has achieved, this will awaken within oneself an inner desire to try to follow in their ways. And even if the reader does not succeed in imitating this great person completely, nonetheless it is not possible that the reader will not be moved even in a small way from their current place to a more elevated place. Such a person will be inspired to choose a life of righteousness and work toward attaining valuable spiritual goals, just as this great person dedicated their life toward.

The practical benefits come about through describing some of this great person's behavior. For example, through telling stories about the unique ways they worked hard, descriptions of the obstacles that stood in the way of developing their greatness; and lastly, how they battled these obstacles and overcame them. (EY, p.23)

One Soul Gives Light to Others
One healthy soul is able to give light, life, and strength to all the souls that are connected to him. This is the spiritual greatness of being connected to *Talmidei Chachamim*/Torah Sages. (KYK 2, Pinkas 5:42)

Great Souls
It is possible to spend time with another person, and as a result, the negative parts of one's soul become pure. A person benefits as a result of the other person's great spiritual strength. This other person helps to transform one's negative drives into a positive force. This is one of the explanations of the mitzvah of *Dveikut B'Talmidei Chachamim*/connecting oneself to Torah Sages. To be sure, this is only referring to the act of connecting oneself to the greatest and highest quality souls. (KYK 2, Pinkas 4:98)

The Ups and Downs of a *Tzadik*

Experiencing all the Good and Bad
The souls of the greatest *Tzadikim* contain everything – all of the good and all of the bad in the world. These people experience the sufferings of everyone, but they also experience pleasure from everyone. They transform all of the bad in the world to good. When they give meaning to their own sufferings, they give meaning to the world's suffering. The *Tzadik's* soul is the root of many souls. The *Tzadik* is their foundation. (SK 1:210, OK 3, p. 153)

An Up-Down Spiritual Perspective

There are *Tzadikim* whose higher spiritual vision prevents them from being able to contemplate practical matters in an efficient way. Such people need to perceive the world in the direction of up-down. In contrast, most people need to push themselves to perceive matters of spiritual wisdom in the direction of down-up; from practical matters to spiritual matters. Such *Tzadikim* are the rare *Bnei Aliya*/spiritually exalted, who perceive the general home of the Jewish people and nation from a higher perception. (SK 2:300)

The Need for Constant Spiritual Connection

A *Tzadik* needs constant spiritual connection in all of their movements and thoughts. This does not exhaust them; just the opposite, being average exhausts a true *Tzadik*. (KYK 2, Pinkas 5:48)

Making Mistakes Does Not Change Your Essence

One who has a very high soul is a *Tzadik* in their essence. Even if this person makes many mistakes, this does not change their essence, and they must return to their foundation. This is true especially when their mistakes do not come from their pure soul, but instead because of the mistakes of humility and a lack of faith in their great spiritual worth. Mistakes in humility sometimes causes both arrogance and low self-esteem. However, at the end of the day, they will merit everything. "The righteous falls seven times and rises again" (Mishlei 24:16). (KYK 2, Pinkas 5:49)

A Great Fall

Sometimes a *Tzadik* will experience a great fall from their normal level. This is in order to help them realize that they do not have anything to fear. "God is always their stronghold" (a paraphrase of Tehilim 59:10). (SK 2:295)

Do Not Assume You Are Flawed

Sometimes when the soul grows spiritually, it feels sick due to a mixture of dirt contained in matters of holiness – in prayer and in the interpretations of the Torah. When a true *Tzadik* encounters such feelings of sickness, one does not assume that the flaw is in the holiness of one's soul. Instead, the *Tzadik* cleanses and transforms the mixture of dirt contained in these matters of holiness. Eventually, the *Tzadik* transforms everything to the purity of heaven. (KYK 2, Pinkas 5:124)

Cannot Focus on Books and Words

Sometimes a *Tzadik* cannot study in the normal style of learning because their thoughts ascend to a more spiritual Torah that is not expressed in any letter or vowel. (KYK 2, Pinkas 5:132)

Unable to Live on a Lower Spiritual Level

There is a type of *Tzadik* who is able to live on a low level of spiritual connection. At such moments, one is in a consciousness of sleep; one is similar to most people on the outside. The insights that reveal themselves to such a person are also on a lower level of spirituality. This type of *Tzadik* lives in a state of restricted spirituality. Nonetheless, their spirit is still strong since they have confidence that it will not be long before the spiritual sun within them will illuminate in all of its glory.

However, there is another type of *Tzadik* who is unable to compromise and adapt to a lower level of spirituality. They are similar to a fish in the ocean who is unable to live anywhere but the water; the great ocean is their place of freedom and paradise. When this great spiritual level disappears from such a person, they feel a great pain and are unable to find inner peace. This will continue until God sees their suffering and revives their spirit; they will go from a deep darkness to a great light. Such a *Tzadik* will begin to sense spirituality in their life in a far greater way. This new insight will repay them for the time spent asleep. "Instead of your shame, you will receive a double portion" (Yeshayahu 61:7). And their honor will be elevated "in the light of the king's face is life" (Mishlei 16:15). (SK 8:150)

Anger is Not Your True Self

The *Tzadik* who is good in their essence, their words and thoughts will only have a good influence. And even if sometimes they are filled with great anger, it will not have a bad influence, since the bad is not their true desire. (KYK 2, Pinkas 5:139)

Anger Rooted in a Higher Perfection

Sometimes a *Tzadik* will become confused and experience great anger toward the world. This is a result of their immense desire for higher perfection and to "dwell within the body of the king"[14] with ultimate perfection. At such moments, angry and judgmental words may come out of the *Tzadik's* mouth – both toward individuals and the masses. Nonetheless, such matters do not come from the *Tzadik's* heart; and they should be considered love wounds. The heart of a *Tzadik* is filled with a great love for all creatures: the righteous and the wicked, Jews and non-Jews, and even toward all animals. This is true both individually and communally. Indeed, the *Tzadik* judges all of them favorably.

Sometimes a person understands that their main personality trait is kindness, generosity and love. Nonetheless, as a result of certain experiences of suffering and pain, their lips may express angry and judgmental words. Such a person needs to calm their mind and return in *teshuva* for every word and thought that was not in line; for anything that was said not according to the true perfection of good traits. A person should not allow one's heart to fall into despair. Regarding this it is said "Blessed is the person who God does not count their sin against them; and whose spirit is found no deceit" (Tehilim 32:2).

---

14. A well-known kabbalistic phrase.

In general, such moments of anger increase after a great light has passed through their soul. Yet an even greater and more penetrating love appears. Then, comes an inner demand to pray for the generation and all of its needs – specifically for the wicked to do *teshuva*. This all takes place in order for the world to be repaired according to the divine ideal. This is the crown of all desires. It is what a heart filled with wisdom and clear human honesty continually and truly yearns for. "The desires of *Tzadikim* are only good" (Mishlei 11:23). (SK 3:170)

The Benefits and Challenges of Being a *Tzadik*

There are *Tzadikim* who are distant from sin. They cannot imagine the true disgust of sin in the same way that *Beinomin*/average people can. These average people are closer to sin and need a greater defense against it. While it is true that the *Tzadik's* distance from sin causes them to have less awareness of the repulsive nature of the sinner. Nonetheless, it also causes the *Tzadik* to be more connected to the trait of kindness and the desire to forgive. It helps the *Tzadik* give courage to people who have given up on themselves, as well as open up the gates of *Teshuva*/growth. (SK 3:342)

Not Falling into Despair

The true *Tzadik* does not fall into despair because of anything. It may so happen that in the *Tzadik's* mind, they fall into despair due to enormous sins, so much so that they have lost all hope. Yet even there, the *Tzadik* will search for the light of God and find it. To be sure, this lack of giving into despair does not mean that they stubbornly oppose the feeling of *Teshuva*/growth. Indeed, such a feeling is planted in the nature of a person in order to purify them from all sins. Rather, this person continues to strive forward to an even more expansive pathway of *Teshuva*.

And even when a person discovers in one's soul that they are surrounded by negative actions, beliefs and traits, they should not be overwhelmed. Such a person should find courage in God that

He will save them from all suffering – whether spiritual or physical suffering. And even though one has immersed oneself in many materialistic matters as well as various fights and disagreements between people, one will discover that they are still ready with all their heart to repair their mistakes, and to return to a life of divine and mindful connection. (YKY 1, Eighty-One Pinkasot from Yaffo, 15)

The Unconditional Positive Attitude of a *Tzadik*

The Root Good Within Everything
The true *Tzadik* does not see any bad in the world; one finds the good root within everything. Just as the *Tzadik* sees a good quality within all creatures, so too, one finds a good quality within all ideas and opinions in the world. The *Tzadik* elevates these ideas from their lowliness and cleanses them from their impurity. (KYK 2, Pinkas 5:130)

The Good Inside Oneself and Inside the World
The main spiritual work of a *Tzadik* is to truly love the inner parts of one's own soul, as well as to uncover the righteous qualities of the entire world. (KYK 2, Pinkas 5:142)

Giving Your Happiness to the World
The *Tzadik* desires to bring happiness to the entire world, to all of existence. One does this by elevating their own inner world, through elevating themselves. This is the joy of God. "God rejoices in His creations" (Tehilim 104:31). (SK 2:113)

Filled with Love
The greatest *Tzadikim* are filled with love. There is no specific thing that can fill their enormous love, since all matters in the world are small compared to their great feeling of love. The only thing that

can fill their love is the divine encounter. Therefore, they love all things in the world, since everything is a manifestation of the divine light. (SK 1:417, OK 4, p. 393)

A Consciousness of Caring for the World

The true *Tzadik* is always thinking about bettering the entire world. One does not let go of this general thought due to any obstacle in the world. The *Tzadik* is always solving problems that are connected to this great thought. By working on finding solutions, one elevates existence to a very high level. (KYK 2, Pinkas 5:143)

I am a *Beinoni* but My Way is the Path of *Tzadikim*

A letter to the Ridvaz, Rabbi Yaakov David Wilovsky (renowned Talmudic commentator, author, educator, and Rosh Yeshiva in Tzfat), June 9, 1912

Due to my own imperfections, I do not deserve the name *Tzadik*. If only God would give me the ability to say with sincerity: "For example, I am a *Beinoni*/ordinary person" (Berachot 62b). Nonetheless, there is no doubt that with the help of God the way that I am trying to follow is the path of *Tzadikim*. Those who follow me and connect to me in the way they study Torah and serve God; those who follow me sincerely with a real faith in the sages, will eventually merit to see the light and truth within this righteous and firm path. (IR 2, p. 197)

Are You a *Tzadik* or a Rasha?

A person knows inside of their soul if they are a *Tzadik Gammur*/great righteous person. That is to say, one has a strong love of God that brings light to all of life – even if it is hidden inside of one's soul. In addition, one has a love of people and a strong tendency toward goodness and kindness that rests inside of oneself continuously.

If so, a person must not abandon this character trait and one's great spiritual desire due to any obstacle in the world. This is true even if a person perceives oneself as a *Rasha Gammur*/great evil person, a sinner, causer of other people to sin, a thief, and in general, full of sins. This principle applies whether one perceives oneself as a sinner *Bein Adam La'makom*/toward God or a sinner *Bein Adam La'chaveiro*/toward other people.

These are merely thorns that surround the higher rose, which is the holy essence of one's inner soul. The truth is that one's essence can never change; it will eventually overcome all obstacles. This person should be continuously involved in finding spiritual and practical ways of how to actualize this higher good. "He will not grow tired or weary" (Yeshayahu 40:28). This person will strengthen one's heart in God. (YKY 1, Eighty-One Pinkasot from Yaffo, 41)

7

Kabbalah and Mysticism

"When is it a good time to study Sitrei Torah, the spiritual and mystical parts of the Torah? When one feels an intense inner desire for closeness to God rising up and getting stronger." (OT 9.1)

RAV KOOK'S MAIN KABBALISTIC TEACHER WAS RAV SHLOMO Eliashav (the Bal HaLeshem), the author of the famous kabbalistic book *Leshem Shevo V'Achlama*. In addition, Rav Kook was heavily influenced by the great Kabbalist, the Arizal. Rav Kook once said of himself, "There is nothing in my thoughts and opinions that does not have its source in the writings of the Arizal" (Nefesh HaRaaya l'Shloshah b'Elul 1:46).

One of the most important insights Rav Kook had about studying Torah was that not all souls are alike when it comes to their spiritual nourishment. Some souls are hungry for Gemara and practical halacha, while others crave the inner wisdom of Kabbalah, Chassidut and Mysticism. There is no reason to argue about which type of Torah is more essential. Instead, God made each soul in a unique way and it is each person's responsibility to uncover a personal connection to studying Torah.

In many journal entries, Rav Kook wrote about how his soul is naturally drawn to the world of Kabbalah and Mysticism. As a result of his own passion, Rav Kook encouraged others who feel a similar spiritual hunger to set aside regular time to study the words of *Sitrei Torah*, the hidden dimensions of the Torah. "The main advice I usually give to my friends and others similar to me is that one must set regular times to learn the more spiritual books of the Torah" (IR 1, p. 339). In this chapter, Rav Kook will explain why some souls are more attracted to Kabbalah and Mysticism than other souls, as well as when and how to study these ancient mystical texts.

Who Should Study Mysticism and Kabbalah?

Torah that Transforms Your Soul

Each person needs to be immersed in their own personal matters, in whatever they are most suited. This is especially true regarding matters of study. In certain situations, it is difficult for a person to stay true to their heart's desire. Nonetheless, they must be courageous and not abandon that which transforms their soul. (OT 9.1)

Torah Study that Fits One's Soul

There is a type of person who notices that they are succeeding in the spiritual parts of the Torah, in the wisdom of truth. In contrast, they notice how difficult it is for them to study halacha in an in-depth way. For such a person, it is an accepted principle that it is one's inner obligation to set aside one's main time for Torah study that fits one's soul.

In a similar way, a person who notices that their study of *Sitrei Torah*, spiritual and mystical Torah, transforms them, raises up their soul, and draws them closer to holiness – in both an emotional and deep intellectual way. In contrast, they notice that these same beautiful fruits do not come about when they study the surface parts of the Torah. In fact, they notice how their regular Torah study does not succeed in uprooting the negative traits that they feel within their soul. If so, it is a clear proof that their *tikun* and spiritual transformation must come about through studying the illuminating parts of the inner Torah, the wisdom of truth.

In fact, a person may reach such a level of inner purity where even studying the surface layer of the Torah inspires them to these holy levels of spirituality. One is then able to expand themselves even greater until they are able to fulfill their spiritual mission of returning to experience the pleasures of studying the highest spiritual secrets. "To eat and be satisfied, to be dressed in elegant clothing"

(Yeshayahu 23:18). Everything will be done for the sake of God, with the purest of intentions. "God does not despise the struggles of the poor" (a paraphrase of Tehilim 22:25). (OT 10.3)

Do Not Be Intimidated by Others

One may find great people connected to the Torah, with fear of God and much wisdom, who are nonetheless not connected to *Sitrei Torah*, the spiritual and mystical parts of the Torah. Perhaps this is because of their great spiritual level; perhaps it is because they have a great amount of material to occupy their spirits in the treasures of the surface layers of the Torah.

Regardless, one should not fall into despair over this, due to the inner feeling, push, and yearning of one's soul for such spiritual secrets. Even if we decide that this inner desire is a result of one's lack of skills in surface layers of the Torah. What difference does this make? Ultimately, this is one's personal gift, and one should rejoice in one's portion. "God is close to all who call out to Him with truth and purity" (Tehilim 145:18). "God does not favor the rich over the poor" (Iyov 34:19). (OT 10:4)

Souls Attracted to *Nistar* versus *Niglah*

The content that distinguishes *Niglah*/practical wisdom from *Nistar*/spiritual wisdom, in both Torah as well as in all types of wisdom, is due to the different personalities within human beings.

A person who is open to *Niglah*/practical wisdom does not need any mystical vision in order to develop and perfect their personality. The sensitive and ethical nature of their soul develops on its own through the spiritual dimension found within practical wisdom. Regarding a Jew or a person immersed in Torah, the Jewish soul has the inner sensitivity and ability to develop and perfect oneself through absorbing various practical wisdoms. One is able to take these practical wisdoms and transform them into rich spiritual material.

At the core of the matter, we are forced to say that there is a certain type of natural spiritual richness found within *BaAlei HaNiglah*/people who are drawn to practical wisdom. They do not feel the need to immerse themselves in spiritual and lofty content. They already contain inside of themselves a dimension of spiritual material that nourishes them. In fact, sometimes it is precisely because such people are already nourished that they experience a sickening feeling when involved in *Nistar*/spiritual wisdom.

On the other hand, these same people often discover inside of themselves that they lack knowledge of practical details. As a result, their life becomes filled with many obstacles due to the lack of practical knowledge. This is part of what pushes them to focus more time involved in practical details.

This is in contrast to *BaAlei Nistar*/people who are drawn to spiritual wisdom. Such people feel that they are already sufficiently nourished in the dimension of practical wisdom; they feel as if the path of practicality is clear in front of them. Any problems regarding practical issues usually become solved without too much energy, often in the moment of action itself. However, these spiritual people feel a continuous need for hidden wisdom and mysterious matters of the spirit in order to develop and complete themselves. They feel a type of intense hunger and thirst for all hidden and enigmatic matters. Questions regarding spiritual meaning, things that exist in the highest and hidden dimensions, leave them no rest. They feel a pressure to be continuously immersed in solving such questions – in their various details and ways of understanding.

It is rare to find someone whose search for *Niglah*/practical wisdom and *Nistar* /spiritual wisdom are equally strong. Usually, there is a contradiction and opposition between the two. However, it may very well be that if a person was influenced by society and helped to see the great value gained by working toward both of these sides, then a spirit of "jealousy of wise people" (Bava Batra 21a) will come upon this person. Such a person will develop the desire to nourish oneself from both of these traits. Even though one will usually come across great obstacles in trying to accomplish this, one will eventually find the strength to overcome them as well.

These rare types of people are constantly busy with the heavy work related to this difficult wisdom. Yet at the end of the day, they bring so much blessing to the world. As a result of their hard work, they create a new world, "where heavens and earth kiss each other" (Bava Batra 74a). In fact, once they have actualized their complex vision, other people are able to benefit from it as well. It is almost as if a new type of stable soul has come into existence, something for future generations, something that is able to fuse together different and opposing worlds. This is a real revelation, a double force of creation. "Wisdom will cry aloud in the street" (Mishlei 1:20). "To reveal to you the secrets of wisdom, for true wisdom has two sides" (Iyov 11:6). "Write down the vision and explain it on the tablets" (Chavakuk 2:2). (SK 2:70, OK 1, pp. 36–37)

The Importance of Kabbalah and Mysticism for the World

A Thirst that Cannot Be Quenched by Limited Substance

When an individual and generation reach a point where a unique spiritual consciousness is being called upon to express itself, they will not be able to quench this thirst with any limited substance.... The secrets of the universe, the secrets of Torah, and the secrets of God, grow stronger and demand a response from the generation.

The stubbornness within people to search for spiritual satisfaction in the surface level of the Torah, weakens their strength, scatters their spirit, and brings their stormy spiritual desire to a place of emptiness and frustration. Eventually, the heart full of despair will turn around and search again for another path.

For this reason, the courageous of strength are being called upon. These are people for whom the divine light is their entire life's essence.

Now, even if they have fallen and broken due to great despair; even if they have fainted due to a lack of faith in themselves; even if they have become exhausted due to constant fighting against the masses – a person who walks with confidence toward the spirit... will never give up trying to repair; they will not give up their enthusiasm.

It is precisely this type of person who holds the flag to the secrets of Torah... to the salvation of the Jewish people and humanity, to the body and the soul... and to the old and the young.

If we speak, but silence takes a hold of us; if we try to articulate ourselves, but the concepts get stuck inside of us; if we feel that we simply don't have the strength to direct our speech and search for the right words; then we will not be intimidated by this and turn back from our fixed desire. A heavy mouth will not stop our strength and higher desire. The word of God has spoken and it will be revealed. To announce peace to those who fight amongst the nation. "'Creating praise on their lips. Peace, peace, to those far and near,' says God. 'And I will heal them'" (Yeshayahu 57:19). (SK 3:317, OK 1, pp. 5–6)

The Importance of Studying Spiritual Matters

When there is no one in the world who will study the highest spiritual values, then the light contained in such values disappears from people. Little by little, the thoughts and desires of human beings begin to descend into the depths of ignorance and evil. People find themselves sunk in the dirt of impurity, sins, and terrible crimes. They become addicted to barbaric lusts that rule over them and surround them like a wall.

Life becomes darkened and people's hearts become filled with bitterness and hatred. Each unique talent only causes more anger and friction between different people, families, social groups, and nations. However, when the great minds of society are focused on seeking as much divine light as possible, their souls are turned upward. It is through their own spiritual elevation that they draw down spirituality to the masses. The idealistic and spiritual desires within the masses strengthen even without them being conscious of it. *Ruach HaKodesh*/the Holy Spirit of calmness and peace expands and flows throughout the world. "The spirit of the King Mashiach" (a kabbalistic phrase used in the Zohar). (YKY 1, Eighty-One Pinkasot from Yaffo, 36)

Spiritual Explorers
There are explorers who yearn to discover new locations in the world in order to enrich the greater world with new sights. As a result, the world is able to enjoy reading about these new discoveries in a peaceful state and benefit greatly. In a similar way, there needs to be people – and they certainly do exist – who act as spiritual explorers. Such people will yearn to discover new sights in the intellectual world and then share their new discoveries with other people. The world will then be able to enjoy these new intellectual discoveries without difficulty and benefit greatly.

It is important that these spiritual explorers do not give up due to the difficulties of their journey and the physical and spiritual sadness that sometimes comes their way. Such people should learn a lesson from these physical explorers. (KYK 1, Pinkas Rishon L'Yaffo 52)

How Spirituality Influences the World
When it comes to the knowledge of the deepest spiritual secrets, the goal is not to publicize them to the world quantitatively, so that many people will know about them. This is something that is impossible. In fact, even if the masses did know about these secrets in their outside form, they would not know about their inner content. This would do more harm than good. Instead, spiritual secrets need to be absorbed into people who possess a higher vision.

Such individuals, in their spiritual stature, elevate the world from its lowliness by their very existence – and not through a direct and visible influence. Indeed, inner secrets should not be revealed, nor is it even possible.

To be sure, their great illumination does have a strong impact, and their influence can be seen in the ways people perceive life, in people's conversations, movements, inner desires, and higher goals in life. Everything is affected, encouraged, strengthened, and sanctified. Similarly, the ultimate goal of the Jewish people influencing the world is not about publicizing ideas in a direct and visible way of studying and educating. Instead, when the Jewish people truly embody the spiritual treasures within themselves, then the entire world will naturally be elevated. (SK 1:253, OK 1, p. 86)

From Inside the Depths of a Person
Prophecy and *Ruach HaKodesh*/the Holy Spirit come from inside the depths of a person, and from there it expands to the rest of the world. (SK 5:127)

When Should One Study Kabbalah and Mysticism?

An Intense Desire for Closeness to God
When is it a good time to study *Sitrei Torah*, the spiritual and mystical parts of the Torah? When one feels an intense inner desire for closeness to God rising up and getting stronger. This inner desire becomes so strong that it doesn't give the soul any rest. At such moments, one is not satisfied with any other spiritual and holy matter in the world. The only satisfaction comes about through studying the inner wisdom that speaks about the secrets of the world. This is the characteristic of a person who is immersed in *Torah Lishma*, Torah for God's sake. Regarding this it is taught "One who immerses themselves in Torah becomes elevated" (Avot 6:2). (OT 10.1)

My Soul Longs
My soul longs for the secret wonders,
For that powerful place of the highest secrets,
And my soul will not find peace by attaining more knowledge,
For such knowledge is only focused on small details.
(KYK 1, Pinkas Rishon L'Yaffo 110:2)

Studying Spiritual Torah Before Midnight
In general, there is a tradition that a person should not study *sitrei Torah*/spiritual mystical Torah before midnight. Nevertheless, if one's soul is feeling dark and needs a type of joy that is connected to the highest light of the inner depths of Torah, then one can be lenient about this. In fact, it is even a mitzvah to do so. "The secrets of God come to those who fear Him; God makes his covenant known to them. My eyes are always focused on God, for only He will liberate my feet from traps and snares" (Tehilim 25:14–15). (SK 6:44, OK 3, p. 303)

Not at All Moments
Not at all moments is a person worthy of experiencing higher spiritual encounters. Most of the time one does not have these higher inspirations; and it is precisely during such regular moments that a person must focus on studying the surface layer, the body of the Torah, as well as practical actions.

Nonetheless, when the light of the soul bursts out, a person must immediately give it its freedom. The soul must be allowed to expand, ponder, imagine, reflect and comprehend. At such moments, one must be permitted to yearn and long for the highest heights, for the Source of one's own source. The life of one's soul; the light of the life of the soul of all the worlds; the light of the higher divine; its goodness and beauty. (OT 10.2)

How to Study Mysticism and Kabbalah

Books Help to Reveal One's Inner Depth

All books and opinions that come from outside of a person – whether holy or secular – are only there to awaken one's inner spirit. They help to reveal what is hidden deep inside. (SK 1:609)

Uncovering the Meaning Within Hints

Every *Remez*/hint contains within it meaning and spiritual foundations. The light of a thought is filled with everything. Therefore, any vessel that is able to receive an insight absorbs a spiritual property. To be sure, one must make the effort to uncover the meaning contained within the *Remez*/hint. The word *Remez* is an acronym for *Re'eh Mah Zeh* – see what is here. (SK 1: 876, OK, 1, p. 109)

The Language of Secrets

Razim/spiritual secrets need to be explained and understood precisely through the language of secrets and not through explicit and open words. This is the basic attitude when it comes to revealing truth. And furthermore, it is incomparably greater than the attitude of translation, which is the numerical value for sleepiness. Deep ideas should be explained precisely through deep language. (SK 6:81, OK 1, p. 108)

Hints Found in a Text are Similar to Great Creative Works

Remazim/hints found in a text can be compared to free-spirited creative works. The way free-spirited creativity functions in the secular world is similar to the way hints found in a text function in the world of holiness. The more the wellspring of genius is filled with the sap of life, the more a person's creativity is enriched with different ways of expression. If the spring is truly great, one is able to create things that are very distant from reality; things that no eye has ever seen and no ear has ever heard. Nonetheless, it is precisely within such great creative works that the wonderous glow of life can be seen. This is the foundation of their creation, this is what the creative soul is laying witness to.

In a similar way, the more a person nourishes themselves from the light and life of faith, the more the *Remazim*/hints found within a text will grow and expand. Hints will be found underneath every sprout, for it is there that is hidden great treasures of ethics, self-development, faith, the beauty of holiness, and its glowing strength. This is the result of an inner divine trust that is drawn from the strength and desires of the Jewish people. "Rejoice all those with an upright heart" (a paraphrase of Tehilim 32:11). "Those who search for God and His strength" (Ibid. 105:4). (SK 5:119, OK 1, p. 109)

Perceiving the World from a Different Perspective

Even a secular artist perceives the world in a completely different way, in a more beautiful way, than all other secular people. This is even more true regarding *Tzadikim*, who perceive the world with *Ruach HaKodesh*/the Holy Spirit. The entire world is perceived by them with a dimension of higher beauty and glory. This is similar to the beauty of "no eye has ever seen God except you. God helps those who wait for Him" (Yeshayahu 64:3) (Berachot 34b). (SK 8:176)

Stumbling Blocks when Studying Spiritual Wisdom

Many people have stumbled in the process of contemplating *Nistarot*/spiritual wisdom. Nonetheless, a person who is capable of studying such wisdom should not turn back from one's continuous desire to contemplate higher thoughts.

In truth, all matters of life are filled with stumbling blocks. Nonetheless, those who walk with pure intentions should trust in their ways, and God will help left them up. This is true regarding spiritual life as well. A person needs to purify their heart, and be disciplined in self-development and ethics. Indeed, this is the inner content of holiness: to do God's will and direct one's heart to heaven. As consequence, one will be guarded from stumbling blocks. A person will walk their path in safety, in Torah and wisdom, contemplating God, comprehending truth and the wisdom of God. (SK 3:144, OK 1, p. 90)

Freedom from Spiritual Chains

My soul requests from me that after all learning, research, reflection, and thought, that I free myself from the spiritual chains, from the prison of detailed description that limits the soul. My soul requests from me that I journey toward the world of freedom, through the hidden insights drawn from all those matters that were learned and described in detail. (SK 8:171)

Big Ideas versus Details

Rational Perspective versus Mystical Perspective

The rational perspective of the world, regarding all things material, practical, ethical, spiritual, individual and collective, swallows up all the details inside of a great and general insight. As a result, the rational perspective is able to elevate itself to the dimension of general principles. However, its flaw is that it does not search deep enough into the smallest details. This happens to the rationalist in both secular and holy realms.

The *Razit*/Mystic, on the other hand, does penetrate into the smallest details. There is no line or point that the Mystic passes over with silence. There is no crown or letter for which the Mystic won't uncover endless meaning. There is no movement, even the smallest vision, that the Mystic won't pour over rays of light, to imagine and describe, to feel and contemplate. To be sure, the *Razit*/Mystic has the danger of sinking too deep into the smallness of details, whereby its expansive wings grab a hold of the fearful rock of the darkness of smallness.

Therefore, a person must always switch between these different strengths. At times, one must absorb the surface and rational dimension. When one is in control of this perspective, it will lift them up. The purpose of the rational attitude is to elevate matters to the most expansive heights, to the highest meaning, with the greatest insights. Nonetheless, even these great insights are considered small details in the context of the greatest insights.

Indeed, at the end of the day, the *Razit*/Mystical attitude will be victorious due to its great strength in God. It will succeed in showing the entire world that there is a higher greatness in everything small. There is no high or low, big or small before God. Everything is both high and elevated as well as small and lowly.

On the one hand, everything is high and uplifted due to the source of life, the illumination of the life of all worlds, which flows into everything. On the other hand, everything is small, low, and miserable when left without the source of light. At such moments, all spiritual dimensions are dark. "When you disconnect from them, they will remain as names alone, like a body without a soul" (*Petach Eliyahu HaNavi*). "For with You is the fountain of life; in Your light we see light" (Tehilim 36:10). (SK 1:614, OK 1 pp. 105–106)

Studying Details First

At first, a person needs to enrich themselves with details. This is in order to give their spirit a type of freedom and expansion that will eventually lead to a more general spiritual understanding. Such an understanding is the true pleasure of a person, a longing for the expansive river of the highest understanding.

After one has reached the balanced level of acquiring details, a person's spirit will then be able to develop more general spiritual values. Such values will raise up above all details. And when these general spiritual values will mature and develop in their own way, their higher understanding will hover above all details.

This can be compared to how a dove hovers above its nest. A person will be able to uncover the hidden life and light within each and every detail... something that give richness to all details, in all their various nuances.

Eventually, one will reach the true greatness of a person, something that demands them not to do any action in a mindless way – *Mitzvot Anashim Mi'lumdah* (Yeshayahu 29:13). Instead, every action and routine; every labor and mitzvah; every emotion and thought; every piece of Torah and prayer, will be illuminated with this hidden light, with this general spiritual light. (SK 1:611, OK 1, pp. 53–54)

Roots versus Branches

The strongest spiritual roots, which are filled with the freshness of life and reality, send forth endless branches. Sometimes when the soul is tired from all the branches, one must hold on to the original root. And as a result, one's strength will be renewed. One is then able to return to take pleasure from the branches with a new perspective. This causes many more branches, sprouts, and flowers to blossom, which previously would not have come to the world. This is the meaning of the principle that the highest spiritual secrets come to strengthen the legal discussion of Abaye and Rabba, and the most idealistic ethics come to strengthen the technical and social world. (SK 3:252, OK 1 pp. 52–53)

The Need to Refresh the Details with Greater Spirituality

The ideal spiritual principles only reveal their power through the many details. These details fit together in an organized system both in one's spiritual and physical life. Indeed, details do not have meaning without being connected to the general soul principles. Therefore, sometimes I feel a great tiredness due to the heaviness of details that bore and weigh me down. At such moments, I need to renew my soul through refreshing myself with an experience of general spiritual principles. When the flash of general spirituality flows its streams of water into the many detailed and carved out buildings, then we are able to return to serve the details with precision and energy. (C, p. 137)

How to Explain Big Ideas with Small Ideas

Sometimes a person explains big ideas through small ideas, taking universal principles and applying them to individual principles. One must be careful not to make bigger ideas smaller, but rather smaller ideas bigger. In the act of contemplating the true foundation of an idea, we discover its greatness. As a result, our souls become filled with a yearning for this greatness from higher worlds. Our ideal life becomes stronger and our inner freedom expresses itself in a pure and holy way. (SK 6:200)

Mystical and Revealed Ideas Need Each Other

Every mystical thought needs many worldly thoughts to express and embody it. Such worldly thoughts will be a shield and roof railing for it. As a result, this mystical thought's illumination will not descend into the abyss of imagination, lies and destruction. On the other hand, every worldly thought needs a spark of mysticism. This helps mature and guard it from the destruction of becoming the source of death. Indeed, the origins of revealed thoughts are none other than the source of life. (SK 1:613, OK 1, p. 112)

Combining Spiritual and Practical Study

We must find a middle path between the most spiritual ideas and the most practical ideas. This will lead to the establishment of a comprehensive new type of learning, a holistic study, which includes all types of subjects. Its style will be a combination of the practical side with the spiritual side in a unifying way. (SK 8:158)

8

Dreams, Death, and Reincarnation

"After a person quietens down the noises of bodily life, the essential flaws of the soul awaken." (SK 7:55)

PEOPLE HAVE ALWAYS SENSED THAT THERE IS MORE TO LIFE THAN just the physical reality. Following the Kabbalistic and Mystical traditions, Rav Kook believed that there is a hidden dimension of reality that the soul experiences. Just as the nature of the body must be studied and given attention to, so too the nature of the soul must be studied and listened to.

> The path of repairing the soul can be very subtle. A person may encounter certain blocks that seem like physical blocks. Nonetheless, their essential roots are very spiritual and exalted. Ultimately, the greatest achievement comes about through spiritually repairing the soul. (SK 7:55)

In this chapter, Rav Kook will describe to us what happens to the soul while we sleep and how we should best interpret and respond to dreams. In addition, he will explain a more holistic perspective toward death and why people have so much fear regarding this heavy subject. Finally, Rav Kook will discuss the spiritual logic behind reincarnation – what happens to the soul once it leaves this world. In general, one of Rav Kook's main educational goals is to encourage a person to identify as a soul and to therefore take seriously the needs and desires of their inner world.

Dreams

Dreams Are the Deeper Reality

The greatest dreams are the foundations of the world. However, there are different levels of dreams. The prophets dream: "I speak to them in dreams" (BaMidbar 12:6). The poets dream while awake and the visionary thinkers dream about *Tikun Olam*/repairing the world. In truth, we all dream, "When God will return the captives of Zion, we will be like dreamers" (Tehilim 126:1).

There is an arrogance to the life of society since it focuses itself only on the material dimension of life. This removes the light of dreams from the dark and gloomy world; it removes the expansive illumination and higher ascent contained in dreams. The world shakes with pain due to the poisonous sting of reality that lacks the illumination of dreams.

However, these pains are the sufferings of love. They cleanse the world and help it clarify how mistaken those people are who praise this imperfect reality. Only the freedom of dreams is the true essence of reality; it rebels against the current reality and its limitations.

Eventually, the vision of dreams will return and it will be a clear vision. "With him I speak face to face–– clearly and not in riddles – and he sees the image of God" (BaMidbar 12:8). (SK 3:226)

The Spiritual Process of Sleep

The act of sleep and all of the natural occurrences in the night that cause sleep and are connected to it have two opposite effects on a person's life. On the one hand, the higher spiritual dimensions of a person can be elevated since one's imagination becomes free from the limits of the physical senses. Therefore, if a person is continuously connected to their intellect with holy desires, they will be able to envision, imagine, perceive, and understand matters that they were unable to do while awake.

On the other hand, if the strength of life within the body has become disconnected from the spiritual side of a person, then the body will function on its own, following its natural impulses in a dark and cloudy way.

Each of these directions will produce parallel results. Pure insights will be produced from the higher soul due to its higher illumination. On the other hand, darkness and dirt will be produced due to the thick shells within the soul and the dark mud that was dwelling inside when it was clinging to the brick of physicality left on its own.

In response to this, each morning we try to focus ourselves on two spiritual goals. On the one hand, to purify and cleanse the spirit of life. On the other hand, to connect oneself to the insights that were gathered from the higher soul of a person. Ultimately, what we desire is to unite both extremes in one greater harmony. (SK 1:660, OK 1, p. 230)

Cheshbon HaNefesh Before Going to Sleep

The negativity of the world finds a resting place inside of oneself. It strengthens and becomes embodied within each person. With every passing day it increases its power and prevents a person from improving and getting better. "A person's negative inclination increases and strengthens each day" (Kedushin 30b).

It is impossible for a person to confront this reality without consistent prayers, one of which is the Viduiim/confessional prayers. Indeed, a person must confess their sins – both public and private sins. They must confess even their most private and hidden sins: the negative desires that strengthen and surround them.

When a person does not forget to do Cheshbon HaNefesh/a personal accounting of one's soul, one will be able to gradually shake off the negativity that has come upon them. That is, before it has had time to form a heavy shell around them, something which is difficult to release oneself from.

The Masters of *Cheshbon HaNefesh* remove negativity from themselves each day. Such people do *Viduiim*/confessional prayers before they go to sleep each night. They confess their own sins as well as the entire world's sins. At the very least, they express their protest against individual and collective negativity, in any place it exists. Such Masters of *Cheshbon HaNefesh* direct their soul toward the presence of goodness and holiness. As a result, they elevate the soul to the source of a life of holiness; they connect the soul to the wellspring of goodness. "I entrust my spirit in Your hands (Tehilim 31:6 and from the bedtime *Shema* prayer found in the Siddur). (SK 1:607, OK 3, p. 302)

Interpreting Dreams

Rabbi Chisda says: A dream that is not interpreted is like a letter that is not read (Berachot 55a).

A letter is an expression of the sender's desires; it is used to achieve the wishes of the sender. On the other hand, if a letter is not read, this does not change the desire of the sender. While it is true that if the letter is read it may motivate the reader to fulfill the sender's wishes. Nonetheless, if the letter is not read, the sender will think of other ways to achieve their original desire.

This principle is also true regarding dreams. Dreams are a permanent law of nature. It is therefore impossible that they do not contain some higher purpose. One of the purposes of dreams is to be an inner motivation to transform and prepare a person for their future....

Using a dream to help transform and prepare a person for their future depends on the wisdom of interpretation. An interpretation must be rooted in the wisdom of the soul, the power of the imagination, and its connection to reality. When a dream is interpreted appropriately, a person is helped by the dream to become transformed and prepared for their future. However, when a dream is not interpreted at all, then additional dreams will not be the source of future changes in the soul. Just as the desire of the sender of the letter does not change when the letter is not read, so too, God's desire does not change in regard to matters that should have happened to a person through the influence of the interpretation. (EA Berachot 2, p. 130)

Good Dreams and Bad Dreams

Rabbi Huna says: A bad dream is shown to a good person and a good dream is shown to a wicked person (Berachot 55a).

The foundation of both good and bad character traits is dependent on the type of self-love a person has. One whose self-love is so extreme that it oversteps the boundaries of righteousness and truth becomes blinded by their love. A person begins to think that all of their ways are perfect and does not believe that they have any imperfections.

… However, this is not true regarding a righteous person whose self-love is built on righteousness, truth and justice. If such a person commits a sin or has a negative trait inside of their heart, they will acknowledge this without self-deceit. The images that come to a righteous person's imagination are filled with self-improvement and self-criticism. Therefore, when a dream comes to such a person through the inner thoughts of their heart, "they are shown a bad dream."

In contrast, there is a type of wicked person whose righteousness and honesty are simply an expression of their bias desires and lusts. Such a person envisions only good things. "Your laws are rejected by them" (Tehilim 10:5). Therefore, "a wicked person is shown a good dream." All of this is included in the principle of "anger is better than folly" (Kohelet 7:3). This is said by the rabbis about the tranquility of wicked people and the sufferings of righteous people (Shabbat 30b). Indeed, there is a type of person who has dimmed their soul so much that even a shade of righteousness and justice will not enter their heart. As a result, they are not shown even the basic insights that the world is run by. That is to say, the usual self-criticism that comes about through dreams that help a person straighten their ways.

In contrast, there is a type of honest person who is pure in their ways and the spirit of God guides them. For such a person, if they make a mistake in something, their good spirit will wake them up and motivate them to return and fix their mistakes. Therefore, the insights of a bad dream will be something that helps them comprehend mistakes and improve their ways. (EA Berachot 2, p. 132)

King David's Dreams versus Achitophel's Dreams

"All of King David's life he never saw a good dream, and all of Achitophel's life he never saw a bad dream" (Berachot 55a).

A person who judges their soul when they do something wrong shows that they are "humble and modest in spirit" (Sanhedrin 88b).[15] Such a person recognizes that they are not clean from mistakes and imperfections. This is how David behaved when Shimi Ben Gera cursed him. David suffered from this and said "God told him to curse" (Shmuel 2, 16:10).

The opposite is true regarding Achitophel. He was over-powered by a love for his own honor. As a result, when Achitophel saw that his advice did not work out, he committed suicide. This was a sign that he did not internalize the idea that he had imperfections and that he should therefore not be so upset when he was not given honor. Achitophel did not comprehend that perhaps rebuke and criticism would actually have helped him improve his ways. Therefore, until such a person becomes humble, they will "never see a bad dream." (EA Berachot 2, p. 132)

---

15. The Gemara states: "Who is a person who will enter the World-to-Come? One who is modest and humble" (Sanhedrin 88b).

All Dreams Follow the Mouth of the Interpreter

Rabbi Bizna bar Zavda said that Rabbi Akiva said that Rabbi Panda said that Rav Nachum said that Rabbi Birayim said in the name of one Elder. And who is he? Rabbi Bena'a: There were twenty-four interpreters of dreams in Jerusalem. One time, I dreamed a dream and went to each of them to interpret it. What one interpreted for me the other did not interpret for me, and, nevertheless, all of the interpretations were realized in me, to fulfill that which is stated: All dreams follow the mouth of the interpreter (Berachot 55b).

We have learned that even when there are disagreeing opinions, they are not truly disagreeing. Rather, each side is judging the matter from their unique perspective. In this sense, one perspective does not negate another perspective.

In fact, even when different perspectives seem to be contradicting each other, one should not conclude that they are truly disagreeing. It could very well be that it only seems like a disagreement because of a lack of research in the matter. However, when a person comprehends the issue in a deeper way, one discovers that there is indeed truth to each perspective, even when they seem to be contradictory.

When every type of wisdom is expanded, there is enough there to have an entire philosophy. Now, since interpreting dreams is dependent on a holistic knowledge of the soul, one must therefore judge a dream from the perspective of the soul as well as its effects on the body.

The Sefer Yetzira says that there are twelve general parts to the soul that correspond to the twelve general limbs of the body.... A person may be wise and comprehend one of the parts of the soul in a thorough way – either from the perspective of the soul or from the body. For example, the eyes. Its physical ability is an entire philosophy that one must specialize in. Yet this is also true regarding the eye's connection to the soul and its various effects on each other. So too, (there is a body and soul wisdom) in all of the twelve parts that the Sefer Yetzira counted.

For this reason, there were twenty-four dream interpreters because each one explained the message based on the specific wisdom they possessed. Just as the soul includes twenty-four parts, a dream also includes all twenty-four messages. (EA Berachot 2, pp. 146–147)

The Interpretation Influences the Fulfillment of the Dream

All dreams follow the mouth of the interpreter. Is the statement "All dreams follow the mouth" sourced in a Torah verse? Yes. As Rabbi Elazar says: From where is it derived that all dreams follow the mouth of the interpreter? 'And it came to pass, just as he interpreted for us, so it was'" (Bereishit 41:13). (Berachot 55b)

One of the main goals of dreams is to communicate what will happen in the future when a person changes their ways. We see that there are many different lessons we can learn from a dream. We must conclude from this that a dream together with an interpretation is one complete system in reality. In a similar way, we could say that the intellect of a person together with shaping the natural elements of the world are one complete system in reality. This was the original intention of God: that people would discover how to manipulate nature through their intellect.

In a similar way regarding the Written Torah and the Oral Torah. The written Torah can be explained in different ways. This was the intended way so that it would be connected with the Oral Torah. The intellect with the rules of interpretation together with the new situations of life teach us how we must uncover all of the hidden lessons.

... This is also true about the principle that "all dreams follow the mouth." We learn this from the verse "Just as he interpreted it for us, so it was." In other words, it is God's intention that there should be many different faces and perspectives. Anything that can be said is permitted to be said. Everything follows the mouth in order to expand the Torah and strengthen it. This principle is true regarding dreams as well, which is considered one-sixtieth of prophecy. (EA Berachot 2, p. 147)

The Limits of Dream Interpretations

Rava said: "This is only in a case where the interpretation is connected to the content of the dream. As it is stated, 'Yosef interpreted each person according to his dream'" (Bereishit 41:12). (Berachot 55b)

The soul that has the dream and the intellect of the interpreter are one single unit. Therefore, perhaps a person might think that possible interpretations can be as abstract and far-reaching as one desires. Indeed, perhaps a certain dream will cause a feeling inside of the interpreter which is connected to certain things in their own life but is not related to the dream at all. Therefore, Rava taught that interpretations should not become too distant and abstract from the dream itself. While it is true that the one who dreams is influenced by the mind of the interpreter, nonetheless, it must always return and be related to what the dreamer actually saw themselves.

This principle is also true regarding the Torah. While it is true that the Torah can awaken many thoughts inside of a person; nonetheless, these ideas should not be considered Torah unless they have a direct relation to the Torah and its principles. However, a person who interprets things in such an abstract and distant way; one who learn things that are only connected to their own personality; one whose character and thoughts are the main thing that caused the Torah to give birth to these thoughts; such a person is close to the prohibition of "teaching matters from the Torah that are not aligned to halacha" (Sanhedrin 99b). (EA Berachot 2, pp. 147–148)

Paying Attention to One's Inner Feelings

Rav Huna bar Ami said in the name of Rabbi Pedat in name of Rabbi Yochanan: "A person who has a dream and it causes one's soul to be troubled, should go and have it interpreted before three people" (Berachot 55a).

The main way to strengthen the righteousness within a person is to train oneself to pay attention to one's inner feelings. The voice of God often calls to a person from within the walls of their own heart. It tells them to turn away from negative ways and not become corrupt. A person should therefore train oneself not to arrogantly crush the inner feelings of one's soul. (By paying attention to these feelings), the intended message will then be able to reach this person from God – the One Who created us with this soul. Such a person will then be able to separate themselves from matters of evil and the various ways that turn one away from the straight path.

"A person who has a dream and it causes one's soul to be troubled." A person should not neglect the call of one's soul, for it is a child of the upper worlds. Letting these feelings pass by in silence without giving attention to the trouble in one's soul will eventually result in throwing away any connection to one's inner goodness and honesty. As a consequence, one of the strongest and most accessible foundations of self-growth will collapse.

Instead, a person should pay attention and process their inner feelings. One should try to transform their troubled feelings into emotions of joy and relief. This can be achieved by surrounding oneself with positive and consoling words of supportive and loving people. (EA Berachot 2, p. 134)

The Thought-Filled Dreams of the Night

Told by Rav Kook's younger brother, Rav Chayim Kook:

One time I traveled to the city of Zemiel and stayed at my brother's house, Rav Kook. In the morning I saw him get up from his bed in a very fast way, wash his hands, make a blessing, and sit down immediately to write in his journal. This was not something Rav Kook usually did. In fact, the way Rav Kook wrote in his journal in a fast and hurried way at such an early hour of the morning awakened my curiosity.

I searched until I found the key to the cupboard where his journals were kept. When I opened the journal, I found a long Kabbalistic essay that began with the verse "Amidst the thought-filled dreams of the night" (Iyov 4:13). (HA, p. 65)

Death

Eternal Existence

Our temporary existence is merely a spark within eternal existence, the glory of eternal life. It is impossible to actualize the potential goodness hidden inside this temporary life unless it is aligned to eternal life. This inner consciousness dwells inside the spirit of all of existence. All the spiritual disagreements in the world cannot remove this truth. These disagreements only prepare the way before it. Even those opinions that disagree with it are in truth helping it.[16] (SK 2:141, OK 2, p. 377)

Connecting Oneself to Eternity Defeats Death

In a deep sense, eternity is the powerful foundation behind all social life. The desire to connect oneself to the glory of eternity defeats death. It wipes away all human tears. The greatest people do small things in great ways. (SK 2:142, OK 2, p. 377)

---

16. Due to the difficulty of translating this piece and the next piece, I was guided by Yaacov David Shulman's wonderful translation, which can be found on his comprehensive website of Rav Kook translations: https://www.ravkook.net/death.html.

Death is a False Vision

Death is a false vision, and what makes it impure is that it spreads a lie. What people call death is in fact an increase in life. However, as a result of immersing oneself in the depths of small-mindedness, people perceive this increase of life in a depressing and darkened way – what people call death. In their holiness, Cohanim do not listen to this lie. The only way to escape while this false kingship rules the world is by closing one's eyes in any place that causes error. "One must not enter a place where there is a dead body" (Vayikra 21:11) "One must not become impure from a dead person amongst one's nation" (Ibid. 21:1). (SK 8:23)

Healing Oneself from the Fear of Death

Fear of death is a sickness of humanity. It comes about as a result of sin. Indeed, sin created death. And *teshuva*/spiritual growth is the main medicine to remove death from the world. All of the efforts of human beings revolve around saving themselves from death. Yet they will only reach their goal through increasing their soul's connection to its inner source.

When a person immerses oneself in the dust of materialism and becomes overly excited by matters of the body, this increases death. It increases fear upon fear.

No matter how much a person tries to stop being afraid from death, this will not succeed. The reason is because one's entire existence is immersed in matters that death controls. It is death that destroys and wipes out all of such matters.

How is it possible that a person's heart will not tremble at the thought of beauty turning into filth, and that which one cherished turning into something of nausea? When life is without a higher goal, death will automatically become terrifying. Fighting death is in vain. Courage will not help. The ultimate and true medicine that will free the world from the slavery of death is hidden in the treasure of life, in the soul of Torah when it reveals itself in all of its glory. Such medicines are hidden away in the strongest place. (SK 1:486)

Death Has its Own Spiritual Purpose

A person should not go to a cemetery dressed with *tefillin* on their head and arm and begin studying Torah. If one does this, they transgress the sin of "Whoever mocks a poor person shows contempt for their Creator" (Mishlei 17:5). (Berachot 18a)

A person should not think that death has no purpose and is absolute nothingness just because death does not possess the same type of perfection that we are familiar with in this world. No, this logic is incorrect. "God is the Creator of all things" (Yirmiyahu 51:19) and "everything that God did is very good" (a paraphrase of Bereishit 1:31). Indeed, God does not create anything completely bad or negative.

A person must therefore recognize that death too has a greater purpose and goal. Regarding this the rabbis said "Behold, it is very good" (Bereishit 1:31) – 'this is referring to death'" (Bereishit Raba 9:6). There is a dimension of reality where the activities of this world stop and a different type of perfection exists. This is true even regarding the best types of activities such as *mitzvot* and Torah study. Therefore, when a person goes to a cemetery, they should not be immersed in Torah study and *mitzvot*. This comes to teach us that there exists a dimension of reality with a different type of perfection that does not fit within our human categories; it is a type of perfection that we cannot reach in this world.

"If a person does this" (wears *tefillin* and studies Torah at a cemetery) then this demonstrates that death is complete nothingness and that there is no other place in a higher reality where we stop the activities of life. Regarding such a person it is written "Whoever mocks a poor person shows contempt for their Creator" (Mishlei 17:5). Indeed, a person must show the perfection of the Creator in all of reality, "because God's ways are higher than our ways and God's thoughts are greater than our thoughts" (a paraphrase of Yeshayahu 55:9). (EA Berachot 1, pp. 88–89)

The Connection Between Life and Death

Rachava stated that Rav Yehuda said: One who sees the deceased taken to burial and does not escort the body has committed a transgression of: "One who mocks the poor blasphemes his Creator." (Mishlei 17:5) (Berachot 18a)

Escorting a dead body teaches us that there is a connection between life and death. It shows us that the actions in this world have an effect on life after death. As a result, a person will be inspired to honor God throughout life to the best of their abilities. One comprehends that their actions will not disappear like smoke, but will rather express themselves in a different form after death. The reality of their actions will continue to give fruit. However, this is not true for a person who does not escort a dead body. Such a person may acknowledge the truth of the eternity of the soul and the revival of the dead. Nonetheless, if they do not recognize how their actions in this world have an effect on life after death... they have not fulfilled the purpose of honoring God, whose main objective is the perfection of His creations. (EA Berachot 1, p. 89)

Life After Death

If a person does escort a dead body, what is their reward? Rav Asi stated: The verse says about them: "One who gives to the poor gives a loan to God, and Hashem will repay them" (Mishlei 19:17). (Berachot 18a)

Escorting a dead body teaches us that accompanying the deceased is more important than matters of the materialistic world. Therefore, regarding a person who escorts the death the verse writes: "One who gives to the poor gives a loan to God, and Hashem will repay them" (Mishlei 19:17). This can be compared to a lender who trusts the one who borrowed. Even though the lender does not yet see the money, nonetheless they faithfully trust the borrower. In a similar way, a person trusts even though they see that life is ending. Nonetheless they appreciate the worth of death since they trust in the righteousness of God. God did not create human beings in vain, to place inside of them a living soul for the sake of some materialistic game. Rather, there is a higher purpose that will come about at the end of life. (EA Berachot 1, p. 89)

Reincarnation

The Essential Repairing of the Soul

From the point of view of reincarnation of the soul, there may be essential flaws in the soul that have nothing to do with the flaws of the body and its temperament. It could also be that as long as the bodily forces are strong and the lusts are intense and overpowering, the essential flaws of one's soul will not be felt or recognizable. The soul's inner flaws will not have a strong impact on a person since there are other forces present – the loud noises of life.

However, after one quiets down the noises of bodily life, the essential flaws of the soul awaken. These are sourced in a previous time period. The time has now arrived to do *HaTikun HaNishmati*/the essential repairing of the soul. All the moral guidance that was focused toward the bodily forces was like an introduction and doorway to this more essential work of the soul. To be sure, the path of repairing the soul can be very subtle. A person may encounter certain blocks that seem like physical blocks. Nonetheless, their essential roots are very spiritual and exalted. Ultimately, the greatest achievement comes about through spiritually repairing the soul. A person succeeds in repairing parts of life that existed from a previous time period. "From generation to generation they praise Your works; they tell of Your mighty acts" (Tehilim 145:4). (SK 7:55, OK 3, p. 237)

Is Reincarnation Logical or Illogical?

From the vantage point of logic, there is no intellectual reason to oppose the spiritual principle of the reincarnation of the soul. Why is it so difficult to imagine that there is a connection between the spiritual soul and the material realm for the purpose of processing, purifying, and concentrating on new traits from the context of an earlier time period? In regards to this work of purification, why is it so difficult to accept that as long as the work has not yet finished, something must return, repeat and reoccur?

To our surprise, we know of a number of logical people who refuse to accept this intelligent attitude. To be sure, the belief in reincarnation has a positive impact on faith and moral development. Yet why should this be considered an intellectual flaw?

There are even most distant reincarnations, including from one species to another, from inanimate objects to plants, to animals, and eventually to human beings. This is all due to the normal progression of ascent and descent due to a mistaken choice. Yet what is so strange about this logic? A similar argument about the essential differences of souls are like chaff in the wind compared to this general attitude of reality. (SK 7:179)

Everything is Connected to One's Essence
It is not inconceivable that every matter that is connected to a person – from one's food, drink, utensils, movements, and possessions – has an inherent connection to one's true essence. (SK 2:71)

Rav Kook's Soul Connection to Rebbe Nachman
During the time period that Rav Kook was the rabbi of the city of Yaffo, Rebbe Nachman's book "Likutei Moharan" would often be sitting on Rav Kook's *Shtender*/book stand where he prayed. Every so often, Rav Kook would open the book and study it. A Breslav Chassid from Jerusalem added and testified to Rav Moshe Tzvi Neria that one time Rav Kook said about himself, "I am the soul of Rebbe Nachman." One time a person spoke in an insulting way about Rebbe Nachman in Rav Kook's presence. Rav Kook stood up and protested against this with full force. (OtR, vol. ii, ch. 25)

9

The Meaning of *Mitzvot*

"How unfulfilled people are who do not know the divine, who do not pray and do mitzvot with the entire congregation of the Jewish people. The spiritual tools of the soul want to be used, yet these people are not responding to the obligations of their soul." (SK 1:20)

THERE IS A DEEP DESIRE WITHIN EACH PERSON TO EXPERIENCE A greater meaning in life, to fulfill their soul's potential, and to connect to God. Yet according to Rav Kook, it is not enough to have a general connection to meaning. People feel unfulfilled when they do not have practical ways of achieving this higher connection. Rav Kook says that *mitzvot* are practical spiritual tools that help a person connect to God and uncover their full potential.

> *Mitzvot* and prayers are the best spiritual tools to expand the inner desire for closeness to God; they come to empower a person's journey toward God in the depths of one's soul. (SK 1:20)

In this chapter, Rav Kook will encourage us to go through a paradigm shift in the way we perceive *mitzvot*. Instead of seeing *mitzvot* as merely rules to follow and obey, Rav Kook will ask us to relate to *mitzvot* as God-given spiritual tools that help structure one's inner life, reveal one's soul's potential and expand one's connection to God. In addition, Rav Kook will warn us about healthy and unhealthy ways of doing *mitzvot*.

The Goal of *Mitzvot*

Clearing the Path from Obstacles

The soul's inner awareness grows and strengthens when a person clears its path from stumbling rocks. These are one's bad thoughts, damaged character traits, and negative actions. The soul naturally elevates itself toward the highest desires: to be good and honest, prepared for the purity of ethics, closeness to God, a sensitive spirit, love of people, charity, kindness and uprightness. Spiritual and practical work, education and good reinforcement, are simply tools to help clear the path from obstacles. (SK 3:10, OK 1, p. 138)

Revealing the Soul

The educational goal of all actions and study is to help reveal the inner strength of the soul. (SK 3:75)

Internal Wisdom

Internal wisdom accesses the depth of something. A person is born with this type of internal wisdom, it comes from one's unique soul. Any type of study should only be used to help a person understand oneself, to reveal to a person their soul. It is the sins of the world that prevent a person from this self-knowledge. (KYK 1, Reshimot M'London 10)

Techniques for Spiritual Consistency

It is impossible to stay consistently on one level of spirituality. Nevertheless, through regular study of Torah in a deep way (*lishma*), daily acts of *mitzvot* with purity, prayer with concentration (*kavana*), and regularity in songs and praises to God, this increases consistency. (KYK 2, Pinkas 5:53)

Natural Faith versus Inherited Faith

Inner *Chassidut* includes within it the idea of natural faith. This is a divine light that pulsates within the soul as a result of its own power. It is not connected to a faith that is the result of the light of the inheritance of one's forefathers and tradition. Tradition comes to develop and accompany the light of this higher faith; it guards it from mistakes and straightens its ways. "Your word is a lamp for my feet, a light on my path" (Tehilim 119, 105). (SK 7:80, MiR, "Emunah" 8)

Mitzvot as Spiritual Tools

It takes great spiritual effort and maturity until a person recognizes God's closeness inside of oneself. All parts of life become aligned when this divine connection awakens in a healthy way. It does not matter which particular way a person comes to a connection to God. It may come about through the path of intellect and logical thinking, or it may come about through the path of inner emotions. What matters most is that a person recognizes the truth of this divine connection inside of oneself.

Mitzvot and prayers are the best spiritual tools to expand the inner desire for closeness to God; they come to empower a person's journey toward God in the depths of one's soul. And therefore, how great and important is the value of each prayer with concentration, each blessing and praise, each mitzvah and good custom. All of these are an established pathway to enable feelings of divine closeness in the heart of a person.

How unfulfilled people are who do not know the divine, who do not pray and do mitzvot with the entire congregation of the Jewish people. The spiritual tools of the soul want to be used, yet these people are not responding to the obligations of their soul. As a result, they feel miserable and dried up inside. Now, even if they try to quench their natural moral thirst through ethical actions, this will not satisfy their desire for closeness to God. This unique type of thirst will only be quenched through divine actions that are designated for Godliness. What is necessary are words of holiness and mitzvot, divine instructions.

We must have compassion on all people, and specifically on our children, those who are our family and kindred spirits. We must help to clear the pathway for them toward closeness to God. This comes about through studying and following the Torah. Indeed, the more we succeed in achieving this important goal; the more we increase good and pure deeds that naturally bring closeness to God in the world, the greater happiness there will be in the world. (SK 1:20)

The Soul's Thirst for Jewish Perfection

The soul's thirst and longing for general perfection can be quenched through any type of spiritual insight that it discovers. However, the particular thirst for Jewish perfection and reaching its unique purpose can only be quenched through the fulfillment of the Torah. (SK 1:349, OT 11.10)

Mitzvot Create our Jewish Character

We need to uncover how the acts of *mitzvot* impact us, how they cause us to feel, and how they build our world – both one's individual and national world.

Tefillin transform our perception. They have the spiritual ability to imprint the essence of the words written inside the *tefillin* on the soul of those who wear them. The letters engrave themselves on the essence of the soul. The inner spiritual essence, which is the purpose of those passages of Torah within the *tefillin*, help build the Jewish soul each day. They build the unique attitudes of the Jewish people. They help give a unique form and color to all parts of life – to the life of the soul, morality, and to the entire Jewish essence.

It was precisely because of this daily spiritual sustenance that the soul of a Jew was developed, the Hebrew spirit awakened – and continued to stay awake and alive – capable of its own unique spiritual powers. This is one of the great educational principles of the Jewish nation: to intentionally shape its spirit to fit with its unique existence.

The Jewish people's food is her food, aligned to her inner spirit. On the other hand, the forbidden food blur and damage her spirit. We do not need to search for this principle of blurring and damaging the spirit in universal ethics. Human universal ethics goes in other directions. It does not need to purify the soul with as much power at the beginnings of its desires. This is something unique to the Jewish people. The forbidden foods pollute the heart and cause the unique imprint of the Jewish people to be lost. Such forbidden foods blur and damage the holiness of the Jewish people. As a result, a person's inner desires and talents do not become connected in a Jewish way. Such individuals become like limbs that do not absorb the inner life of its people in a deep emotional way. Their souls become clouded and damaged.

An individual Jew does not have a separate soul apart from its people. Rather, it is drawn from the great Jewish nation. This is the spiritual power of "one nation in the land" (Shmuel 2, 7:23). Whoever uncovers this "hidden face" will see and understand how much one must honor every law and rule. (SK 1:161)

Staying Loyal to the Jewish Tradition

There is an organic spiritual network within each soul that is influenced by the lifestyle, actions, and thoughts from previous generations. A person may desire to disconnect one's way of life, thoughts and feelings, and all the more so one's faith, from the lifestyle of Avraham, Yitzchak and Yaakov. Even though such a person may feel that they are lacking nothing, nonetheless they are actually ripping their soul into pieces. Indeed, a time will come when they will awaken from their spiritual slumber with great suffering.

In contrast, there is a person who trusts in God, the God of our forefathers…. Such a person may not yet feel the great pleasure and hidden joy within this lifestyle. Nonetheless, a time of physical and spiritual change will eventually come when their soul will be awakened. A storehouse of kindness will be revealed to them as a result of their path of simplicity. "Many are the sufferings of the evil, but God's unfailing love surrounds the one who trusts in God" (Tehilim 32:10). (SK 3:85)

Making the Mitzvot a Natural Part of You

The ultimate perfection is when the righteous ways of God (the mitzvot) become so strong inside of a person's heart that they are similar to one's natural desires. Such natural desires exist as an eternal convent. As a result, the ways of God will have two virtues. The first virtue is a freedom that is rooted in choosing. The second virtue is the strength of anything that is engraved and permanent within nature. Regarding this it is said, "I will put my law in their minds and write it on their hearts" (Yirmiyahu 31:33). (KYK 1, Pinkas Rishon L'Yaffo 68)

Natural Spirituality

Those who argue that we should follow the natural and free instincts of a person forget that the spirit within a person and the spirit within the entire world also has a nature. And this spiritual nature also desires its freedom of expression. The foundation of morality and Torah is none other than this natural spirituality. (SK 1:552)

Doing Mitzvot at Specific Times

We need a sensitive spiritual understanding that explains the importance of doing mitzvot at specific times. This is most relevant in relation to the exact times of when the Shema and prayer are said. A superficial spiritual understanding downplays the divine importance of doing mitzvot at specific times. We must protect ourselves from such a spiritual perspective that downplays the great faith in the truth of the Torah. (KYK 1, Reshimot M'London 20)

Great Spiritual Insights Should Illuminate Small Details

All of the greatest wisdom and spiritual insights do not release us from the necessity of caring about actions in a very real and concrete way. These great insights should help illuminate the way we do actions. The greatest ideas in the world do not move us away from the necessity of small details. This is similar to how the greatest things in the world do not exempt us from the smallest physical needs. Spiritual insights help guide a person to receive the purest light in a way that the smallest details can be elevated to the greatest significance. (KYK 1, Reshimot M'London 26)

Spirituality Should Not Undermine Practical Details
One needs a very balanced and expanded mind in order to have a spiritual attitude where the greatest and loftiest ideas do not undermine the smallest and restricted details. (KYK 1, Reshimot M'London 18)

Healthy and Unhealthy Ways of Doing *Mitzvot*

Religious Actions Should Not Weaken You
When religious actions are linked to a weak spirit, it causes such actions to look ugly. A person with a strong spirit simply cannot bear to see weak sentimentality. Not only do religious actions need to be rooted in sophisticated beliefs, but even actions that are emotionally intelligent to all – when they are connected to a weak spirit – turn people off. Society needs to find ways to preserve religious actions, while at the same time, remove the damaging ways that people tend to carry them out. (KYK 1, Pinkas 5:35)

Religion Not Motivated by Reward in Heaven
Sometimes the negative inclination comes to a person to prove to them that they have no hope for the next world. This person should know with confidence that they are about to be elevated to a very high spiritual level: to connect to God without the desire to receive reward. Instead, to be motivated by a pure intellectual love. (KYK 2, Pinkas 5:100)

A Special Spiritual Talent

When a person recognizes in oneself that one doesn't desire at all to receive a reward for doing *mitzvot* and serving God, a person should not take for granted this special spiritual talent. One should work hard at developing this special sensitivity, until one truly arrives at the lifestyle of "serving one's master not for the sake of receiving a reward. The awe of heaven will then be upon him" (Pirkei Avot 1:3). This shining level of consciousness is fitting for the seeker of God. (SK 8:27, OK 3, p. 306)

Atheism that Helps Religion

The atheist's denial of reward and punishment in the next world educates people to be motivated to do good actions for the good itself. The more that people do good for good's sake, the less need there will be for the belief of atheism, which is nothing but a cultural means to arrive at this consciousness. (KYK 2, Pinkas 5:110)

The Natural Faith of the Soul

Deep spirituality includes within it a spark of natural faith, a divine light that pulsates within the soul, something that comes from its own power. This is something that is outside the light of Torah and the tradition of our forefathers. The ancient tradition travels and accompanies this higher light of faith, protects it from mistakes, and directs it on its path. "Your word is a lamp for my feet, a light on my path" (Tehilim 119:105). (SK 7:80)

Nullified versus Exempt

"*Mitzvot* will be nullified in the future times" (Nidah 61b). Note that it is written "nullified from *mitzvot*" and not "exempt from *mitzvot*." The idea of something being nullified is similar to the nullification of prohibited non-kosher food. When extra kosher food is added, the prohibited food can no longer be tasted or recognizable on its own.

In a similar way, in the current times, the taste and reason of the *mitzvot* are often lost inside of the actions of the *mitzvot*. Yet in the future times, the taste and reason of the *mitzvot* will be so recognizable that the actions of the *mitzvot* will be lost inside of the taste and reason of the *mitzvot*. To be sure, it is impossible to experience the light of a mitzvah without doing the concrete practical action of the mitzvah....

Now, since the nations of the world will not be able to experience the taste and reason of the mitzvah without the practical actions of the mitzvah, therefore converts will search for ways to attach themselves to the concrete actions of the *mitzvot*. Concerning the mitzvah of *tzitzit* it is written, "And you will do in action all of My *mitzvot*" (Bamidbar 15:40). Therefore, "all the nations will grab a hold of the corners of people's clothes" (a paraphrase of Zechariah 8:23). (KYK 2, Pinkas 1:61)

The Importance of Non-Idealistic Motivations
Sometimes it is beneficial for a person to begin their immersion in Torah study *Lo Lishma* – without idealistic motivations. By doing this, the desire to study Torah will become fused together with physical and illusory motivations. As a result, when a person does eventually succeed in transforming themselves so that they study Torah *Lishma*, with more idealistic motivations, then everything rises up. However, if a person begins their immersion in Torah study *Lishma*, with purely idealistic motivations, then their lower physical desires are not connected with the higher spiritual motivation. As a consequence, one's spiritual connection will always be above their body.

To be sure, this idealistic motivation too has its benefits due to its purity and clarity of Torah insights. Nonetheless, its flaw is that it lacks the dimension of being natural. However, there does exist a dimension of existence with the highest level of holiness, where the expansive mind pours through the thickest clouds. It is here where physical motivations are strongly connected with the highest spiritual images. This was the spiritual level of "Rabbi Shimon Bar Yochai and his friends, who made Torah their livelihoods" (Shabbat 11a). (SK 5:11)

Uncovering the Individual Meanings of Mitzvot

Taamei Mitzvot

There is a great matter that has not yet been sufficiently explained. When one researches it, one discovers much spiritual wisdom as well as great and holy insights. This is none other than the study of *Taamei Mitzvot*/the spiritual meaning of *mitzvot*. To be sure, the phrase *Taamei Mitzvot* does not refer to investigating why God commanded us to do a mitzvah. It is this form of investigation that our great teacher the Rambam already attempted to do. Nonetheless, it seems like the rest of the wise men of Israel did not agree with this attitude. Indeed, this form of investigation is not beneficial, since it is above the limits of human intellect and is related to the spiritual principle that forbids trying to "investigate the essence of God" (Iyov 11:7). To do this, we would need to investigate what God was thinking when He chose to give us these *mitzvot*. However, we do not know if we have a ladder that ascends to the peak of such a high mountain.

Instead, what we mean by the study of *Taamei Mitzvot* is the study and comprehension of *Segulot HaMitzvot*/the spiritual quality of *mitzvot*. Certainly, if God commanded us to do these *mitzvot* and said that our perfection and the perfection of everything is dependent on following the *mitzvot* of the Torah, then each mitzvah has its own *Segulah*/spiritual quality that relates to each soul within God's people who are all obligated in these *mitzvot*.

We should not attempt to understand why God chose to place this specific spiritual meaning in this mitzvah and another spiritual meaning in another mitzvah – this is above our intellect. However, we can certainly investigate these *mitzvot* and see what practical spiritual qualities and insights God placed inside of them. We must attempt to understand the quality of their effects, their different spiritual powers – in all their details....

Even regarding this, we cannot understand everything on our own. For what are our limited intellects able to comprehend when it comes to matters of such great worth? Instead, we must search in the words of the Torah, prophets, and *Kitvei HaKodesh*/Holy Writings. With the help of their insights, will we begin to understand.

We will research the words of Chazal, the Gemara, and the Midrashim that are scattered in various places. We will develop such insight with logic, just as we use logic for understanding *halachot*. Indeed, God has already helped us uncover the inner logic of halacha and we have seen that by doing this we have reached the ways of truth in every matter and law. In a similar way, uncovering the inner logic within *Segulat HaMitzvot* will help reach, with the help of God, the ways of truth in every intellectual investigation.

To be clear, the goal of uncovering the meaning of *mitzvot* is not simply for the sake of hinting at and remembering correct ideas. Indeed, this is not the pathway to perfecting God's will that we see in the rest of existence. Rather, *mitzvot* are real acts that help actualize important spiritual goals in the divine order. The effects of these *mitzvot* are set rules just like all other set rules of existence that God created within nature and above nature. (MaR, p. 540)

Six Different Ways to Explain a Mitzvah

Mitzvot include inside of them every single type of explanation. This is because *mitzvot* are one organic unit that contains many different details that depend on each other. Therefore, we need to find inside of each mitzvah all the different types of explanations and how they interact with each other.

1) There is a desire for simple individual meaning. From this desire comes all the rational explanations of *mitzvot* and anything that brings happiness and expansion to the mind.

2) There is a desire to experience all of existence as one unified whole. From this desire comes all the visionary ideas and higher eternal goals.

Then there are four desires that fit in between.

3) There is a desire for divine connection inside the Torah and the search for God, the Creator and Sustainer of everything, the Master of all worlds, the God of all souls.

4) There is a desire for unwavering ethics that yearns for righteousness, quality of life, honesty, and justice for all.

5) There is a desire for religion, to sanctify oneself through all the different religious actions and holy customs....

6) There is a desire for... nationalism, whereby a person finds happiness and fulfillment through a deep connection with one's people. Such a person desires the continued wellbeing of one's nation and its unique inner nature.

To be sure, the most essential desire is to express all of these specific desires: the individual, divine, ethical, and religious.... We must be careful to direct each mitzvah in the right way. There are some *mitzvot*, where one of these six desires express itself in a stronger way, while the other desires are less significant. There are also some *mitzvot* where a variety of desires are expressed simultaneously.

The way we experience *mitzvot* is also dependent on the specific time period in history. Sometimes we find that a certain desire is expressed in one mitzvah or a group of *mitzvot*, while the other desires are hidden away and not able to express themselves. However, after a few generations have passed, we sometimes find that another desire is able to express itself through this mitzvah, while a previous desire is now hidden away. Such historical changes can also impact the experiencing of specific details in each mitzvah.

It is our duty to search for all six different ways of explaining each mitzvah. Sometimes we will find all six explanations in a clear and obvious way. At other times, we will find only certain explanations in a clear way, while other explanations will be more hidden. (KYK 2, Pinkas 1:2)

Collective Spirituality

10

Community

"Society is always blessed when those free-spirited personalities...
focus their attention on the needs of community." (SK 4:67)

SOMETIMES THE SEARCH FOR INDIVIDUAL SPIRITUALITY AND
self-introspection is so powerful that it overtakes everything else.
The deeper one enters oneself, the less one hears the sounds of the
outside world. "How can I experience more happiness?"; "How can I better heal myself?"; "How can I reach the ultimate meaning of life?" Rav
Kook believed that there is a hidden temptation within free spirited,
deep, and introspective souls to separate from the needs of the community and focus all of their energy on their individual spiritual growth.

According to Rav Kook, a person who has focused a lot on self-
growth and individual spirituality must push themselves to be involved with the community. The spiritual insights gained while being
alone can have a tremendous impact on transforming the world. Instead of turning internally and ignoring the outside world, one must
take what spiritual and psychological truths one discovered and share
it with the outside world. There is a story told about Rav Kook that
when he was younger the Chofetz Chaim requested that he become
a community rabbi. Rav Kook replied that it would distract him from
his studies. The Chofetz Chaim told him that "community needs take
preference." (SHR, p. 81)

In this chapter, Rav Kook will encourage us to take time away
from individuality and focus on the needs of the community. He will
be honest and discuss the difficulties of being involved with the often dry and technical details of communal issues. Ultimately, this is
one of the most reoccurring questions in Rav Kook's writings: "How
can I be committed to my own individual spiritual growth while also
being involved in the important and holy needs of the community?"

To Increase Good in the World

After all the noise and drama that comes from sophisticated thoughts that have caused endless damage; after all the deepest study in the structure of secrets and the hidden mysteries of existence, we reach the following conclusion. A person's efforts should be focused on developing their actions in order to increase good in the world – toward individual people as well as toward all of existence. A person's mind should be focused on the many clear thoughts that give an illumination of life to anyone who is involved in them. The righteous actions of each individual will eventually impact the masses. This will transform people each in their own way from the scales of guilt to merit. As a result, the world will become more exalted and elevated. (SK 1:631, OK 3, p. 315)

Holy Worry

Deep down inside of each person with a pure and sensitive heart and soul exists a type of holy worry. It worries about how to help the greater community. This type of worry is a divine spark within the soul. When it is developed and perfected through proper methods and correct study it will be a great illumination that transforms a person. If such a person merits, they may even reach *Ruach HaKodesh*/the Holy Spirit. Therefore, it is very important for one to develop these pure emotions. If one is a person of wisdom and learning then one should not ignore those moments of goodness when one's soul feels and yearns to break out and give more than one is capable of. (LD 19)

There is a Reality Beyond Yourself

A person needs to work very hard until they comprehend how there is a reality beyond themselves. Only when a person truly understands this will they be able to comprehend their Creator. Therefore, just as the verse "And you will love your neighbor as you love yourself" (VaYikra 19:18) encompasses the entire Torah, so too it is the foundation of truth and knowledge of God. (KYK 1, Pinkas Rishon L'Yaffo 76)

Empathy
Empathizing with other people's suffering refines the spirit of a person and purifies their mind. It makes the soul clearer and closer to the higher compassion of God, Who is the life of all worlds, Who has compassion on all creatures. (PR 2, p. 217)

A Pain Inside the Soul
There is a pain inside the soul that cannot be repaired until the entire world is repaired – in its total completion. (PR 4, p. 331)

Private People Who Help Transform Society
By nature, spiritual seekers are not usually social people. Their personalities can be compared to the ancient free-spirited personalities, whose social sensitivities were distant from their hearts. It is precisely because such people's thoughts were not distracted by social issues that they were able to focus on inner transformation. Indeed, the inner world of a person is of far greater spiritual value than mere social logistics. However, as a result of the inner transformation of such individuals, the entire society becomes transformed. Society is always blessed when those free-spirited personalities – who are above the norms of society – focus their attention on the needs of society. Society will then gain the quality of life that such enlightened souls have clarified for themselves, to live according to the light of life. (SK 4:67)

The Balance Between Privacy and Community
Sometimes idealistic thoughts cannot sufficiently develop and expand due to the soul's desire to guide the masses. As a result, an inner desire is born to separate completely from all types of social structures. However, by distancing oneself from the structure and spirit of the masses, this causes an exhaustion of natural instincts, which is often found in spiritual people. These types of people

need to strengthen their souls by allowing themselves to be influenced by the simple purity of the masses who follow their natural instincts.

Even though the masses contain much darkness and unsophisticated knowledge, nevertheless, they also contain many holy and powerful desires. These virtues are worthy of being the spiritual foundations of people with the most sophisticated wisdom. A spiritual thinker must stand in the middle of these two principles that oppose each other – separation and connection. From the first principle, a person is able to develop their mind. From the second principle, a person will receive natural strength found in simplicity. (SK 8:10)

Social Interaction Purifies a Person

It is very hard to endure social interaction, to be involved with simple people whose entire essence is absorbed in another world completely. Indeed, people who are absorbed in deep spiritual growth, in great ethical yearnings, feel no connection to normal social interaction.

Nevertheless, precisely this pain of social interaction purifies a spiritual person and elevates them. A deep person's spiritual influence on society, which comes about through regular social interaction, purifies society, and brings the beauty of holiness and freedom to anyone who comes in contact with them. In addition, the energy of holiness then returns and affects the spiritual person in an even more powerful way then the one receiving it. One becomes a social being filled with depth and holiness. This is an even higher character trait than the holiness of being alone with oneself, which is normally the fate of a person whose immersion in spirituality is the foundation of their life. (SK 3:315, OK 3, p. 271)

Does Socializing Strengthen or Weaken a Person?

When a person socializes with many different types of people and greets them in a positive way, this strengthens one's ethical character. To be sure, this only happens when a person has first strengthened their mind and has a sincere desire for honesty and righteousness. However, when a person does not have clear ethical goals, then socializing with people can be damaging. A person becomes pulled in the direction of any opinion or value that comes their way. In such cases, the more external influences one has, the more one's inner character becomes damaged. And when a person does not have a strong sense of self, they also do not have a firm foundation for truth and righteousness.

In contrast, there is a type of person who develops a clear mindset and a strong willpower through devoting themselves to good character traits and the ways of God. For such a person, socializing with external opposition actually strengthens one's inner character and talents. Indeed, this is the nature of tension and opposition: it has the ability to strengthen a person and increase their power and courage. (KYK 1, Pinkas Rishon L'Yaffo 33)

Spiritual People Who Care for Others

People who are capable of experiencing the highest levels of spirituality, holiness, and understandings of the mystical parts of the Torah, should not compare themselves to the majority of people. Their way of life needs to be a higher path; their minds need to be focused on higher values, removed from the busyness of the world, and continuously turned toward the holy. Through doing this, they contribute a great goodness to the entire world; they increase an energy of happiness, holiness and peace; they warm people's hearts and illuminate people's souls through their own uniqueness.

When they hold back and neglect their high level of spirituality, a great spiritual fall occurs in the world. Even though their path of holiness needs to be done in an extreme way, nevertheless, they also need to focus their minds on the needs of the masses. They must know "that there is a time for every desire" (Kohelet 3:1). They must learn to strengthen the meaning inside of life itself and to develop a deep knowledge of the world. Inside of their souls, such people must develop a strong connection and love toward society. Only then will they be truly well-rounded. *Tikun Olam/* Repairing the World will then be worthy of coming through their hands. Such people's deep sense of humanity will then be beautified, and they will be elevated to the greatest level of good. Beauty and *Ruach HaKodesh/*the Holy Spirit will come upon them with pleasantness and joy. (SK 6:26, OK 3, p. 268)

Expanded Self-Love versus Self-Absorbed Love

From the perspective of the oneness of existence, the entire dilemma of self-love disappears. While some have seen self-love as the beginning of sin, others have seen it as the foundation of ethics. However, in truth, there is only such a thing as a love of everything, which is actually the most enlightened form of self-love. In contrast, distorted self-love is something that loves only a tiny detail from its narrow perspective; it hates the essential self. This is a form of blindness, which is no less foolish than it is wicked. (SK 3:6)

Spirituality Causes a Love of People and Nature

The more natural it is for a person to perceive the world through the lens of spirituality, the more they will be able to perceive all people and nature with a great love and respect. The spirituality that lives within all people and nature is very precious and important. Therefore, the clearer one's spiritual perception, the greater will be one's ability to see the inner value within all creation. The materialistic perspective cannot experience such a deep level of respect, even when it is filled with an external appreciation of creation. It simply cannot be compared to the level of perception of the spiritual person, who perceives even the smallest spark of spiritual value within people and creation. The love of life and the love of nature; the love of the individual and the love of society; the love of the nation, the family, and the inner essence of each thing continuously develops and expands. (SK 4:79)

Spirituality and Practicality

Understanding and pondering the greatest spiritual truths does not distance a person from the real and practical world. This is simply the result of misconceptions that have been mixed with spiritual truths; and it is the main obstacle that prevents spiritual truths from being united with the practical world. The forefathers (Avraham, Yitzchak, and Yaakov) were immersed in both spiritual and practical issues. They were able to do this because they cleansed their misconceptions from the pure spiritual truths. In fact, Moshe Rabbainu's great level of prophecy – which usually causes prophets to lose connection to one's physical senses – did not cause him any obstacle at all. Moshe would speak to God "as a person speaks to their friend" (Shemot 33:11). This was because of his clear grasp of spiritual truths, which was devoid of any misconceptions.

Therefore, understanding lofty spiritual truths is not an obstacle, but actually strengthens one's connection to the practical world. This is similar to how divine wisdom impacts the world even though it is infinitely elevated. "Who is like Hashem our God, the One who sits enthroned on high, Who comes down to look on the heavens and earth?" (Tehilim 113:5–6). All the contradictions that exist between the spiritual and physical are rooted in the number of misconceptions in one's mind. The more clarity that one has in one's mind, the less disagreements will exist and peace will come about.

"*Talmidei Chachamim* (Torah Scholars) increase peace in the world, as it is written, 'All of your children are students of God' (Yeshayahu 54:13)" (Berachot 64b). This is referring to lofty spiritual truths. "And there will be great peace for your children" (Yeshayahu 54:13). This is referring to practical wisdom. "Do not read the words as *Banayich* [Your Children], but rather *Bonayich* [Your Builders]." This refers to all acts of transformation – whether spiritual or physical. "Rabbi Yehudah HaNassi would say: Which is the right path for a person to choose for oneself? Whatever is

harmonious for the one who does it, and harmonious for humanity" (Pirkei Avot 2:1). (KYK 1, Rishon Le'Yaffo 71)

Help the World Even Before You Are Perfect

The regular pathway toward self-perfection is moving from one
level to the next. At the start, a person should perfect one's actions
as much as possible, fix one's character traits, and only after this ascend to even higher levels. However, a pathway of gradual growth
only applies to an individual person who was not created to do
great and enormous deeds for the greater community. Yet there is
a type of person who is an *Adam Klalli*, a person of the community, one who is dedicated to greater social issues. Such a person
must always – and even more so than all other people – guard their
ways, fix their actions, and character traits. Nonetheless, if they
find themselves on a specific level of growth, this should not cause
them to give up their most idealistic goals and actions.

Such a person should not say that they have yet to reach this
level of growth and must first fix themselves regarding more ele-
mentary obligations. Rather, the needs of the masses are always the
highest priority. Private matters – even matters of the soul – must
not hold one back. Before David completed his ideal level of *Teshuva*, he sent a message to Yoav "Continue to attack the city and destroy it" (Melachim 2, 11:25). (YKY 1, Eighty–One Pinkasot from
Yaffo, 21)

Feeling the Pain of Each Individual

A person cannot truly feel the pain of the community unless one
first feels the pain of each individual. And one who truly feels the
pain of each individual will not cause pain to other people. Such
a person will follow all the laws about not damaging others (Bava
Kama 30a)[17] with a spirit of purity and with a heart full of honesty
and love. (HA, p. 336)

---

17. "Rav Yehuda said: One who wants to be a *Chasid* (pious) should observe the

Feeling the Pain of the Community is Itself a Reward

It is impossible for a person to truly feel the pain of the community unless they transform their ways, repair their character traits, and fully return to God. Attaching oneself to the pain of the community in the depths of one's heart is itself the reward of the mitzvah. Only the purest souls, those who walk in the path of the divine Torah merit to achieve this. (OTs 13:4)

Sharing Spiritual Wisdom with Others

A person who is truly righteous and virtuous needs to think about the following matter. There are an unmeasurable number of souls who feel and think. When their minds are clear and enlightened, filled with honesty and inner peace, they experience an inner happiness in their own life and bring happiness to others. This illumination of happiness grows and expands when people are fed with this inner goodness and it becomes accessible to everyone.

However, when people's minds remain dark and murky, they experience tremendous sadness. Their world is dim and all of existence is experienced as a prison full of suffering. It is therefore the greatest and holiest obligation of those individuals who are *Masters of Good Spiritual Thinking* to share their goodness with others. They must try to use all of the various means and tested methods to share this spiritual nourishment with any soul with the breath of life inside of them. This will bring happiness to all. (HA, p. 331)

---

matters of tractate Nezikin" (Bava Kama 30a) so as not to cause damage to others.

11

Love

"Love needs to be overflowing in one's heart constantly toward every-thing." (KYK 2, Pinkas 5:62)

RELIGION IS OFTEN ACCUSED OF CREATING JUDGMENTAL FEELINGS toward people. And unfortunately, there is a lot of truth to this accusation. "Why are you not following the laws of God?" "Why are you not eating, dressing and behaving according to the rules of Torah?" Yet Rav Kook didn't accept this judgmental form of religion. Rav Kook tried to help his students recognize that the stronger one's faith is in God, the stronger one's love should be of people. "Faith and love are always connected when they exist inside the soul in a perfected way. The perfected light of one side awakens the second side" (SK 1:221). For Rav Kook, love is not only something that two people share in a romantic relationship, but also a spiritual trait that one must develop toward all people and creatures in the world. "The character trait of love dwells within the souls of *Tzadikim*/righteous people. It includes all creatures, and does not exclude anything – nation or language" (KYK 2, Pinkas 5:126).

To be sure, Rav Kook was not naive about love. He not only understood how important it is to develop love but also how dangerous love can be without having the proper boundaries. This was Rav Kook's constant dilemma: Is there a way I can love people without being taken advantage of? Is there a pathway toward being open and vulnerable to others without them damaging and hurting me? In this chapter, Rav Kook will explain to us how love is the essence of Judaism and faith and therefore how important it is to overcome obstacles that prevent us from loving others. On the other hand, Rav Kook will be honest about the difficulties and dangers of love; he will give us guidance about how to develop love within healthy boundaries.

Faith and Love

Faith and Love Are Always Connected
Faith and love are always connected when they exist inside the soul in a perfected way. The perfected light of one side awakens the second side. It shines out of the depths of the soul in all its fullness. (SK 1:221, O. "HaTechiyah" 17)

The Greatest Power of a Person
There is no spiritual power that a person is capable of actualizing in all its fullness like a person's ability to actualize faith and love. This is proof that these strengths are the foundations of reality. (SK 1:222, O. "HaTechiyah" 17)

All of History
Everything that the individual and society does in history comes to perfect faith and love. (SK 1:223, O. "HaTechiyah" 17)

Nothing Remains Without Faith and Love
All spiritual light that illuminates the world comes through faith and love. Faith and love are the essence of life, both in this world and in the next world. When we hold back the light of faith and love, nothing else remains in life. (SK 1:224, O. "HaTechiyah" 1)

The Sickness and Medicine
The world's present culture is built on atheism and hatred. These two values deny the essence of life. The only way to overcome this sickness is through revealing all the treasures of faith and love. This is the ultimate goal of the mystical parts of the Torah. (SK 1:225)

The Jewish People Must Focus on Faith and Love
Torah produces love and *mitzvot* produce faith. These are the vehicles that enable faith and love to come into the world constantly. As the Jewish people awaken to its national life, it needs to focus its spiritual and physical culture on this twofold center of unity. Two

that is really four: the Torah and *mitzvot,* faith and love. (SK 1:226, O. "HaTechiyah" 17)

A Love that Overcomes Obstacles

Natural Love and Not Externally Commanded
The love toward all human beings needs to break forth from the source of kindness. It should not be motivated because of an external commandment. It will then lose the clearest part of its illumination. Rather, love toward all human beings should be a strong inner movement in one's soul. This love needs to stand strong in the face of many difficult obstacles and contradictions that are scattered like stumbling blocks. Such obstacles include individual statements found within the Torah, the outlook of certain *Halachot*/laws, various spiritual attitudes that come from the limits of the surface layer of the Torah, as well as national ethics. It must be made clear that when love distances itself from its divine source, its flower begins to wither. (SK 1:564, OK 3, p. 318)

Divine Love Overcomes All Obstacles
Sometimes there are obstacles and contradictions that hold back love due to nature or words of Torah. Love then needs to be purified until it is elevated to the divine love that created all creatures, which also sustains all creatures at all moments. (KYK 2, Pinkas 5:127)

Overflowing Love
Love needs to be overflowing in one's heart constantly toward everything. (KYK 2, Pinkas 5:62, MiR, "Ahavah" 1)

Good to All
The main spiritual service to God is training oneself to be good to all. (KYK 2, Pinkas 5:128)

Hatred of People is Hell
Hatred of people is the essence of hell and the root of idol worship.
(KYK 2, Pinkas 5:129)

Love of All Creatures
The greatest *Tzadikim*, the warriors of God, lift up the natural love
of their family until it reaches the entire Jewish people. And from
this light they are filled with a glowing love toward all creatures on
earth. (SK 2:37)

Love Without Exception
When the light of faith illuminates a person in all its purity, one
loves all people and creatures without any exception. All of one's
desires are for the sake of bettering and transforming the world.
Even the specific ways that one helps people are full of ethics and
honesty. It all depends on the amount of faith that shines in one's
heart. (SK 2:42)

The Struggle with Amalek
The character trait of love dwells within the souls of *Tzadikim*/
Righteous People. It includes all creatures, and does not exclude
anything – nation or language. Even Amalek is only wiped out
under the heavens; but through purification, Amalek is elevated
to the root of goodness, which is above the heavens.[18] The *Tzadik*

---

18. When Rav Kook uses the phrases "under the heavens" and "above the heavens" he is referring to the Torah commandment to wipe out Amalek found in the book of Devarim: "You shall wipe out the memory of Amalek from under the heavens" (25:19).

However, it is unclear what Rav Kook means in this piece. One possible explanation could be that according to Rav Kook, "under the heavens" and "above the heavens" represent two states of consciousness toward evil. "Under the heavens" signifies the limited human perspective that experiences Amalek/Evil as nothing but negative, and therefore desires to wipe it out. "Above the heavens" signifies a more divine and spiritual perspective that perceives some higher divine purpose to evil.

includes everything in his love. However, one needs great strength and purity to achieve this spiritual unity. (KYK 2, Pinkas 5:126)

Removing Anger from One's Heart

It takes a lot of hard and insightful work to totally remove anger from one's heart. That is to say, to truly look at everything with a positive eye, with an attitude of compassion and kindness that has no limits. In order to emulate the higher eye, the eye that is totally free, one must have compassion on the fact that people are drowning in the slime of evil. This must also be applied toward the actions of evil people – even the most wicked. One must find their good qualities and help them lessen their negative qualities.

One must strengthen the trait of judging people favorably even regarding those wicked people who the Torah says "do not have mercy upon them nor shield them" (Devarim 13:9). For this verse is only referring to those times when their actions must be judged and trialed. However, from the point of view of the inner world, one must search for the hidden good intentions that exist even in wicked people. When one finds a good point, it removes the poisonous force inside of the wicked. The negative force gradually decreases until eventually such people become repaired.

We must contemplate the following Talmudic statements: "We learned Torah in Jerusalem from the grandchildren of Sisra," "We learned Torah in Bnei Brak from the grandchildren of Haman" (Sanhedrin 96b). From these statements we are able to comprehend the depths of kindness and how we must not be pulled after the forces of hatred – even regarding the biggest enemies. From this we can learn how to relate to those people who cause us suffering due to their differing beliefs and destructive behavior. From their perspective, they are doing these actions with a positive goal in mind. This is even more true when those positive goals become actualized and cause positive things in the world. While it is true that together with this good there is an element of bad and de-struction, nonetheless, the bad does not cancel out the good. (SK 3:158)

Forgiving Oneself and the World

A person who is always pained over one's own mistakes and the mistakes of the world, needs to continuously forgive oneself and the entire world. By doing this, one brings forgiveness and the light of kindness to all of existence – to God and people. At the begin-ning, one needs to forgive oneself; after this one is able to bring a universal forgiveness to everything. Whoever is closer to such a person's root soul receives forgiveness first – one's family, close friends, nation, generation, world, and eventually all worlds.... Such a person uncovers the hidden goodness contained inside of everything. This is the spiritual consciousness of Avraham. And every generation contains someone like him. (SK 2:150)

Love that Causes Humility

The highest form of love causes humility since its love is directed toward "*Ishtaba B'Gufa De'Malka*," Dwelling in the Body of the King (a kabbalistic term taken from the Zohar). This great love comes from the consciousness of dissolving the individual self which perceives itself to be a separate and distinct entity. Such con-sciousness has infinite depth. Even if one had all the days of eterni-ty, one would still not be able to draw out all of its water. (KYK 1, Reshimot M'London 14)

The Dangers of Love

The Danger of Being a Loving Personality

The desire to do kindness needs a great shield. A person with the personality of kindness, who yearns to influence everyone, is also more likely to be influenced by everyone. This is the law of influ-ence: that the one who influences will also be influenced.

... However, this is the strength of the greatest givers of kindness... that bad people will only be influenced and not influence... God promised Avraham a shield in order that his influencing good and bad people would not damage himself. He is the role model of this greater type of kindness. "I will be a shield for you" (Bereishit 15:1). (SK 7:23, OK 4, p. 499)

A Shoe for the Soul

Whenever a person lacks the trait of "hating wicked people," it is very possible that negative actions and beliefs will affect and damage them. While it is true that through the great power of kindness one is able to sweeten and illuminate wicked people, a person should also develop the trait of *Gevura*/holding back. This trait acknowledges an inner hatred toward the greatest wicked people who lift up their hand against the Torah. This trait of *Gevura* can be compared to a shoe for the soul, which prevents one's feet from getting dirty due to the mud of spiritual negativity. This trait of *Gevura*/holding back protects the soul and keeps it pure. (SK 1:473, OK 3, p. 334)

Does Love Include Loving Wicked People?

The attitude of loving all people includes everything. Therefore, sometimes a wicked person is also included in this love. Nonetheless, this attitude of love does not take away from the trait of hating evil. In fact, such love actually strengthens the hatred. An attitude of love includes the wicked not due to their inner evil, but because of their inner good. Indeed, love states that this inner good exists within all matters. Therefore, when one separates out the good quality within the wicked in order to love it, the remaining evil is despised in all its intensity and absoluteness. (MiR, "Ahavah" 8)

Loving a Person's Divine Image, Despising their Flaws

A destructive person should only be despised for their flaws. However, they should be respected and loved for their inner divine image. It is important to understand that a person's positive qualities are more essential to them than their negative traits. Therefore, the Gemara says that a person should tear open a fool like a fish from the back (Pesachim 49b).[19] However, one should not tear them open from their face, since this is where the divine light exists. (MiR, "Ahavah" 9)

Connecting a Lowly Desire to a Higher Love

All human lusts need to be connected to a higher love. Such higher love elevates the living spark within the lust and improves it. As a result, the lust becomes a refined strength, having a positive effect, creating pleasantness and a renewal of life. Eventually, this lust becomes something that illuminates existence and increases the divine light in the world. The lust for money, food, honor, and sex – in all of their many details – are connected to a higher love. In truth, these lusts are sediments of love, sparks of holiness that have fallen to the shells. (YKY 1, Eighty–One Pinkasot from Yaffo, 69)

Sexuality Detached from Higher Goals

When the human spirit becomes so immersed in the lust for sex that it becomes totally submerged, then its ideals and morals become blocked. It creates the spiritual trait of the foreskin. This pathological attitude causes the body to have a lust for sex outside the realm of idealism and removes it from any higher ethical goals.

To be clear, this pessimistic attitude toward life causes moral decent; and it is one of the forces that separates the lust for sex from its idealistic values. The reason for this is because when the world is perceived in an overly negative way, then why would there be an ideal to increase these unfortunate human beings? According to this pessimistic attitude, the entire lust for sex is not rooted in any

---

19. "Rabbi Shmuel bar Nachmani said that Rabbi Yochanan stated, 'It is permitted to tear open a fool (*Am HaAretz*) like a fish.' Rabbi Shmuel bar Yitzchak said: 'And one may tear him open from his back'" (Pesachim 49b)

form of idealism. Rather, the lust for sex is simply motivated by the desire to break out and express itself. In stark contrast, there is a positive perspective toward the world, an optimistic philosophy of "And God saw all that He had created, and it was very good" (Bereishit 1:31). This optimistic perspective connects idealistic values to the lust for sex.

Nonetheless, the flesh of man and the human spirit has fallen so much until it has developed a foreskin. In response to this, the human spirit must create a spiritual path of repairing the *Brit Kodesh*/holy covenant through the *Brit Milah*/covenant of removing the foreskin. As a result, all of a person's desires and strengths will be directed toward a greater, holier, and more idealistic goal. "From my flesh I will see God" (Iyov 19:26). And God will sanctify the holy Jewish people. God is one. (SK 1:497, OK 3, p. 301)

The Power of Sexual Desires

The sexual desire has the danger of uprooting a person from the connection they have with their own life. The reason for this is because the sexual desire is rooted in the desire for a continuation of life for all future generations. However, when the sexual desire is connected to holiness, then the holiness of the *Brit*/covenant is able to be elevated to the spiritual level of "the righteous one for all generations." (SK 1:357, OK 3, p. 298)

Be Fruitful and Multiply

We know that life is not easy, that life in this world is full of pain and suffering. In fact, the sages concluded that it would be better for a person not to have been born (Eiruvin 13b). How then can we bring children into such a world? It is not for the flawed world of the present, nor the cruel world of the past, that we procreate and raise children. Rather, we bring new souls into the world to advance the universe towards the infinitely bountiful world of the future. Through the mitzvah of "be fruitful and multiply" we actively participate in the world's gradual progression. (OR vol. II, pp. 518–519)

12

Good and Evil

"Just as there exists a desire for the destruction of the world, so too, there exists a desire to build, elevate and develop the world." (SK 5:45, OK 2, p. 475)

THE WORLD IS MADE UP OF MUCH GOODNESS AND DIVINE LIGHT. AS each day passes, babies are born; soul mates meet and fall in love; loyal friendships are built and developed, people overcome their fears; moments of prayer, insight, and creativity are experienced. One of the main themes of Rav Kook's writings is to encourage a person to stop being negative and to instead focus on the divine goodness within the world.

Yet if we are being honest, the world is also filled with much darkness and evil. As each day passes, the news report countless cases of emotional and physical abuse, rape, shooting and terror attacks, and even national wars. There are many pieces where Rav Kook is honest with his readers and describes the very real darkness and evil contained within people and the greater world. "There is no doubt that there exists an evil force in the world that desires to do evil. It creates terror in the world; it is a tyrant, full of power" (SK 6:244).

Rav Kook believed that a person of faith does not need to deny the existence of evil. Instead, if God is the source of all, then God is the source of both good and evil. There must be a divine purpose to evil. "We can see that despite all its negativity and evil, it eventually serves a purpose – even if this is a temporary purpose" (Ibid.).

In the first half of this chapter, Rav Kook will explain from a kabbalistic and philosophical perspective why God created a world that contains both good and evil. In the second half, Rav Kook will deal with evil in a more practical way. He will give us advice on how we should relate to the negative desires we find inside ourselves as well as how to deal with people who are toxic and commit evil actions.

Evil Has a Divine Purpose

Evil Helps to Develop Good

Chachmat HaRazim/Mystical Wisdom explains the reality of spirituality and the world in all its different expressions – the good and the evil. When we look through the lens of spirituality, we can see how the depths of good is the true cause for the depths of evil. It is evil that helps the good become enhanced and reach its greatest level of fullness and perfection. Therefore, all of existence contains the desire for evil – evil morals and evil actions.

Just as there exists a desire for the destruction of the world, so too, there exists a desire to build, elevate and develop the world. The greatest divine wisdom guides us not to follow evil but rather to raise up a person as well as the entire world from the depths of evil to the highest good. This is the purpose of both the entire world as well as the individual person. This is also the purpose of evil itself: that it will be elevated and transformed into good. This will happen when we understand that the very desire for evil is intended to help develop and enhance the good.

In truth, the branches of evil that strayed from the roots of goodness are nothing but an illusionary reality. The appearance of evil exists only as long as the light and beauty of goodness has not yet been uncovered from the depths of evil. However, after this light of goodness appears in the world, evil will no longer be needed in order to improve goodness. People will then recognize that evil does not have its own inherent existence. "The spirit of impurity will be removed from the earth" (Zechariah 13:2). "The idols will totally disappear and God alone will be exalted on that day" (based on Yeshayahu 2:17–18). (K 5:45, OK 2, p. 475)

The Temporary Purpose of Evil

We can see evil inside of the individual person as well as in society. We also can see that despite all its negativity and evil, it eventually serves a purpose – even if this is a temporary purpose. Evil contains a special power, strength of will, depth of life, that is needed in order to enhance and develop honesty and goodness in the world.

We have confidence that at the end of time evil will be removed and the individual and greater world will purify itself. Everything will then stand on the foundation of goodness and evil will finally disappear. The universal desires for evil, terror, murder, arrogance, and anything similar will "disappear like smoke" (Tehilim 37:20).

There is no doubt that there exists an evil force in the world that desires to do evil. It creates terror in the world; it is a tyrant, full of power. This force exists as long as the world needs such negativity... until the world learns to purify itself and a new spirit, a spirit of the life of purity is blown into all people. Holy souls will be awakened to do acts of true salvation. We will be protected in a kingdom of higher holiness. And everything that is said in the ancient words of the rabbis and their hints about evil in existence; about its temporary power and influence; about evil being destroyed and its ultimate destruction at the end of days – everything is written with words of truth. (SK 6:244, OK 2, p. 478)

Evil is Not Random

We see the universal existence of evil on a collective and individual level. Evil exists within the inner character of a person as well as in one's practical actions. When we examine any manifestation of evil, we can see an organic order and structure. It is impossible to say it is simply random. This basic principle enables a person to perceive the essence of evil as an active, living and conscious force in the world. This also enables a person to recognize evil in all its specific movements and levels of influence. There is a Godly kindness, goodness, power, ability, wisdom, and guidance, which fills everything. It is impossible that this Godly force could give an empty space in the world for random evil. So too, it is impossible for this Godly force not to wipe out evil from the face of the earth and to protect existence from its destructive force.

From this we can recognize that the foundation of evil in this world is a creation of God. "I form light and create darkness; I bring peace and create evil. I, God, do all these things" (Yeshayahu 45:7). Now, since we understand that evil is a part of creation and made from God, we can know with certainty that this evil was created to help transform the universe toward a greater collective and individual goodness. Indeed, without the creation of evil, the world would not be able to actualize its ultimate potential. From this we can recognize that the essence of evil is good, and the essence of this good is very deep and profound. (SK 7:126, OK 2, p. 479)

The World of Separation versus the World of Oneness

When a person sins, they are in "the world of separation."[20] Each detail stands separately on its own. Evil stands on its own; it therefore has an evil value and causes damage. However, when a person returns to God from a motivation of love, the illuminated existence of "the world of oneness"[21] shines on them immediately. Everything is connected within one greater unit. Indeed, from an all-encompassing context, there is no such thing as evil. Evil is merely joined to good in order to add flavor to it and elevate good to an even greater significance. This is how sins truly transform into merits. (SK 2:97, OTs 12:5)

Absence Precedes New Existence

The principle of absence preceding new existence can also be applied to beliefs and values. When we see the spirit of humanity filled with turbulence; when well-established beliefs are falling apart, we should immediately expect the creation of new innovations in the spirit of humanity. There is no doubt that these innovations are for a beneficial purpose.

---

20. A well-known kabbalistic phrase.
21. Ibid.

The power of creation was that God built worlds and then destroyed them, built more worlds, and then destroyed those too. Regarding the world that was suitable for the goal of doing good, God said: "This one pleases me" (a paraphrase of Bereishit Raba 3:7). Such is how the attribute of creativity develops and bursts out. In a similar way, as times and generations progress; as many negative aspects become gathered together in the realm of spirituality – even when these are very holy and elevated – there always needs to be a type of destruction for the sake of expansion. This is the sign that a new spirit is giving birth: the creation of new and even more perfected buildings than ever existed before.

And so, our spirit should not fall when we see many crises and destructions in humanity that are damaging much of the good that already exists. Crisis does not announce destruction but rather a type of renewal of form and overall purification. When this task is completed, it will contain such strength that it will be able to remove all the dirt and negativities, to purify the vessel, and make it totally pure. "Yet her profit and her earnings will be set apart for God... Her profits will go to those who live before God, for abundant food and fine clothes" (Yeshayahu 23:18). (KYK 1, Pinkas Yerushalayim 21)

Good and Evil are both Necessary

If there were only good smells caused by beautiful flowers and fruits, then there would be no bad smells in the world at all. A person would not be able to bear the sweet smells since it would be overbearing and intoxicating. There is therefore the need for bad smells in the world. On the other hand, if there were no good smells in the world then a person would be overwhelmed by the bad smells. Indeed, the good fragrances balance out the bad smells.

This principle is also true regarding beliefs and character traits. Without evil and foolishness, the material world and the private world of the individual would not survive – they would be destroyed by the great longing for spirituality and collective belonging. On the other hand, without divine holiness and purity sourced in the image of God found deep within each person and founded in the Torah, then the world would certainly be destroyed due to the power of evil, the filth inside of atheism, and the arrogance of wickedness. It is not possible to get rid of all the evil of existence. Rather, a person must fix as much as possible; distance evil from its extreme expression; cover the filth; and place it outside of the camp. (KYK 1, Pinkas Rishon L'Yaffo 89)

Looking at the Long-Term Effects of an Action
The good and evil value of something is not only discerned and judged by the specific action itself. Instead, we must judge the consequence of repeated acts of goodness. We must judge how these good actions affect the masses and their long-term effects. In a similar way, we must judge the long-term effects of evil actions. The power of ethics spreads out from the general to the specific; it gives a beautiful form for good actions and an ugly form for bad actions. In general, looking at the long-term consequences of a specific act gives one a sign if something is evil and destructive. This is also true for judging if something is good, especially when something is really good. (KYK 1, Pinkas Rishon L'Yaffo 19)

The Good and Evil Within People

Are Human Beings Good or Evil?
Even if we decide that human beings are evil and that if a person was given the opportunity to follow one's desires, they would destroy everything. Despite this, and perhaps precisely because of this, we would gain clarity about the need for a higher ethics. With all the evil within a person, one still discovers a desire for good inside of them. Even though such a person has a desire for destruction, nevertheless, they would still prefer that their desire be to repair and fix.

A person would be happy if underneath the desire for destruction would be buried an inner desire for creation and productivity. Indeed, there is a hidden desire within a person for morality. Each human being contains a deep desire for a quality of life where one's essence transforms into good. A person desires that instead of having a lust for evil and destruction, they will develop a desire for good, wholeness, and transformation – to influence the world for the good. And in truth, the entire belief that the natural desire of a person is evil is only one side of the truth. Yes, a person has a tendency toward evil. Yet one also has a powerful tendency to do good. The essential desire of a person is that the good desire will strengthen and overpower the evil desires and that the evil lusts will be ruled by the good desire. This is not only what a person desires for oneself, but for all people, for all of existence. The essential desire for good to overpower evil is the goal of a life of faith and a connection to God. (KYK Pinkas 2:10)

The Good and Evil Within a Person and all of Existence

We see good desires inside a person that are aligned with morality, which lead to building the world in all of its perfection and beauty. Yet we also see evil desires inside a person that are aligned with destruction, shattering, filth and dirt. This principle is also true regarding all of existence. To be sure, from the point of view of existence itself, there is no filth or dirt, destruction, or shattering. Indeed, absence enables existence, and dirt enables beauty. However, such filth and destruction do exist from the limited perspective of existence that includes good and bad, beauty and dirt.

The inner desires of a person are one of the revelations of existence. Each person has the ability to direct the dirt inside of themselves toward beauty and the destruction inside of themselves toward fixing and repairing. Sometimes a person is pulled after their lowly and enslaved nature, and the desire toward negativity overcomes them. As a result, many damaged actions, feelings and movements are expressed. When this person is sustained by the negative forces found in existence, this damages a person even further.

At such moments, a person goes through an immense struggle until their inner force of good takes control, and the elements of freedom overcome the elements of slavery. This person heavily immerses themselves in Torah and everything holy in order to liberate their inner self. (YKY 1, Eighty–One Pinkasot from Yaffo, 37)

Each Desire Wants to Be in Control

We see two general desires inside the soul of a person. They have two opposing goals. On the one hand, there is a desire to fulfill all the longings of evil and all of the lowliest lusts – both physically and spiritually. At times, this desire strengthens, expands and confuses a person, such as in the cases of jealousy and hatred. On the other hand, we cannot close our eyes to the inner desire for good that expresses itself in the spirit of a person. The whole world is worthy in its eyes; it desires to give wisdom, goodness, and fill the world with kindness, love, and light.

Each desire wants to live on its own, be in control of the heart of a person, and fill up all of one's spirit and soul. The tension between these two desires creates a storm inside of one's heart and fills life with anguish. One continuously tries to create an inner harmony and do anything to remove this pain in one's soul. While it is true that peace is created by one side subduing the other side, nonetheless, there is a higher path than this: the path of making a covenant and uniting together. In this second path, one side transforms and joins the other side it is fighting with – bringing with it all of its great strengths and talents.

There are therefore two main paths to align one's desires so that the foundations of a person's life will be built upon them... The first path is the way of descent. That is to say, to guide a person toward an attitude of life whereby the voice of God in one's heart is drowned out and no longer present. As a result, one is able to give in to one's material lusts – including the evil inclination of anger, lust, hatred, and cruelty within the soul. This is the general attitude of evil which takes up a great part of the collective groups within humanity.

The second way is the path of elevation. That is to say, to educate a person toward the highest goals. The voice of God will be heard in one's heart; and the goodness of light, kindness, and love will be one's portion. This pathway comes about slowly and gradually, with small measured steps and in a way of modesty and quietness. (O. Orot Yisrael 1:6)

Two Souls

A person is spiritually made up of two souls: a good divine soul and an evil animalistic soul. This principle is one of the most important foundations for understanding the essential spirit of human beings; and it gives the clearest path to creating the ideal moral life.

Through this principle, a person is able to find continuous inner peace – whether in times of ease or in times of suffering. When a moment of goodness occurs, a person should connect their mind to the divine soul in order to expand, elevate, and strengthen it. When a moment of difficulty occurs, a person should focus their mind toward the evil animalistic soul in order to purify it of any dirt. Such a person should rejoice over the pain that the evil animalistic soul is currently experiencing, since this is how it becomes pure.

In general, a person should train themselves to look at one's negative qualities as something that is external to one's essence. By doing this, one will judge oneself in a just and correct way. (SK 1:809, OK 3, p. 235)

Responding to Evil with Calmness or Anger?

From a higher perspective, there is no reason for anger and frustration. We recognize that every event helps to bring the ultimate good and desired goal. Nonetheless, it is impossible to run the world with this mindset alone. Therefore, on the one hand, there is a need for anger. On the other hand, we must always be influenced from this higher perspective. We must strive with all of our energy toward actualizing the ultimate good, and not get frustrated due to any obstacle or failure. Indeed, it is the obstacle itself that helps us move toward the ultimate good.

This spiritual principle guides us toward a deep tolerance for humanity. However, most of the world is not able to accept this spiritual truth. They argue that if we accept everything with positivity, then we won't abandon evil and strive toward reaching the greatest good. Yet the truth is that precisely because of a person's higher awareness, they will strive toward abandoning evil and pursuing good with all of their heart and soul. In addition, due to a person's belief that the ultimate goal will be actualized regardless of all the obstacles and disturbances, they will experience inner peace constantly. When there is an expanded consciousness, there is also a greater level of tolerance. This consciousness expands until it spreads over everything. (KYK 1, Rishon Le'Yaffo 139)

Seeing the Good in a Thief

One Shabbat night a thief was caught in Rav Kook's home by the members of the house. They did not want to hand over the thief to the British police and instead brought him to Rav Kook. Rav Kook asked the thief: "Why did you steal?" The thief apologized, returned the silver candlesticks that were in his hand, and swore to Rav Kook that he would not steal again. Rav Kook then allowed the thief to leave. Not long after, they realized that Rav Kook's gold pen (that he had received as a gift from his trip in America) had gone missing. Two years later a package arrived in the mail – the pen was in it. (SHR, p. 286)

The Ideal World versus the Real World

The desire to break past the limits of human understanding causes a person to blur the differences between good and evil, purity
and impurity. To be sure, this desire is motivated by a great light
and holiness. For in such a realm, everything really does return to
goodness and holiness where there is no Satan or damaging forces.
Nonetheless, in the limited world we live in there truly is great evil
and impurity. Therefore, on the one hand, we are obligated to be
connected to loving goodness, purity, and holiness; of becoming
conscious of all its glory and beauty. On the other hand, we are
obligated to focus on being conscious of the disgust of evil and impurity, and despise it. (SK 3:288, OK 3, p. 130)

Hatred of Evildoers Must Come Before Hatred of Evil

When a person hates evil in a deep and powerful way, this hatred
must begin with a hatred of the evildoers themselves. Only afterward can this hatred become focused and clarified through wisdom
until it reaches a higher purity, where only a hatred of evil itself exists. Only at such moments can a person develop compassion and
mercy for those who are attached to evil – to the evildoers themselves. "The sins will be wiped out and not the sinners" (Berachot
10a).[22]

---

22. Rav Kook is referring to a story from the Gemara where Rabbi Meir prays
that the wicked people of his neighborhood be wiped out. His wife Bruria criticizes his prayer and instead instructs Rabbi Meir to pray that these evil people's
sins be wiped out and not the sinners themselves. Here are the original words of
the Gemara: "There were some lawless men living in the neighborhood of Rabbi
Meir, who used to cause him pain. Once Rabbi Meir asked of God that they
should die. His wife, Bruria, asked, What are you thinking? Is it because it is
written (in the book of Tehilim), 'Let the sins be wiped from the earth?' Does the
text write sinners? Rather, it is written 'Sins.' Also, look at the end of the verse,
'And let evil be no more' – i.e. when 'Sins will cease,' then 'The evildoers will be
no more.' Rather you should ask God that these evil doers repent and stop being
evil. Rabbi Meir asked God on their behalf and they repented" (Berachot 10a).

However, if a person begins in a very idealistic way, to focus only on the essence of an abstract evil, then a hatred of evildoers themselves will never come about. This is because a lack of hatred toward the evildoer blurs and confuses the hatred of evil. This would lead to the danger of much goodness being lost. This would be a stumbling block for many people. Indeed, there are those who have fallen because they began with an idealistic hatred of evil. Such people's lack of hatred toward the evildoers themselves eventually caused them to be lovers of the evildoers, and as a result, they fell into the mistake of loving evil itself. Therefore, one's initial attitude must be rooted in the trait of judgment and only afterward in the trait of compassion which comes to sweeten it. (SK 8:228)

Individual Dirt versus Universal Dirt

There is dirt that gathers up inside the soul of a person and breaks out and expresses itself through negative character traits, twistedness, lowly lusts, anger, and hatred. These are all symptoms of a general dirt in the world. There are individuals who work on cleansing the dirt inside the depths of their heart and soul. They accomplish this through character development or even more powerfully through the light of Torah and the elevation of prayer. This act of individual cleansing rises higher and cleanses the general dirt of the world; the universal judgment sweetens through this holy light. (SK 8:108, OK 3, p. 234)

13

The Jewish People

"We need to think Jewish, feel Jewish, live Jewishly, and to see the joys of the Jewish people." (O. Orot Yisrael 3:5)

FOR RAV KOOK, IT IS NOT ENOUGH FOR A JEW TO FEEL SPIRITUALLY connected to God on an individual level, one must also strive to be connected to one's nation, to feel rooted in the Jewish people. Many of Rav Kook's writings center around the theme of how a Jew should aspire to acquire for oneself Jewish spiritual traits – to think, feel, speak, and live Jewishly. A Jew should feel such a strong connection to one's people that they would perceive other Jews as their family, and would therefore defend and stand up for all Jews – no matter whether they are religious or secular, right-wing or left-wing.

On the other hand, Rav Kook was aware of the dangers of extreme patriotism toward one's nation and how easily this can turn into a self-absorbed nationalism that ignores the greater world. Rav Kook therefore spends a lot of time in his writings trying to help his readers recognize how one of the main goals of the Jewish people is a universal morality whereby the nation does not neglect the outside world but instead uses one's resources and wisdom to care for the world. In one piece, Rav Kook says that any Jew who acts immorally causes a disconnect between themselves and the Jewish people. "The ideal soul of the Jewish people is absolute ethics. Therefore, any ethical imperfection found inside of an individual causes a separation from the soul of the Jewish people" (O. Orot Yisrael 2:2).

In this chapter, Rav Kook will encourage us to develop a deep connection to the Jewish people but also warn us about the dangers of a self-absorbed nationalism.

Connecting Oneself to the Jewish People

To Feel, Think and Live Jewishly

The thirst to be swallowed up in the spirit of the Jewish people needs to increase. We need to think Jewish, feel Jewish, live Jewishly, and to see the joys of the Jewish people. This is the deepest, highest, and most expansive goal. (O. Orot Yisrael 3:5)

The Goal of Acquiring Jewish Traits

A Jew who desires to experience the true light of life needs to make an inner agreement with oneself: to root oneself in the Jewish people with all of one's emotions, senses, physical, and spiritual strengths. A person should make it the goal of their life to acquire Jewish character traits and beliefs to the best of their ability. Of such matters, the main thing is the acquirement of Torah in all of its breadth and details. However, one should also try to acquire anything that is connected to the wisdom of the Jewish people. Through the elevation of the Jewish people, the entire world's source of life will be elevated. (O. Orot Yisrael 3:6)

A Love of the Spiritual Possessions of the Jewish People

The precious love a person has toward the spiritual possessions of the Jewish people expresses the same thing that the simplest "fear of heaven" and pure faith does. It is only due to a lack of understanding that causes people of "confused articulation," to think that they contradict. (O. Orot Yisrael 4:7)

The Torah is a Spiritual Land

Just as the Jewish people can only actualize their potential in the land of Israel, so too, an individual Jew can only actualize their spiritual potential through the Torah. The Torah is the spiritual land for the unique potentials of the Jewish soul. Therefore, when it comes to growing and developing the Jewish soul, all non-Jewish knowledge is similar to the diaspora. (SK 3:123, OT 12.7)

The Individual's Contribution to the Jewish People

When an individual elevates and purifies themselves, they infuse their spiritual qualities with the entire nation.... Therefore, the spiritual strength of the nation is dependent on the individual growth of each person. (O. Orot Yisrael 6:2)

Is the State the Source of One's Happiness?

A state is not the source of ultimate happiness for a person. This statement can be said about a normal state. Such states are simply a big responsible organization with many ideas that are the crown of human life. These great ideas hover above the state but do not penetrate it. However, this is not true for a state whose entire foundation is idealistic and its essence is engraved with idealistic content. This truly is the ultimate happiness of a person.

A state like this is the highest rung on the ladder of happiness. Such a state is our state, the State of Israel, the foundation of God's throne in this world. Its entire foundation is to make God one and His name one. This truly is the ultimate happiness. (O. Orot Yisrael 6:7)

A Language Comes from the Spirit of the Nation

A language comes from the spirit of the nation. Therefore, the more the language is used in its life and writings, the more the nation's spirit will be imprinted onto the people. This is a general principle: the growth of the branches strengthens the root; it enables the roots to give off life and moisture. From this we can learn about all matters that come from the general spirit of the nation. The more things branch out the more they strengthen the foundation of the nation and its essence. (O. Orot Yisrael 7:11)

The Inner Philosophy of a Language

Each language comes from a specific philosophy toward reality. The philosophy of the Jewish people is one of holiness. This specific philosophy creates the language of Hebrew, which is truly a holy language. When one distances oneself from the philosophy of holiness one removes the light of this language. It is possible to give many speeches praising the Hebrew language due to various logical reasons. Nonetheless, if this is done in a way of life that turns its back on the greater philosophy of holiness, then a hidden hatred of the spirit of the language exists.... Therefore, the language will only express itself clearly when it is used to communicate the name of God to the world. To be sure, the specific reasons given that praise the holiness of the language should be accepted. Nonetheless, they must join together for the ultimate goal and eternal purpose. (O. Orot Yisrael 7:12)

The Revival of the Language and the Land
A letter to the Mizrachi Movement, March 18, 1914

In my opinion, we need to stand firm by the principle of taking the good elements from all places and movements. This is true all the more so when it comes to our national movement, which will always be rooted in holiness. This is because its main focus is on the well-being of the holy nation. In our eyes, the revival of the language, just like the revival of the land of Israel, will never lose its honor. This is true even though most people who are involved in such matters are unfortunately connected in an unideal way. Nonetheless, it is for this very reason that we need to put even greater effort in taking part in these big changes that are growing and rising. We must know with clarity that it is the word of God that is redeeming His people and bringing them – "little by little" (Yerushalmi Berachot 1a) – the light of salvation. (IR 2, p. 281)

Loving all Jews

The Spiritual Work of Defending Jews
Loving Jews and the spiritual work of defending the community as well as each individual, is not simply emotional work. Rather,

it is a great expertise within the Torah and a deep and expansive wisdom. Loving Jews has many branches and all of them grow out and are drawn from the energizing dew of the light of the Torah of kindness. (O. Orot Yisrael 4:1)

Unconditional Love toward the Nation

The unconditional love we have toward the nation, toward the mother of our people, cannot decrease due to any reason or imperfection in the world. "God does not look at the negative in Yaakov; God has not seen perversity in Israel. Hashem his God is with the Jewish people, and he has the King's friendship" (Bamidbar 23:21).

We come with a loyal love and deep respect. We come in the most committed way with a warm spirit and soul. It is specifically from this motivation that we call out to the nation to do *Teshuva*, return to the Torah and do *mitzvot*. It is specifically from this motivation that we call out to the nation to return to a life of holiness, faith, the inheritance of our ancestors, and our ancient tradition. And it is specifically from this motivation that we call out to the nation to return to the light of God, to the God of Israel. Indeed, God places His presence on His people and land forever and ever with His mighty strength.

We must distance ourselves from any resentment. We must rise above any small-minded thinking and feelings. We must elevate ourselves above any hatred and frustration. Instead, we must open ourselves up to a pulsating love rooted in its purest source. (EC, p. 59)

With You My People

With you my people, my nation, my mother, the source of my life, I fly to the ends of the world. With your eternity I live a life of eternity. With your beauty I am filled with glory and beauty. With your poverty I am filled with pain. With the suffering within your souls I am filled with deep sadness. With the wisdom and understanding inside of you I am filled with wisdom and understanding. (SK 1:163)

Feeling the Pain of One's People's Pain

The attempt to be totally joyful in this world without any mixture of sadness is in vain and even impossible. In fact, the forced effort to try to attain that which is above the limits of reality actually lowers a person to the very opposite trait that they were trying to achieve.

"It is forbidden for a person to fill their mouth with joy in this world" (Berachot 31a). This prohibition rests in the nature of every sensitive and wise soul. The enormous suffering of the world that includes all different hardships of life can be sensed in the heart of any person with a clear awareness. It is felt by any Jew who connects the awareness of the world's suffering with the painful struggles of their own nation, whose pain is as tragic and broken as a great ocean. (HA, p. 342)

Shedding Tears for Jewish Soldiers

From an essay Rav Kook wrote in response to two Jewish soldiers being killed in the Galil in 1911

We have new tears for new deaths, for young deaths, whose blood was shed by foreigners here in the land of our ancestors. And not just any young people, but young people full of heart, whose souls were on fire, who came to revive the Jewish people in its land. Such people let go of all other ideals of life, and chose to focus on building the Jewish nation in its return to the land of Israel. For such dear children of Zion...whose heart would not melt? Whose eyes would not shed a tear?!

I did not have the chance to know these young men who died fighting for the land of Israel... However, I was told that one of the young men... in the last hour of his life after being shot, when he knew that he was going to die, calmly expressed that his soul was at peace, that he had died serving to revive the Jewish people in its land. This young person's heart... found a moment of calmness in the flickering moments between life and death, with the knowledge that he had died in order that the Jewish people would be able to live in its land. In the face of this horrific vision; in response to this powerful soul, both heaven and earth call out: Holy! (MaR, pp. 89–90)

The Jewish People Must Be Ethical

The Ethical Goal of the Jewish People

We the Jewish people desire to live precisely because of the greater ethical purpose of existence. We recognize that our own focus of life is this greater ethical purpose. As a result, we are confident that we will help to complete this higher purpose. If we suddenly lose this greater ethical purpose of existence, then we would also lose our desire for life. Our life would collapse without any way of repairing itself. However, we will never lose this greater ethical purpose. Indeed, all it takes is one small spark hidden in the depths of our soul to bring back this greater desire.

We love this higher ethical purpose of existence just as we love ourselves. In fact, we love this desire more than we love ourselves. Deep inside we feel a small spark of this greater purpose which includes everything. And the beloved goal of loving all of life is more precious to us than our own individual spark. (O. Orot Yisrael 1:5)

Immorality Weakens One's Relationship to the Jewish People

The Jewish people is rooted in a higher divine morality. Therefore, any moral strength that is found in its individual people increases strength to the Jewish people. In contrast, depending on how much dirt and wickedness is found inside of a person, any moral drop and wickedness weakens the Jewish people as well as that individual's connection to their nation. (O. Orot Yisrael 2:1)

Jewish Imperfections versus Universal Imperfections

The ideal soul of the Jewish people is absolute ethics. Therefore, any ethical imperfection found inside of an individual causes a separation from the soul of the Jewish people. This includes any general ethical imperfection as well as any ethical imperfection that the Jewish people would consider an imperfection or sin. (O. Orot Yisrael 2:2)

The Religious Do Not Focus Enough on Ethics

Why do the secular currently run Israeli society and not the religious? It is because those who follow the Torah do not focus enough of their attention on defending the rights of the worker and many other ethical issues. Indeed, this must be fixed. (SR, p. 377)

14

Exile, Redemption, and Aliya

"To begin with, there are barely any chapters in the book of the Zohar that don't speak about redemption and the Land of Israel." (IR 2, p. 91)

FOR THOUSANDS OF YEARS, THE JEWISH PEOPLE WERE EXILED from the land of Israel and scattered amongst the nations of the world. Rav Kook believed that the Jewish people's return to their ancient homeland was not simply a geographical change but a part of a much greater spiritual and ethical redemption taking place in front of our eyes.

One of the main questions Rav Kook struggled with was what was the spiritual purpose of exile? Why was it necessary for the Jewish people to spend so many years cut off from their homeland? Was there a hidden purpose to exile connected to the ultimate redemption of the Jewish people? In Orot, Rav Kook writes:

"We were forced to leave world politics. Nonetheless, this contained within it a hidden desire" (O. Milchama 3).

In this chapter, Rav Kook will deal with fundamental questions such as: What does it mean for the Jewish people to be redeemed from exile – both physically and spiritually? Is the current secular State of Israel the ideal version of redemption, or is there a greater vision we are still striving toward? And lastly, how should a person make Aliya?

Exile and Redemption

All of History is One Continuous Redemption

Redemption is always progressing and moving forward. The redemption from Egypt and the future completed redemption is, in fact, one movement that never stops. This progression forward of the "mighty hand and outstretched arm" (Tehilim 136:12) began in Egypt and continuously expresses itself in all events in history.

Moshe and Eliyahu are the redeemers of the very same redemption. The first began it and the second will finish it; the first opened it and the second will close it. Only together will they complete the task. The spirit of Israel is sensitive to the movements of redemption, which continues to express itself in every event in history. This will continue until it expresses the light of redemption, in all its fullness and goodness. (SK 5:109, O, "Orot Yisrael VeTechiyato" 28)

The Redemption Can Happen in Many Different Ways

A letter to Rabbi Pinchas HaCohen Lintup (Kabbalist, author, rabbi of the Chassidik community of Birzai, and study-partner of Rav Kook in his youth), February 13, 1908

I will not hold back from pointing out to you... that we need to be practically involved in building our nation in the land of Israel. "We should not get into the habit of rejecting everything" (a paraphrase of Pirkei Avot 4:3). Just the opposite, we should criticize those "small of faith" who limit the hand of God to follow the vision that they imagine is correct.

The Baal Shem Tov says that "a person must serve God in all the different paths" (Keter Shem Tov 91). In a similar way, one must anticipate salvation, which is one of the foundations of serving God, and something that a person will be asked on the day of judgment (Shabbat 31a). However, a person must anticipate salvation in all the different paths. In truth, one path does not contradict another path.

We must merely clean out all the different paths; and with all our strength we will remove all the thorns and stones that are on the way. However, in their inner essence, all these different paths lead to the ultimate destination. (IR 1, p. 142)

The Present Moment Does Not Have All the Light
If a person comes along and says that they experience all the light of Torah and *mitzvot* in the current time period, do not believe them. It is a sign that such a person does not understand the depths of *Tzfiyat Yeshuah*/anticipating redemption. (O. Orot Yisrael 7:6)

Forced Out of World Politics
We were forced to leave world politics. Nonetheless, this contained within it a hidden desire. We longed and dreamed of a time when we would be able to run a state without wickedness and barbarism. To be sure, in order to actualize this vision, we will need to utilize all of our strengths; to use all of the necessities that the time calls for. In truth, these necessities will be guided by the hand of God, the Creator of all the worlds.

The delay is necessary. Our souls were disgusted by how governments ran their countries during difficult time periods; when they committed terrible sins. However, it won't be long before the time has arrived and the world will have evolved. We must therefore prepare ourselves. We will then be able to run a government based on righteousness, wisdom, honesty, and clear divine guidance. (O. Milchama 3)

The Tribes Were Forgotten
The forgotten connections to the tribes are a preparation for unifying the nation. If we would have remembered how the tribes were divided up, each tribe would have been completely separated from

the nation during exile. The poison of foreign influence would have crushingly penetrated each group while they were alone.

To be sure, due to this forgetting, there was an increase in confusion. Not only a confusion regarding which special prayers were appropriate for each tribe for the sake of repairing the world. Also, all the values of life, internal and external; all the different colors of emotions, studying styles, customs, and guidance were mixed up. When each of these is in their right place it increases light and life for the specific type of soul contained in each tribe; it builds its world. In contrast, when each tribe is mixed up with another type of order that is not fitting for them then this dirties and contradicts its development.

However, all of this caused pain and suffering only temporarily. Yet, in the inner dimension of life, the general soul of the nation was actually given life through the wiping out of the specific divisions.... Ultimately, through this mixed-up oneness, filled with confusion and a lack of order, will come a type of life that is fixed and ordered, something that will eventually reveal the light of redemption and salvation. The people of Israel will return to its home and each tribe will return with a harmonious oneness. "Flocks will again pass under the hand of the one who counts them (Yirmiyahu 33:13). (O. Yisrael veTechiyato 27)

Is the Current State of Israel the Ultimate Redemption?

Zionism Cannot Be Separated from God

The spirit of the nation has currently been awakened and many of its followers are saying that they don't need the spirit of God. If they could really establish a national spirit like this within the Jewish people, then they would succeed in creating a nation rooted in impurity and destruction.

However, what these people want, they do not know them-selves. The spirit of the Jewish people is inherently connected with the spirit of God. Therefore, even if such people say that they don't need the spirit of God, once they have said that they desire the spirit of the Jewish people, the divine spirit dwells inside their inner point of desires automatically. While it is true that the in-dividual person can separate themselves from the Source of life, this is not so regarding the entire nation of the Jewish people. The spirit of God dwells within all the possessions that are considered precious in the eyes of the spirit of the nation – its land, language, history, and customs.

And if there comes a time when people will be inspired to say that all of these possessions are connected only to the spirit of the nation, and try to separate these possessions from the spirit of God... how should the *Tzadikei HaDor*/the righteous of the gen-eration respond? To rebel against the spirit of the nation and to despise its national possessions – even just with words – this is im-possible to do. The spirit of God and the spirit of the Jewish people are one unit. Instead, the righteous of the generation need to invest great effort to uncover the light of God and holiness within the na-tional spirit and its possessions. This work must continue until all people who are connected to thoughts of the nation and its pos-sessions will naturally recognize that they are already standing im-mersed, rooted, and living a life of Godliness, shining with holiness from a higher strength. (SK 1:71, O, "*HaTechiyah*" 9)

The Jewish People Can Never Be Totally Uprooted from God

A covenant was made with the entire Jewish people that they will never become totally impure. To be sure, such impurity can influ-ence and damage them. Nonetheless, it can never totally uproot the Jewish people from the source of a Godly life. (SK 1:70, O, "*HaTechiyah*" 9)

A Protest Movement Within the Jewish People
A letter to the Mizrachi Movement, August 15, 1913

The Mizrachi movement needs to be to Zionism what the Jewish people are to the nations of the world: a constant force of agitation and disruption. It must be a force that never stops its unique efforts and protests. It must continuously voice its demands and hopes until the fulfillment of its greater, spiritual, and ancient beliefs.

... The dream of our people is not simply being good or even expert students of European culture (whose well-being is itself in great doubt). Zionism needs to return to the original source of its people's life. It is impossible that Zionism has nothing to do with religion.[23] This is a shameful belief and even worse than the desire to change the location of the Temple, which can be found in the book *Tel Aviv*.[24] Indeed, Achad HaAm was justified when he was outraged at the Zionist movement over such things.

Mizrachi needs to continuously demand that the disgraceful line "Zionism has nothing to do with religion" be wiped away from the Zionist program. In its place the following line should be written: "Zionism is established on the foundations of the national revival in its own land based on the Torah." This line should be understood in the most expansive and deepest way. (IR 2, p. 209)

Not Everything Modern is Correct
A letter to Rabbi Dr. Moshe Seidel (professor of Bible studies at Yeshiva University and one of Rav Kook's closest students), February 1, 1918

Zionism cannot find complete justification since it is a modern movement and not everything modern is correct. The cruel war

---

23. A quote associated with the secular Zionist Max Nordau.
24. The original name of Herzl's book was "Altneuland," and was translated into Hebrew as "Tel Aviv."

that is going on in the world is also a result of the modern movement and much evil exists within this. (IR 3, p. 157)

The State of Israel Must be Characterized by Jewish Qualities
A letter to Rabbi Dr. Moshe Seidel, January 29, 1914

The main thing is this: The State must be "the land of Israel." The unique Jewish qualities – in their most ideal form – will lead the country. Even though the State struggles with various conflicts, eventually peace will come about through the Soul of the life of all worlds, Who is reviving His unique people in His precious land. While such matters may seem sentimental at the moment, they will eventually become matters of necessity filled with the courage of life. They will be considered the foundation and main work of the nation. (IR 3, p. 159)

Aliya

Repairing the Sin of the Spies
A letter to Rabbi Dr. Moshe Seidel, January 1, 1905

"A small group in the land of Israel is more precious than a large *Sanhedrin*/Rabbinical Court outside of Israel" (Yerushalmi Nedarim 6:8). The root of exile and the negativity that comes to the world as a result, is because we do not proclaim the worth and wisdom of the land of Israel. Indeed, we have not repaired the sin of the Spies who spoke negatively about the land. To fix this, we must do the opposite: to proclaim to the whole world the land's glory and beauty, its holiness and honor. Let us hope that after all our praises that perhaps we have succeeded in expressing even one ten-thousandth of the incredible loveliness of the land; of the glorious light of its Torah; of the elevated illumination of its wisdom; and of the holy spirit that pulsates inside the land.

To be sure, there are many levels when it comes to *Kedusha*/holiness and *Chol*/secular matters. "Each one is burnt up due to the closeness of one's friend" (Bava Batra 75b). Nonetheless, there is a type of light and bliss of holiness that exists in the land of Israel that truly does not exist in the diaspora. This is especially true for Torah scholars who actively seek God. Even in my smallness, I know this principle to be personally true. (IR 1, p. 102)

It is a Mitzvah to Taste the Sweetness of Israel

It is a mitzvah to taste with an open mouth the pleasures and sweetness... of the land of Israel. "For you will nurse and be satisfied from her comforting breasts; you will drink deeply and delight in her overflowing abundance" (Yeshayahu 66:11). We need to inform the entire world, including the dark and miserable exile. The channel of life, filled with spiritual light and sweet holiness has begun to flourish in our beautiful land. The buds are beginning to be seen in the land. (SK 3:335, O. Orot Yisrael 9.9)

A New Type of Love for the Land of Israel

When a true *Tzadik* lives and develops roots in the land of Israel, he loses the type of love that he had toward the land of Israel when he lived in the diaspora. In the place of this old love, a new emotional and intellectual love grows: he senses that his birthplace could only be in the land of Israel. (KYK 2, Pinkas 5:149)

Kabbalistic Books about Israel and the Redemption

A letter to Asher Ben Yisrael (teacher, journalist, and scholar of Kabbalah), August 4, 1912

You have requested something that is difficult for me to do. I am currently dwelling in the city of Rechovot, without many books. Therefore, it is difficult for me to write down a list of Kabbalistic books that discuss the Land of Israel and *Geula*/the ultimate redemption.

Nonetheless, the truth is that there are barely any Kabbalistic books that don't discuss the Land of Israel and *Geula*. Indeed, Kabbalah is entirely focused on anticipating the ultimate redemption.

As is fitting for higher wisdom, it does not make concessions with the imperfect present reality. Instead, with the spirit of God, it elevates itself to a perfected future reality that is illuminated with holiness. Connected to this, the wisest of the Jewish people were unable to speak about this higher vision of truth and wonder without the Land of Israel and *Geula*/the ultimate redemption.

To begin with, there are barely any chapters in the book of the Zohar that don't speak about redemption and the Land of Israel. In addition, such topics are mentioned throughout the books of *HaTikunim, Megaleh Amukim,* and many places in the *Shlah* (especially in the first section). In addition, the topics of redemption and the Land of Israel are discussed in the books of the Maharal of Prague (especially in *Netzach Yisrael*), who should be counted amongst the Kabbalists, even though his style differs from kabbalists of his time.

The books of *Chassidut* speak a lot about the Land of Israel, specifically in many of Rebbe Nachman of Breslav's books and conversations. In addition, these topics are discussed in *Shaar Ha-Shamayim* (6:9) by Rabbi Avraham Iriri; *Dat Tevunot* by Rabbi Moshe Chaim Luzzatto, and *Pitchei Shearim* from the late Rabbi Yitzchak Isaac Chaver.

It is difficult for me to tell you the exact places without having the books in front of me. My advice for you is that you should look through the *Sifrei HaErachim* such as *Erchai HaKinuim* from the author *Seder HaDorot, Kohelet Yaakov* from the author *Maleh Roim,* as well as *Midrash Talpiot.* In all these books you will find many pearls that should be placed in the crown of the revival of the nation. These books will become something of great beauty and honor when a person of expertise researches and analyzes them. Please forgive me that I cannot fulfill your honorable request. "Be strong and brave" (Yehoshua 1:7) in your important and honest work regarding books. This work is vital for the building of the nation and its honor. May your portion be one of the loyal builders, masters of pure heart and honorable spirit. May God be with you. (IR 2, p. 91)

Those Mountains Did Not Speak to Me

Told by Rav Yitzchak Hutner:

I once traveled with Rav Kook in the mountains of Israel. He was amazed by the mountains. One other person was present with us. He asked Rav Kook, "What is so amazing about these mountains of Israel? Is it not true that you have been to the Alps?" Rav Kook responded, "That is true, however, those mountains did not speak to me." (SHR pp. 254–255)

Questions about *Aliya*

A letter to Avraham Soyer (author of children's books, teacher, and study partner of Rav Kook in a *Chavruta* in his youth), May 20, 1912

My dear friend, I have tried to reply to your questions as fast as I can... I pray that God will help you succeed in all matters. May God liberate you from the depths of pain and stand you firm on your feet. Now, let us turn to your questions.

1) Will you be able to find enough money in the land of Israel? It is impossible to say without first trying. Many people have come without any goals or plans. Nonetheless, over time they have managed to settle in a steady way. On the other hand, there have also been many people who have come with clearly laid out plans and goals. However, at the end of the day, they did not find stability and were forced to leave Israel. May God save us.

2) Living expenses in Israel are similar to those in a large city in the diaspora. In the region of Galilee, expenses might be a little less than in Judea. In general, in the smaller cities, food expenses for meat, fish and milk are similar to those in other smaller cities.

3) In Judea, an average apartment for a middle size family is approximately one hundred and fifty Russian Rubel per year...

4) In our schools, there is good education for national values. On the other hand, religious education is completely ignored. This depresses the heart of anyone who has not yet emptied out their feelings of holiness, which is "the inheritance of the community of Yaakov" (a quote from the Siddur).

5) In my opinion, any person who has become involved with the question of aliya, is first and foremost obligated as a Jew to at least try and see if they can live in Israel. And if, God forbid, they are unsuccessful and are forced to leave to live in another location, they have nonetheless benefited greatly from fulfilling their obligation. They have connected themselves in a spiritual way to our place and home.

I finish this letter with blessings and feelings of friendship. May God help you and the rest of His people who are longing for His salvation. Your good friend, just like we have always been, Avraham Yitzchak HaKohen. (IR 2, p. 81)

Each Person's Unique Relationship to *Aliya*
A letter to Rabbi Shimon HaKohen (religious teacher and preacher in the the community of Mitoi),[25] March 11, 1913

Your precious letter arrived last month, on the 13th of Tishrei. It is very difficult for me to reply to your questions. They are dependent on many side issues, such as the specific time and person. There are people who come to the Holy Land without any money and succeed in having a respectful job. There are people who purchase a small property with not much money and succeed in living in it. And then there are people who come with money and it diminishes and fades away. To be sure, everything is dependent on divine providence.

And so, how can a person from the side give advice on such matters? Whether to encourage a person to bring one's family into

---

25. Mitoi is Yiddish for Riga, Latvia.

such an uncertain situation, or to dissuade them from making *Aliya* to holiness. This is all very difficult. Therefore, it is impossible for me to answer your question. May God guide you with good wisdom and align your path before Him. (IR 2, p. 141)

Aliya for Each Individual versus an Entire Community
One time Rav Kook made the following distinction. If an individual comes and asks you whether or not they should make *Aliya* and live in Israel, you should answer them according to their personal situation. However, any person who dissuades an entire community to live in the land of Israel is considered as one of the "The Spies" who speaks negatively about the land of Israel. (SR, p. 271)

The Pain of Leaving Israel
A letter to the Ridvaz, Rabbi Yaakov David Wilovsky, March 28, 1913

I am shocked by your piece of advice for me to leave Israel to the diaspora in order to receive a rabbinical position. Truly, if someone would give me all "the secret treasures of the world" (Bava Matzia 49a) in exchange for one moment of breathing in the holy air of the land of Israel; or on the other hand, if someone would give me all the silver and gold in the world in exchange for one moment of breathing in the impure air of the diaspora, I would despise both of them (paraphrase of Shir HaShirim 8:7).

The only exception would be if there was a great need for the sake of some communal holiness. In such a situation, the spiritual holy ones have promised us that when we leave Israel to the diaspora in order to return – as the Torah commands – then the air of Israel follows such a person who is connected with a deep love to the land's holiness. In addition, it is understood in a spiritual way that the place that this person stands in the diaspora contains a small dimension of the holiness of Israel.

On the other hand, I was shocked when I read this piece of advice, especially when it comes from the mouth of such a great man like you. Indeed, to leave our place and life's home, and to go to the diaspora which is compared to "someone who is worshiping an idol" (Gemara Ketuvot 110b). (IR 2, p. 154)

A Difficult Decision
A letter to Rav Tzvi Yehuda Kook (Rav Kook's son), April 1, 1914

It is very difficult for me to decide what to do regarding the Agudat Yisrael's invitation to travel to Berlin for the rabbinical conference.[26] On the one hand, you know, my son, how heavy it is for me to leave Israel – even temporarily. On the other hand, knowing that my actions could have a great impact on the rabbinical gathering may lead me to make the difficult decision to leave Israel. My soul is unable to make a decision regarding all this. As a result, the decision keeps getting pushed off. I feel a lot of pressure and I do not know how God wants my heart to respond. May God guide me with His great compassion, with good and honest advice. (IR 2, p. 275)

How Long Will This Continue
A letter to Rabbi Dr. Moshe Seidel, June 23, 1915

It is very difficult for me to endure this situation; I do not even know how long this will continue due to the chaos of war. I only hope to God that He will not abandon me. (IR 2, p. 331)

---

26. In 1914 Rav Kook was invited to speak at Agudat Yisrael's Knessiah Hagedolah (Great Assembly) in Frankfurt, Germany. After debating with his family and students whether or not he should leave Israel for an entire month, eventually he decided that he must go, since it was an incredible opportunity to help strengthen diaspora Jewry's love of the land of Israel. Shortly after Rav Kook arrived in Germany, World War I broke out, and all paths of transportation back to Israel were cut off. Here are excerpts from a letter that describes Rav Kook's struggle to decide if he should make the trip to leave Israel, and then another letter describing his frustration after he became stuck in Europe due to WW1.

On Condition I Can Return

When Rav Kook was exiled in Europe due to WW1, he was invited to be the rabbi of the *Machazikei HaDat* congregation in London. Before accepting the position, Rav Kook made one condition. When the war finished, he would be permitted to leave them and return to the Holy Land. (SR, p. 164)

God Desires It, But Do You?

One time a person said to Rav Kook: "If God desires it, we will make *Aliya* to the land of Israel." Rav Kook replied, "God certainly desires it. The main thing is that you will desire it." (SR, p. 270)

Do Not Overthink It

One time a Jewish tourist from the diaspora came to Rav Kook and asked advice regarding the possibility of living in Israel. Throughout the conversation, the tourist calculated different calculations from each perspective whether or not it is worth it to live in the land of Israel. Rav Kook said to him "Before the Jewish people entered the land of Israel, they killed Sichon the King of Cheshbon" (BaMidbar 21:24). This comes to teach us that a person should come to the land of Israel without "Cheshbon" – which literally means calculations. (SR, p. 270)

The Ultimate Redemption of the Jewish People

It is almost impossible to taste true service of God as long as a person does not study and clarify to oneself the great worth of the individual soul, the Jewish people and the Holy Land of Israel. So too, it is almost impossible to taste true service of God as long as one does not comprehend the proper longing each Jew should have toward rebuilding the Temple, the greatness of the Jewish people and its elevation in the world.

... The verse says "And you will serve God with all of your heart" (Devarim 11:13). Chazal interpreted this to mean "Service of the heart is prayer" (Taanit 2a). If prayer is a type of service, then it is not service unless one has knowledge of the awe of God, until matters of prayer are close to one's heart.

… If a person does not know the great value of the Jewish people, then how will they pray with a complete heart about their redemption? When saying the prayer "Redeem the Jewish People," it is certainly not the ideal intention to simply pray about the sufferings of one's own individual soul due to the burdens of exile. The words of the blessing indicate that its main intention is the great worth and holiness of the Jewish people. If a person does not comprehend the great worth of the Holy Land, its special qualities and holiness, then how will one pray for the rebuilding of Jerusalem? Indeed, prayer must come from the depths of the heart, from a feeling that something is lacking. (MA Intro, 3)[27]

---

27. Due to the difficulty of translating this piece, I was guided by Rav Moshe D. Lichtman's wonderful translation, which can be found in *An Angel Among Men* pp. 248–249.

15

A New Guide for the Perplexed

"This is the obligation of the truly wise of our generation: to follow the path of the ancient sages of caring for the perplexed. We must help expand their minds in response to modern discoveries and teach them how all the greatest truths can be seen through the lens of the Torah."
(PR 2, pp. 18–19)

JUST AS EACH GENERATION HAS ITS OWN UNIQUE INSIGHTS AND wisdom, so too every generation has its own unique struggles, doubts, and perplexities. Rav Kook believed that it is wrong to simply complain about the questions of the new generation and call the youth of the day lazy, undisciplined, and lacking faith. Instead, one must strive to understand the source of their struggles, to respect their sincere questions, and to provide spiritual wisdom that will speak in a language they can comprehend and relate to. Just as the Rambam wrote *The Guide for the Perplexed* for his generation, Rav Kook took it upon himself to write words of spiritual wisdom that would help guide the perplexed of the new generation.

In this chapter, Rav Kook will discuss various pathways to respond to the honest questions of the generation. In addition, Rav Kook will encourage us not simply to preach and complain, but rather to create new religious and spiritual schools (Yeshivot, Midrashot, and various other educational institutions) that will provide Torah and spiritual wisdom that speaks to our current generation.

"This will be achieved not through preaching, nor through protest activities, but rather through developing our strengths and establishing institutions..." (IR 2, pp. 12–13).

Lastly, Rav Kook will describe the unique struggles that will take place in *Ikvata De'Meshicha*/the generation leading up to the times of the Mashiach.

A New Guide for the Perplexed

This Generation is Made up of Contradictions

Our generation is an extraordinary generation; a generation that is a total mystery. It is difficult to find something similar to it in all of our history. It is a generation that is complex and made up of many contradictory forces. Darkness and light are mixed up together. The generation is both lowly and elevated; guilty and innocent. In order to help it out, we need to comprehend its unique quality. (EY, HaDor, p. 108)

Is There Anyone Who Will Reply to their Questions?

It has been many days now that I have been contemplating what the Jewish people are doing regarding the growing cultural storm of destructive opinions and ideas.... My heart whispers inside of me and my thoughts burn like fire: Is there no hope for the Jewish People, God forbid? We know that every generation where negative words were said against the holy Torah and the foundations of faith, there were always great Jewish thinkers who filled this breach with words of logic and wisdom. As a result, all the mocking words were returned to those who originally said them. However, in our generation, haters of God have risen up but there is no one to reply to them. (Ginzei Raaya 3)

Following the Path of the Ancient Sages

The Ancient Sages/*Chachamim HaRishonim* such as Rav Saadia Gaon and the Rambam, saw that the books of atheism were increasing in the world, and how this was causing great confusion in the hearts and minds of people concerning the foundations of the Torah. As a result, they invested much effort in liberating people from their confusions and perplexities. These ancient sages attempted to clear a path for their generation, to teach them that the greatest truths cannot contradict the foundations of the Torah, not even a small part of it, God forbid. Instead, they taught us that we must use the wisdom of interpretation in order to understand the deeper meaning of the Torah. This was a great act of kindness they did for us, because we were then able to come to the point of truth in understanding the Torah.

From the time of the ancient sages (*rishonim*) all the way up until our generation, different opinions have increased, and new ideas have expanded that often deal with faith. This has caused people who do not understand the depth of Torah to find new areas of perplexity. The ancient solutions do not satisfy their questions since the ancient sages did not know the specific reasons that would bring about these new perplexities and confusions.

Therefore, this is the obligation of the truly wise of our generation: to follow the path of the ancient sages of caring for the perplexed. We must help expand their minds in response to modern discoveries, and to teach them how all the greatest truths can be seen through the lens of the Torah. There is no doubt that any person who works on this matter with a pure heart and mind will be successful in one's efforts.

There is much work to be done. Not only do we need to explain to our generation how to understand new matters… we also need to do an even more important thing: to help them understand all the wisdom and matters of faith that was said by our ancient rabbis like Rav Saadia Gaon, the Rambam, the Kuzari, and others. However, sometimes we find in these ancient words ideas that can no longer be said due to modern discoveries. And when a person with a simple understanding of the Torah sees how a small and inconsequential detail of these ancient thoughts is no longer relevant, he assumes that we cannot rely on the most essential ideas of these ancient thinkers, which are actually rooted in the great truths and are eternal.

Therefore, we must combine all the different ways of education in order to show how old spiritual ideas do not contradict the new discoveries of modern times. This will help our generation be liberated from their many perplexities, and find peace and faith in the pure Torah of God. (PR 2, pp. 18–19. #2)

Morality Matters More Than Philosophy

In our generation, ideas have become very confusing and philosophy has lost its level of importance for most people. The way to heal the hearts of the perplexed will not come about merely through abstract intellectual proofs and lofty matters of thought. Instead, we must focus our main attention on something that is eternal, something that no person with a trace of humanity can deny: morality and righteousness.

Morality and righteousness are the depths and foundations of wisdom. Only through morality can we confront a person, because there is no person who isn't obligated in morality and righteousness. Therefore, as a gateway to enter a lifestyle of Torah and awe of God, we must explain all the obligations of the Torah – whether obligations of the limbs or obligations of the heart – as a pathway toward morality and righteousness. In order to explain this, we will be greatly helped by examining the meaning of the Torah, and specifically, the national aspect of it.

When a person follows a lifestyle of Torah through the lens of seeking morality and natural righteousness, they will grow higher and higher. Eventually, this person will become aware of the importance of awe and love of God.

We must create a space for the search for morality and righteousness so that our people will be able to return to the Torah of God and protect its covenant with God. In order to do this, we must remove any possible obstacles related to morality and natural righteousness that have to do with the Torah. We must do this by giving sophisticated explanations of concepts that seem to contradict natural ethics due to an inadequate understanding of the Torah. This is similar to how the ancient sages tried as much as possible to equate the discoveries of the philosophers with the Torah, such as the theological problem of God being described as physical and having emotions.

And thus, when writing books in order to repair our generation/*Tikun HaDor* we must focus our main attention on explaining the meaning of the Torah and *mitzvot*, and showing its parallels to natural morality. This is the main spiritual work we must do in our generation. (PR 2, p. 20, #3)

Confronting Foreign Beliefs

Our minds are overwhelmed by the foreign beliefs that come and go in the world. Such foreign beliefs either come from total atheism or outside religions – Christianity, Islam, Buddhism, or plain idol worship. These beliefs break into our camps, steal the hearts of many, and corrupt people's paths.

Those people who are the guardians of beliefs in general and Jewish beliefs specifically, raise their voices with complaint, invalidate negative beliefs, and attempt to expose their twisted and deceitful nature. However, it is highly doubtful whether such people will succeed in stopping the volcano that has already begun to erupt.

What we need is a more nuanced perspective to this phenomenon. We need the combination of a more all-encompassing perspective together with a more detailed perspective in order to uncover the inner depths of these beliefs and attitudes of faith in the world. A spark of light exists within everything. The general desire of a person longs for goodness, truth, and spiritual happiness – in the deepest sense. Nonetheless, wickedness and ignorance has distorted these general desires and ways. The spark of goodness, divine illumination, light of lights, cannot be articulated and clothed in any letters – not even in the form of an idea. It is hidden and concealed in the depths of the most superficial shells.

The world will continue and develop, the honest intellect will grow and expand, the healthy logic and the many experiences of life will clean away the stumbling blocks on the pathway. Little by little the mistakes will decrease and the confusion of the wild imagination will gradually break apart. (SK 1:167)

Uncovering Jewels from Foreign Ideas

The great *Tzadikim* become elevated in their holiness when they sometimes look into the world of chaos, at various foreign beliefs, into the ways of imagination of idol worshipers and all their confusion. By descending into these darkened dimensions, *Tzadikim* are able to rise up precious jewels "comparable to fine gold" (Eichah 4:2). Eventually, these ideas become the filling pieces for the crown of the holy of holies. (SK 8:147)

A New Yeshiva

Combining the Good Within the Old and New Yishuv

A letter to Rabbi Meir Bar-Ilan (Secretary of World Mizrachi, founder of the Hebrew newspaper *HaIvri*, and the son of the Natziv), March 11, 1911

When I first arrived in the Holy Land, I began to realize that we need to create a new path for the revival of Judaism. This is the true revival of the Jewish people in the land of Israel. I witnessed the lack of strength and life in the institutions of the Old Yishuv, which are the pillars of Torah and Judaism. On the other hand, I witnessed the emptiness and filth of idol worship contained in the institutions of the New Yishuv, which calls itself *Ivriot*/Hebrews, and sometimes doesn't even bother to give itself this label.

My heart has melted inside of me due to the brokenness of our people. This is happening precisely at the time of the nation's healing, at the time of the ingathering of the exiles. It was then that I made a decision inside of me. Despite all the distractions that surround us from the right and left, I am being called upon to raise up a flag that embraces the good and healthy elements in both the

Old and New Yishuv, as well as to do battle with the unhealthy elements in both.

This will be achieved not through preaching, nor through protest activities, but rather through developing our strengths and establishing institutions that combine the good elements of both. As a natural result, the negative shadows will fade away. (IR 2, pp. 12–13)

The Central and Universal Yeshiva

An open letter written to rabbis and Torah scholars around the world, September, 1922

The Central and Universal Yeshiva will be established in Jerusalem. It will be a higher and greater Yeshiva location in our holy place that will be dedicated for the sake of the entire nation – including all those scattered amongst the different lands. This Yeshiva will help our national revival so that it does not become swallowed up in the waves of secular culture that is currently surrounding it. In addition, this Yeshiva will be a point of light for the life of spirituality and true religion for all our people in the diaspora.

This Yeshiva will accept young people from the age of sixteen to twenty-two. The educational program will be set and firm to teach Torah in its various fields: The Written Torah and Oral Torah, Mishna, Tosefta, and Agada; The Babylonian and Jerusalem Talmud, Midrashei Halacha, the Early and Late halachik authorities; Jewish philosophy and mysticism, the Mussar Giants and Masters of Midot; as well as any fields of study that expands the Torah and its knowledge. In addition to all of this, there will be a focus on educating the students with good character traits, guidance toward physical and mental health, as well as a simple and pure awe of God.

The higher part of the Yeshiva will be dedicated to the older students of the Yeshiva. These are the *Talmidei Chachamim*/Wise Scholars who have already finished their studies and are capable of being involved in creative Torah projects. These people should work in a special department focused on creating books and pamphlets that are necessary for the generation – in all the different expertises of the Torah.

The goal of the Yeshiva is that it will bring a sanctification of the name of God, the Torah, the Jewish people, and the land of Israel in the world. The desire of establishing the Yeshiva is that as time goes on it will spread all around the world. It will become known that there exists a higher and special place that includes the wisdom of Torah, religion, and the Jewish people – in their most expansive form. All of this will be situated in this Universal Yeshiva in Jerusalem. (IR 4, pp. 134–138)

Writing Spiritual Books
An open letter to the youth of the Holy Land who love Torah, 1905

The pen is conquering the world, it is ruling thoughts, emotions, and actions. With confidence it is succeeding, shooting arrows and swords with ease. Do you really think we have permission to be silent and not acquire for ourselves this modern weapon? ... Why are we not using the pen? Have our minds dried up, God forbid?... Thank God, we are involved in Torah and the body of the laws. But we need to recognize that these laws are pathways to inner thoughts and the treasure chest of the awe of God.... Our ancestors have given us an inheritance of great treasure from the depths of their hearts and souls. It is a wellspring that we have always drawn from and added to in each generation. Yet we are only using the surface-level parts without even searching out the ancient ideas. In fact, we must add, expand, and innovate, to give a new language to our thoughts and emotions in a way that will help people understand.

... This is most relevant for students in Yeshiva, who dwell in the tent of Torah all their life. Such people do not have any of the obligations of formal teaching or the distractions of society. Their entire goal is to be completely immersed in Torah – whatever field of Torah that may be. These students of Yeshiva have the greatest obligation to give honor to God and Jerusalem through creating an educational curriculum involved in understanding and experiencing God. Through doing this, there will develop authors, innovative thinkers, and spiritual thinkers who focus on the good qualities of the Jewish people, Torah, and the land of Israel. Eventually, the entire people of God, who are thirsty for the word of God, will recognize that from "Zion Torah and light is produced" (a paraphrase from Yeshayahu 2:3). (IR 1, pp. 24–26)

The Need to Spread Torah into English
A letter to Rabbi Pinchas HaCohen Lintup (Kabbalist, author, rabbi of the Chassidik community of Birzai, and study partner of Rav Kook in his youth), October 4, 1922

I am overjoyed regarding the hope of publishing your books in the English language. It has certainly reached the time that your clear and holy words need to be heard throughout the world in the language of the nations for the wise of our generation. Your words describe a Jewish and human vision of the world sourced in the Torah and all its depths. English is the language used by the greatest amount of the Jewish people and therefore they are in need of it. We must help them return to their mother's home. (IR 4, p. 143)

The Footsteps of the Mashiach

Being Influenced by Previous Generations
The generation of the footsteps of the Mashiach/*Ikvata D'Meshicha*, which is the current revolutionary generation, has enormous talent when it comes to releasing from itself a life of strength, passion, and structure. However, since it is so focused on releasing light from itself it is not able to make space for the inherited light that our ancestors passed down from previous generations.

This will continue until the nation elevates itself to a higher consciousness whereby it is able to release light from itself without exhaustion. It will then be like a well-spring overflowing from its natural self. The nation will be free from the chains of its limited individual self and be able to open its heart to receive lights from previous generations. (SK 3:296)

Face to Face: Freely Choosing God

The ability to live in complete opposition to a life of holiness is the only thing that will create the possibility for the most mature and perfected desire to be produced. However, as long as the desire for good is not developed in the world, there is also no real possibility to disconnect oneself from it. Only in the generation of the footsteps of the Mashiach/*Ikvata D'Meshicha* will the world evolve until one's inner desire will be directed toward the greatest good. Yet at the very same time, there will be an increase in the ability to separate completely from the ideal goodness. Only then will choosing to align oneself with the ideal Godly goodness be with absolute free choice.

When the process of separation completes itself then there will be a real possibility to build a world of eternity. This spiritual secret will be revealed in the generation of the footsteps of the Mashiach/*Ikvata D'Meshicha*. In truth, some of this secret has already been revealed. There are people with a deep vision that are already able to grasp this light – a light that consoles and is eternally strong. No longer will we be like Adam HaRishon who was created back-to-back. Rather, God will speak to us face-to-face. (SK 1:643)

Rebellion Against Spiritual Matters

We have a tradition that there will be a spiritual rebellion in the land of Israel and within the Jewish people when the nation begins to return to its land. The material security that will come to parts of the nation will cause a decrease in its connection to matters of spirituality and they will think that they have reached their ultimate goal. There will come a time when they have no desire for matters of the soul.

The desire for lofty and holy ideals will fade away and matters of spirituality will decrease. This will continue until a storm and revolution comes about. It will then be seen how the true strength of the Jewish people is in eternal matters, in the light of God and His Torah; in a passion for the spiritual light. This is the greatest strength since it overcomes all types of worlds and powers.

This rebellion is necessary since it gives birth to a desire for physicality. It must happen in a dramatic way because the nation was disconnected for many years from any need or possibility of being involved with the material world. To be clear, when this desire for physicality comes about it will burst out and create an enormous storm. These are the birth pangs of the Mashiach that will build the world through its sufferings. (O. HaTechiya 44)

16

Agada

"Agada texts were written down not simply for their own literal mean-ing, but also so that by connecting to the logic of a text, a person may be inspired with many deep and subtle insights." (Intro to Ein Aya, Berachot 1)

FROM A YOUNG AGE, RAV KOOK IMMERSED HIMSELF IN THE STUDY of the Gemara. By the age of 19, it is said that Rav Kook was study-ing 60 pages of Gemara a day. Over time Rav Kook realized that he felt a special connection toward the more spiritual and philosophical parts of the Gemara, what is usually called Agada.

> Inside my soul, I know that my ideas concerning halacha, while they may be accurate explanations, do not form a new path that stands out from books already written. On the other hand, con-cerning the world of agada, philosophy, and mysticism, even though I have only invested a small amount of time in them, I can see that with the help of God, I have already found a unique path. In fact, I have not come across books that contain ideas at all similar. (*Midbar Shor*, introduction)

Rav Kook felt that when people study the Gemara, they often neglect the spiritual lessons contained inside the Agada and focus almost ex-clusively on the study of Halacha. As a way of balancing this out, Rav Kook dedicated many years of his life to writing spiritual interpreta-tions of the Agada sections found in the Gemara. His hope was that he could create a revival of the study of Agada. Rav Kook called his book of interpretations *Ein Aya*. In this chapter, Rav Kook will begin by instructing us how to study the spiritual writings of Agada. After this, he will guide us one by one through individual Agada texts. He will first quote the Agada text and then teach us a spiritual lesson contained inside of it.

How to Study Agada

Explanation (*Peirush*) versus Interpretation (*Biur*)

The writings that try to uncover the spiritual light within the words of *Ketuvim*[28] or the statements of the ancient rabbis, we usually call explanations (*Meforshim*) or interpretations (*Mevarim*). These two names symbolize two different styles of interpretation. Each style needs to be perfected in its own way. The foundation of a person's spiritual growth is built on one's ability to interpret (*Biur*) or explain (*Peirush*). The words of the ancient rabbis, which come to illuminate future generations, need to be written in a concise and shortened form. They are something small which contains something great. However, they need future generations of rabbis who will expand their words; either by interpretation (*Mevarim*) or explanation (*Meforshim*). This is also true regarding the need to expand on the words of Torah, Prophets, and *Ketuvim*.

It is normally assumed that the entire task of explanation (*Peirush*) or interpretation (*Biur*) is full of uncertainties and doubts. Indeed, there is always a doubt whether the writer achieved one's goal, whether this person understood the true intention of the essay or statement. Based on this standard of evaluation, our heart turns sour concerning the idea that the holy task of interpreting the Torah... is rooted in such doubt and uncertainty. If the interpreter understood the true intention of the paragraph, great, but if not, the interpreter's effort is in vain, God forbid.

The Ancient Rabbis (*Chazal*) said "interpret and receive reward" (Sotah 44a). It is therefore our obligation to search each statement for the spiritual lesson contained inside. Indeed, as a result of doing this we will receive a reward. When we think deeply about this matter of interpretation, we will discover that the entire

---

28. *Ketuvim* refers to the third portion of the Tanach that includes the more philosophical and spiritual writings such as Tehilim, Mishlei, Kohelet, and Shir HaShirim.

issue is connected to the foundation of faith in the wonders of divine providence and divine oneness.

Explanation (*Peirush*)

A written statement can be read in two different ways. The first way is to correctly understand the text in a straightforward way in all of its details. This is the way of explanation (*Peirush*). The word *Mefurash* is connected to the word *Paras*/spread out. "They will spread out their hands in it like swimmers spread out their hands to swim" (Yeshayahu 21:11). This is a way of expanding the core message that already exists inside of a text. Since the core idea is folded up inside of the text, it is our duty to expand the creases in order to understand the full meaning of the text.

Interpretation (*Biur*)

But there is another way to read a text. There are ideas that are logically and associatively connected to a text. Any way that the details of a text can inspire the mind of a person to create new ideas – such ideas are considered a part of the text. To be sure, such new ideas are not a part of the specific intention of the text. Nevertheless, these newly inspired ideas are a part of a Godly power that created the human mind with the ability to continuously expand ideas for its own needs. In this way of interpreting a text, ideas are taken in a more expansive way. In relation to this way of interpretation, the rabbis said "The Torah's secrets are revealed to a person, and one becomes like an ever-increasing wellspring and like an unceasing river" (Pirkei Avot 6:1).

This is the higher type of interpretation. *Biur* (interpretation) comes from the word *Be'er*, which refers to "a well of flowing water" (Shir HaShirim 3:15). In this path of interpretation, new water is drawn each morning from every insight of wisdom that was inspired from the tradition of our holy ancestors. These new insights come from both the words of the ancient rabbis as well as the words of Torah. "'Is not my word like fire,' declares God, 'and like a hammer that breaks a rock into pieces?'" (Yirmiyahu 23:29). Interpretation (*Biur*) receives its message not from the literal intention of the text, but from the Godly guidance contained inside the text. Inside these holy words, God has prepared for us many messages that come to bring us true happiness and success, to illuminate our soul with the divine light of truth, and to give us spiritual sustenance.

Interpreting Agada versus Halacha

This second way of reading a text, of interpretation (*Biur*), is used more often in relation to agada than in halacha. The goal of halacha is to produce a practical structure. Therefore, the main way of reading halachik texts is the literal and straightforward meaning of the text. Even when a person needs to combine several halachik texts, the ultimate goal is to produce one single practical action.

However, this is not true in relation to agada. ... Agadic texts were written down not simply for their own literal meaning, but also that by connecting to the logic of a text, a person may be inspired with many deep and subtle insights. Therefore, when we approach the texts of the ancient rabbis from this perspective, from the way of interpretation (*Biur*), we must be focused on something much greater than the specific details of the text. We must recognize that by studying these holy texts, we are in fact dealing with divine providence; that through these texts God desires to help us uncover spiritual nourishment that will bring health to our souls.

Both Explanation and Interpretation are Important

Through these two different ways of reading a text, of explanation (*Peirush*) and interpretation (*Biur*), we achieve the spiritual act of studying the Torah. We are confident that we will receive a reward for our efforts even when we don't always understand the specific intention of the author of the text. Indeed, the main thing is that we have pure intentions and that the text we are studying inspires and expands our minds. If we do not explain (*Peirush*) the text, we are at least interpreting (*Biur*) the text. By doing this we are "drawing water with joy from the wells of salvation" (Yeshayahu 12:3). And as Targum Yonatan translates this verse, "You will receive a new Torah with joy from the students of *Tzadikim* (Righteous people)." (Introduction to *Ein Aya*, Berachot 1)

Commentaries on Midrash Have Forgotten the Main Goal

I have realized that most books written about Midrash do not focus on expanding wisdom and spiritual growth (*Musar*). Instead, they have simply tried to explain the famous and important words of the Midrash according to the words of the Ancient Rabbis (*Chazal*) and the Torah. Of course, this too is good, since expanding the words of the Midrash will help a person internalize them and affect their nature and character. However, something is wrong when the spiritual wisdom – which is the main goal – has been neglected.

It seems to me that any person amongst our people who God has given the understanding to enrich the treasure chest of spiritual wisdom, has a holy obligation to give this light to the masses so that they can see it and increase in wisdom. (MS Introduction)

Interpret the Maximum of Meaning

Interpret God's Intention and Not the Author's

The main principle of interpreting the Torah and the Ancient Rabbis (*Chazal*) is that through interpreting the text it will teach us important ideas that transform and enable us to expand our wisdom and talents. The interpretation does not need to be built on the specific intention of the author. It does not need to be the precise intention of the prophet when he was prophesizing these words, nor the exact intention of the ancient rabbis when they said these words. The proof for this principle of interpretation is that even regarding the interpretations of the holy Torah it is said that Rabbi Akiva innovated ideas that were never revealed to Moshe

Rabbeinu. Rabbi Akiva's ideas were built on the ultimate purpose of the divine will Who helped to align and develop his interpretation.

Examples of Non-Literal Interpretations

Therefore, we must not abandon anything in the world that has the potential to transform us; we must find a way to uncover its hidden potential. Sometimes the ancient rabbis explain the name of a city, such as Tiveriah as *Tov Re'eita* – good for seeing – in order to praise the cities in the land of Israel. The rabbis interpreted it like this even though they understood that the city was historically named after the Roman Emperor Tiberius. This is also the reason why Rabbi Meir would find meaning in the details of a person's name. Indeed, a person is able to draw out benefit and meaning from everything in the world. This benefit and meaning that a person draws out from something is certainly included in God's intention. Therefore, in many non-Jewish languages and ideas we can always find meaning.

Learning to Interpret Everything with Meaning

It is true, there is nothing that compares to what can be found in the holy Torah. However, in the times of the Mashiach, we will expand this ability to understand all the details of the Torah, which has no end. "The land will be filled with the wisdom of God" (Yeshayahu 11:9). This ability to find meaning in all the details of the Torah will expand so that a person will be able to uncover meaning within every detail of the world. Indeed, all actions are really God's creation.

... To be sure, a person must first attempt to interpret the straightforward meaning of the text based on the original intention of the author. Nevertheless, we must not criticize the looser interpretation that is not connected to the original intention of the author. While the interpretation may not be closely connected to the original intention of the author, nevertheless, it is certainly not far from the intention of God. Indeed, it is God who caused this text to come to us and Who has inspired within us an interpretation that is beneficial to our lives. We must understand that all spiritual meaning is precious and valuable. An event which helps us increase a small amount of money is not random, because God "gives bread to all people, and satisfies all the living" (from Birkat HaMazon). In a similar way, it is important to recognize that there is no such thing as randomly receiving a spiritual benefit.

Interpretations that Affect Practical Actions

To be sure, this principle of interpretation needs to be examined when it comes to practical actions. Such things need Great Wisdom (*Bina Yateira*). Rabbi Meir was so wise that "people could not fully understand his thoughts" (Eruvin 13b). He was worthy of interpreting people's names to produce practical actions. One must be careful when it comes to this principle of interpretation; and indeed, the Rambam complained about his generation's sickness of interpreting a text in a way the author never intended. Nevertheless, the ancient rabbis did attain such a great level of wisdom. And it is built on the truth of the wisdom of God. "God has spoken. Who will not prophesy? (Amos 3:8) (KYK 2, Boisk 1:21)

Divine Ideas Never Become Old

Divine ideas never become old. In every generation, people dress up divine ideas in the new colors they perceive. And in every new change of color, these divine ideas are given new life. This elevates life in general, and the individual life in particular. (KYK 1, Pinkas 5:32)

Uncovering New Insights from Old Texts

"If you listen to the old, then you will hear new matters" (Berachot 40a). A person must train themselves to comprehend well-known concepts in an independent and internal way, and not simply interpret the words in a literal and childish way. As a result, one will be inspired with many new insights. This is the meaning of the

statement "If you listen to the old" – if you listen in an independent way, "then you will hear new matters." However, as long as a
person is lazy and does not attempt to draw out the meaning of the
old words through one's own independent and inner logic, then
a person will never reach new and clear insights. (KYK 1, Pinkas
Rishon L' Yaffo 50)

Words Should Not Block the Mind

All words spoken or written down should not be allowed to block
one's logic and intellect. This is an important spiritual principle in
the Torah that applies to both spiritual concepts and small details.
(SK 1:278)

Obstacles to Studying Torah

There are three types of obstacles when it comes to *Shkeida*/study-
ing Torah in a disciplined way. The first is when a person is involved
in superficial matters that are beneath the dignity of studying Torah. As a result, one is not able to focus their mind while studying
Torah.

The second is that a person is drawn toward things that are
more exalted than what one is currently studying. For example, a
person is drawn to poetry and philosophical and spiritual wisdom.
In contrast, one's regular Torah study is focused more on simple
matters. Consequently, a person doesn't find much satisfaction in
them. The third is when outside influences overwhelm a person's
physical and spiritual strength. As a result, one loses the pleasantness and pleasure of discovering wisdom. Concerning this it is said
"The more one adds, the more one takes away" (Sanhedrin 29a). In
each of these obstacles, one needs to ponder and examine. (KYK 1,
Pinkas Rishon L' Yaffo 110a)

Uncovering the Spiritual Lessons of Agada

Praying for Other People

> Abba Binyamin says that if two people start praying together and the first person finishes and doesn't wait for the second person to finish, the first person's prayer is snatched away from him. (Berachot 5b)

The lesson we learn from this is that a person's prayers are not desirable as long as one's intention is simply to attain benefit for oneself. Therefore, when a person doesn't wait for one's friend to finish praying, this is a sign that the person didn't focus one's prayers on the needs of one's friend at all. As a consequence, this person's prayers are snatched away from them, and one causes the divine presence to be removed from the Jewish people. God's presence only dwells in a place where true peace exists; where each person seeks to do good for one's friend – either spiritually or physically. (EA, Berachot 1, pp. 19–20)

The Importance of Having Wise Scholars to Learn From

> Rabbi Yehoshua ben Levi said: Whoever makes negative comments about *Talmidei Chachamim*/Wise Scholars after their death, is cast into *Gehenom*/hell. As it is written, "But those who turn to crooked ways, God will lead them away with the people who sin. Peace be on Israel" (Tehilim 125:5). Even at a time when there is peace upon Israel, God will lead them away with the people who sin. (Berachot 19a)

The mitzvah of "You should judge in righteousness" (Vayikra 19:15), which instructs a person to judge every person in a positive way (Shavuot 30a) is one of the foundations of ethical and spiritual growth. By judging a *Talmid Chacham*/Wise Scholar in a favorable way, one also judges their words of wisdom in a positive way. When a person perceives these wise scholars with a sense of awe, one is able to appreciate the depths of their thoughts. The holy words that come from people of truth become a light for one's footsteps, and one becomes motivated to walk in the path of goodness.

The Rambam writes (MT, *Hilchut Teshuva* 4:2) that one of the main things that blocks a person from *Teshuva*/Spiritual Growth is insulting *Talmidei Chachamim*/Wise Scholars since a person will no longer have someone to learn from. When a person judges a *Talmid Chacham* in a negative way, one has no ethical foundation to stand on. In fact, these wise people's words become a stumbling block. "The ways of God are straight; the righteous walk with them, but the sinners stumble in them" (Hoshea 14:10).

Now, since in every generation there are chaotic events that bring ethical and spiritual challenges, every person is likely to make mistakes and stumble. Therefore, one who has become accustomed to judging wise scholars in a negative way will go from one sin to another. Such a person will violate the words of Torah learned from the rabbis, from whom we receive our very life – even under non-dangerous circumstances. Therefore, even when there is "peace among the Jewish people" and the generation is "in awe of God and ponders His name" (Malachi 3:16), "God will lead them away with the people who sin." (EA, Berachot 1, pp. 94–95)

A Drunken Person Should Not Pray

"And Eli thought Chana was drunk" (Shmuel One, 1:13). From this we learn that it is forbidden to pray while being drunk. (Berachot 31a)

Even though the foundation of prayer is built on emotions, and one's emotions often strengthen while being drunk… nevertheless, a person will not reach the ultimate goal of prayer unless one's emotions are connected to the mind. When a person is drunk their emotions rule on their own and the influence of the mind is damaged. This is not fitting for prayer.

In addition, the obligation of prayer does not only concern the moment of praying but also to make sure that praying affects one's behavior long after prayer is finished. A drunken person may feel goodness and righteousness in the present moment, but he will not be able to direct his emotions in order to have a consistent influence on the goodness and righteousness of his behavior. In order for a person to develop ethical strength, he needs a calm and relaxed mind in order to distinguish between the sacred and ordinary, between the pure and impure. However, for the drunken person, the entire world seems the same, and is therefore unable to recognize the damage of his incorrect actions. And thus, the drunken person is forbidden to pray. (EA, Berachot 1, p. 133)

Praying in a House with Windows

Rabbi Chanina says a person should only pray in a house that has windows. As it is written, "Daniel went home to his upstairs room where the windows opened toward Jerusalem" (Daniel 6:10). (Berachot 34b)

Prayer is a spiritual practice inside of the soul of a person. Nevertheless, in order for prayer to transform and affect the person praying, it is necessary that one develops a strong awareness and sensitivity to the outside world. Prayer will then transform both the person and other people. However, a person will not reach the ultimate perfection of prayer if their own spiritual growth causes them to be disconnected from the outside world. The goal of prayer is to bring life to a person, to be inspired by the divine spirit, and eventually do acts of righteousness and honesty. Therefore, "a person should only pray in a house that has windows." The ability to physically see the external world will awaken within a person the obligation toward the outside world one lives in. (EA, Berachot 1, p. 168)

The Importance of Details

> Rav Ashi and some say Chanina Bar Papa said: Take care of going to the bathroom before you stand to pray before God. (Berachot 23b)

This warning contains in it a spiritual insight about walking in a balanced and logical way. A person should not say to oneself that since one has reached a high spiritual level in Torah, wisdom, ethics, and action that one no longer has an obligation to focus on the details of *mitzvot* and ethics. This is not true. Sometimes, even the smallest flaw can cause great damage. Therefore, even the wisest person needs to focus on the smallest actions and details. One must take care that each detail is aligned to Torah and *mitzvot*. One should not belittle these details. As it is written, "a person who sanctifies oneself down low is sanctified up above" (Yoma 39a). The more a person purifies one's actions, the greater light and wisdom of God will illuminate one's mind and elevate one's soul. (EA, Berachot 1, p. 106)

The Stability of a Congregation

> Ravin Bar Rav Ada said in the name of Rav Yitzchak: Where do we know that God is found in the synagogue? As it is written, "God stands in the congregation of the divine" (Tehilim 82:1). (Berachot 6a)

There is a great power contained in a congregation. Therefore, the rabbis have warned us "not to separate ourselves from a congregation" (Pirkei Avot 2:4). One of the powers of a congregation is that once it is founded on a good path, it will not easily change. Such change only happens to individuals. However, when it comes to the general masses, things do not easily change and they remain faithful to God. As it is written, "My Spirit, which is on you, will not depart from you, and My words that I have put in your mouth will always be on your lips, on the lips of your children, and on the lips

of their descendants – from this time on and forever,' says God"
(Yeshayahu 59:21).

The reality of God does not change. As it is written "I am God,
I did not change" (Malachi 3:6). Where can we find this trait of
"non-changing" in our own life? In the synagogue, where there is
a gathering of the masses. This is in contrast to an individual who
does not stay in one mood. Therefore, Hillel connected the two
verses "Do not separate yourself from the congregation" with "Do
not trust yourself until the day you die" (Pirkei Avot 2:4). This was
in order to teach us about the trait of stability found in a congregation. (EA Berachot 1 pp. 22–23)

Thanking God

> Rabbi Yochanan said in the name of Rabbi Shimon Bar Yochai:
> From the day God created His world, no one thanked God until
> Leah came along and thanked Him. As it is written "This time I
> will thank God" (Bereishit 29:35). (Berachot 7a)

There is a difference between a blessing and saying thank you. A
blessing can refer to anything good that comes about even though
it wasn't intended. For example, one might say, "This boy is a blessing, his growth is a blessing." However, the act of saying thank you
comes about as a result of goodness that was freely chosen – either
to give or not to give. Until Leah came along, there was no one who
made the effort to teach people that even though God is the ultimate source of all blessings, nonetheless, things do not come from
God automatically – as certain philosophers believe. Instead, God
freely chooses to give. This is why we say thank you. (EA, Berachot
1 p. 32)

Internal Enemies

> Rabbi Yochanan said in the name of Rabbi Shimon Bar Yochai:
> Bad behavior inside of a person's home is more difficult than
> the war of Gog and Magog. As it is written "A Psalm of David,

when he fled from his son Avshalom" (Tehilim 3:1). Then it is written, "God, how numerous are my enemies, many have risen up against me" (Tehilim 3:2). (Berachot 7b)

There is both an individual and national lesson here. The individual lesson is that each person has various external opponents and enemies who want to damage them, for example, natural forces of nature, weather conditions, and seasonal changes. Nonetheless, these external enemies are not so strong that one would be unable to guard oneself from damage. In contrast, the inner enemy, the *Yetzer HaRa,* which is a person's negative desire, is continuously damaging one's body and soul. From such inner enemies, a person needs great protection since they are so near. As it is written in *Chovot HaLevavot,* "Each person has an enemy between their ribs" (Shaar Yichud HaMaaseh, Ch 5).

The national lesson is that the Jewish people have been damaged by many external enemies and negative cultures. Nonetheless, the mixed multitude in every generation, who are the minority of the Jewish people, have damaged us more. They have filled the Jewish people with hatred toward their Father in heaven, by giving them incorrect beliefs and negative character traits. Therefore, God has promised us, "I will thoroughly purge away your dross and remove all your impurities" (Yeshayahu 1:25). Then it is written, "Afterward you will be called the city of righteousness" (Ibid. 1:26). (EA, Berachot 1, p. 35)

Serving a Torah Sage

Rabbi Yochanan said in the name of Rabbi Shimon ben Yochai: Service of a Torah sage is greater than learning Torah itself. As it is written, "Here is Elisha son of Shafat, who poured water over Eliyahu's hands" (II Kings 3:11). The verse does not say that Elisha learned Torah from Eliyahu, rather that he poured water for Eliyahu. This teaches that serving a Torah sage is greater than learning Torah itself. (Berachot 7b)

The Torah is called "Torat Chayim," the Torah of life. Therefore, the main goal is how a person should act based on the Torah's ways and values.

However, it is impossible to accurately explain the great attributes of a holy person who is connected to Torah – not through words and certainly not through writing. Therefore, only a person who sees with their own eyes the holy ways of a Torah sage will comprehend the value of Torah and how it impacts people who are connected and in love with it.

Therefore, "Service of a Torah sage is greater than learning Torah itself." A person is able to see the holy behavior of a rabbi with their own eyes. This is much greater than any form of learning Torah. (EA, Berachot 1, p. 36)

Praying During a Time of Desire

What is the meaning of the verse: "May my prayer be to You, God, in a time of desire. God, in Your great mercy, answer me with the truth of Your salvation" (Tehilim 69:14)? When is a time of desire? It is at the time when the congregation is praying. (Berachot 8a)

The foundation of prayer... is to help a person perfect themselves and their needs. Prayer helps a person develop their morality, elevate their soul, focus their mind, and strengthen their spiritual side. In general, the main concern for morality would not be so important if a person lived alone on their own. Morality is rooted in the fact that a person is involved with other people. This principle applies to the present moment as well as to the future, toward one's home, family, as well as toward all of society. Therefore, a person needs to internalize this important principle. A person should be careful not to damage other people as a result of too much self-focus.

This is why the main type of prayer is when the congregation comes together. If a person only wanted to perfect themselves, to comprehend correct ideas, it would be enough to study Torah on their own without praying in a congregation. However, the life of morality, which is a necessity for the life of society, is impacted by prayer. Communal prayer is the main type of prayer; while individual prayer is beneficial when it is connected to the community. Therefore, the main "time of desire," when prayer comes closest to reaching its goal is when the congregation is praying. (EA, Berachot, p. 36)

The Trait of Refusing

> The rabbis taught: There are three things that are negative when used too much but are positive when used in small amounts. They are: Leavening, salt, and the trait of refusing something. (Berachot 34a)

There are two types of refusal. The first is to stand up for one's opinion and not to nullify oneself to someone else's opinion. This is a good quality when done in the right way, when another person or many other people want to transgress the line of morality and righteousness. In general, it is good for a person to trust one's own opinion and not always bow down to the words of others.... This is the meaning of something is "positive when used in small amounts."

However, sometimes the line is crossed regarding standing up for one's opinion. A person refuses to change their opinion and agree with someone else even when it is the right thing to do. This refers to "something negative when used too much." There is also another dimension to the trait of refusal. Sometimes a person refuses to change their opinion in such a way that they even want the other person's opinion to fit with their opinion. Regarding this situation, we can also apply the principle of "something positive when used in small amounts." However, here one must be even more careful than the first type of refusal.

Indeed, sometimes when a mistake in the trait of refusal persists, a person can get caught up in big disagreements. Many negative things may happen that become difficult to fix. This is why the Gemara first writes "leavening" and only afterward writes the trait of "salt." This comes to teach us that yeast has the power to change the very nature of dough.... When yeast is used too much, it ruins the dough and then it can no longer be eaten. Even if a person would attempt to add more dough, this would not fix the food. The excessive amount of yeast has simply damaged the dough too much. In a similar way, sometimes when a person tries to change someone else's opinion in an excessive way, one will cause such negative damage that it will be difficult to fix.

In contrast, salt does not change the nature of a dish. Rather, salt simply adds taste by making its own flavor felt in a small way. To be sure, if the taste of salt stands out too much then the dish will be damaged. Yet there is a simple way of fixing it by adding more of the original dish so that it creates the correct balance. In a similar way, there is a type of person who even though they do not want to change their own opinion, they also do not desire to change the other person's opinion to fit with their own. There is no doubt that this can be a negative and damaging quality, nonetheless, it can be fixed in an easier way just as an excessive amount of salt can be fixed in an easier way by adding water and other ingredients. (EA, Berachot 1, p. 163)

A Good Name

When Rabbi Yochanan would finish studying the book of Iyov, he would say the following: A person will ultimately die and an animal will ultimately be killed, and all are destined for death. Happy is the person who grew up in Torah, whose efforts are in Torah, who gives pleasure to one's Creator, who grew up with a good name and who left the world with a good name. Regarding such a person King Solomon said: "A good name is better than fine oil, and the day of death than the day of one's birth" (Kohelet 7:1). (Berachot 17a)

The purpose of a name is not for its own sake. Indeed, a person only needs a name in order for other people to call them by it. Therefore, the phrase "a good name" refers to the positive effect a person has on other people. We can also learn this principle from the book of Iyov. There is an obligation for all great people to not only perfect themselves but also to be involved in helping to perfect others. This is the meaning of "a good name."

A person's positive influence grows and strengthens as history progresses. Sometimes the words of a wise person are not appreciated in their own generation. The people of that generation did not value this person's worth and did not sufficiently try to comprehend the depths of their words. As a result, this person was not able to influence and perfect their own generation in the way that would have been fitting. However, as history progresses and the jealousy from people's eyes becomes removed, the person becomes better understood. Eventually, people walk toward their light.

Regarding this, King Solomon said in his wisdom, "A good name is better than fine oil" (Kohelet 7:1). That is to say, fine oil is a sign of anointing someone. Every generation agrees to anoint someone. Yet sometimes the appointed person only affects their own generation. In contrast, for a truly wise person, whose main efforts are focused on helping and perfecting the masses, "the day of death is preferable than the day of one's birth" (Ibid.). Only when such a person passes away are they able to shine their light in the most powerful way. This comes about through the words and books left behind as well as through their students who drew from the source of their wisdom. (EA, Berachot 1, p. 83)

17

Kodesh and *Chol* (Religious and Secular)

"There is a world of Chol (secular) and a world of Kodesh (religion). In fact, there are many worlds of Chol and many worlds of Kodesh."
(SK 8:73)

ACCORDING TO JEWISH CONSCIOUSNESS, *KODESH* AND *CHOL* REPRE-sent different levels of spirituality and connection to God. For example, Shabbat is considered *Kodesh* while the week is considered *Chol*. The spiritual connection one encounters on Shabbat is different from the experience of the week. In a similar way, Torah study is considered *Kodesh*, while secular studies are considered *Chol*. There is a unique spiritual power and connection that a Jew experiences when studying Torah that does not happen when they study secular subjects. In truth, Rav Kook says that there are many worlds of *Kodesh* and *Chol*: soul/body, spiritual/physical, Israel/diaspora, form/material, light/darkness.

In this chapter, Rav Kook will encourage us to develop a holistic attitude to *Kodesh* and *Chol*. Instead of telling us to choose *Kodesh* and reject *Chol*, to study Torah and give up secular knowledge, Rav Kook will instead challenge us to learn from the unique qualities of *Kodesh* and *Chol*. "Where is the correct place for each one to be used? When do they need to stay separate within their own boundary? And finally, when do they need to unite for the sake of the greater building of society?" (MoR p. 408). In addition, Rav Kook will de-scribe how *Kodesh* and *Chol*[29] should be applied on a national level as the Jewish people come back to their ancient land of Israel.

---

29. It is difficult to translate the words *Kodesh* and *Chol*. *Kodesh* could mean anything from holy, sacred, religious studies, spiritual, separate, or special. *Chol*

The Relationship Between *Kodesh* and *Chol*

Does *Kodesh* and *Chol* Contradict?

There is a world of *Chol*/Secular and a world of *Kodesh*/Religious. In fact, there are many worlds of *Chol* and many worlds of *Kodesh*. These worlds contradict each other. However, this contradiction is from our subjective perception. A human being's limited perception is not able to bridge the gap between *Kodesh* and *Chol*; one is not able to find their common value. Yet the *Kodesh* and *Chol* do indeed harmonize in the highest world, in the place of the *Kodesh HaKedoshim*/Holy of Holies. (SK 8:73, OK 2, p. 311, MaR p. 400)

What Should One Take from *Kodesh* and *Chol*

Together, *Kodesh*/Religious and *Chol*/Secular influence the spirit of a person. One becomes enriched by absorbing from each one what is fitting. From *Kodesh*, a person should take the light of life and the inner essence. From *Chol*, one should take the vessel and external attitude that provides a platform for grasping the inner content. *Chol* gives a person material for metaphors, explanations, and perspectives that help understand the ways of the world and good character traits.

There is indeed a richness and benefit that comes about through distinguishing between *Kodesh* and *Chol*. This benefit becomes clearer and clearer in the act of gathering together all the richness of diverse sources. *Chol* strengthens and illuminates the soul, until it eventually reaches the inner realms of the Torah. The cloudiness of *Chol* helps to shine light into the rays of Torah. Out of the midst of darkness, lights are revealed in their full force and beauty. (SK 5:134, OK 1, pp. 67–68)

---

could mean anything from secular knowledge, regular, ordinary, and profane. Due to the multi-dimensional meaning of the words *Kodesh* and *Chol*, I have left the terms mostly untranslated and in their original Hebrew. Occasionally, I will translate the words to remind the reader of a possible meaning in that specific piece.

Material and Form
Kodesh needs to be built on the foundation of *Chol* because *Chol* is the material and *Kodesh* is the form. The stronger and more prepared the material is, the greater the form will be. (SK 8:90, OK 1, p. 145, MaR p. 400)

The Need to Have Clear Boundaries
The entire world suffers from a mixture of *Kodesh* and *Chol* without a proper order. This lack of order causes these two foundations to oppose each other, whereby *Chol* apposes *Kodesh* and *Kodesh* apposes *Chol*. This opposition also causes certain concepts to become confused. In fact, it can become so confusing that it is sometimes difficult to distinguish what is *Chol* and what is *Kodesh*.

The work of a wise nation needs to be focused on clarifying these two foundations. Indeed, it is through the combination of *Kodesh* and *Chol* that the world will be built, human civilization will be formed, and all eternal and present dreams will be fulfilled. We need to clarify the following matters about *Kodesh* and *Chol*: What is each one's boundary and unique worth? Where is the correct place for each one to be used? When do they need to stay separate within their own boundary? And finally, when do they need to unite for the sake of the greater building of society? (MaR p. 408)

Kodesh and *Chol* Need Each Other
We need to uproot the widespread mistake on both sides of the extreme. We need to clarify and communicate the reality of both of these sides in our life. We must explain why it is impossible to deny or even abandon any one of these two sides. *Kodesh* and *Chol* are the two foundations of our life. Both demand from us the correct development and appreciation, treatment and support; and ultimately, the correct synthesis. By developing and improving each side of *Kodesh* and *Chol*, the entire world will be elevated to a higher dimension – to the beautiful power of *Kodesh Kedoshim*/Holy of Holies).

If *Chol* says it desires to separate itself from *Kodesh* and abandon it, this will only damage *Chol* itself. And if *Kodesh* says it wants to separate itself from *Chol*, this will deaden all values of life as well as *Kodesh's* own worth and influence – for its own sake as well as for the entire world. *Kodesh* and *Chol* are brothers; they need to travel together holding hands – each one on its own unique path. This is true for the journey of life in general, but it is especially true for the sake of giving true vitality to our national revival. (MaR p. 404)

Chol Must Come Before *Kodesh*

In every stage of life *Chol* must awaken first and only afterward can *Kodesh* come and complete it. *Kodesh* comes afterward to refine and prevent *Chol* from its possible dirt and destruction. Woe to *Chol* if it tries to forcefully use its firstborn status and… say: "Me and no one else" (Yeshayahu 47:8). Woe to *Chol* if it does not desire to know about the precious light contained within *Kodesh* and its illumination. In a similar way, woe to *Kodesh* if it says: "Since *Chol* came out first to the world, it has attempted to replace me. I will therefore fight against it; destroy what it has built; and uproot what it has planted." When a person clarifies the depth of life and existence, one sees things in a totally different way. Indeed, this is the fate of existence: *Chol* is the first to enter into the platform of life. (MaR pp. 404–405)

The Need to Seek Worldly Knowledge and Emotions

Rabbeinu HaGra (1720–1797) would say to his household: Whatever a person is lacking in worldly knowledge, they will be lacking ten times more in Torah wisdom.[30] Therefore, together with

---

30. See the introduction of Rav Baruch Schik of Shklov's (1744–1808) book *Euclidus*, where he writes that he heard from the Gra: "Whatever a person is lacking in secular knowlege, they will be lacking one hundred times in Torah wisdom, because Torah and wisdom are studied together." Among other things, Rav Baruch Schik of Shklov is famous for translating many scientific works into Hebrew upon the request of the Gra, the Vilna Gaon.

strengthening Torah wisdom it is an imperative to expand worldly knowledge as much as possible. And even if it is impossible for all Torah scholars to become official experts in all the fields of worldly knowledge, nevertheless it is possible for a person to become familiar with general worldly knowledge and its effects on the world. Such knowledge will enable a person to comprehend the overall style and spirit of the generation. As a result, a person will be able to sustain and help the generation.

To be sure, in order to understand the Torah, it is not enough to have knowledge that sustains the mind. The Torah also includes emotions – and perhaps even more so than knowledge. Indeed, emotions are the inner moisture and essence of life. Therefore, in order to comprehend the essence of life in a quality way, a person must not be alienated from the emotions of life that exist in the world and that are present in the current generation. While a person can understand intellectual ideas through in-depth study, in order for one to comprehend the emotions of life, a person needs physical and mental health. Therefore, the first obligation of Torah scholars – and specifically in our generation – is to follow a lifestyle that brings health, joy, and a normal healthy state for the body and soul. (EY p. 129)

Kodesh Affects a Person's Inner Desires

Spiritual wisdom is greater than any other type of knowledge. It affects a person's inner desires and character traits and brings them closer to the spiritual heights of its content. This is not true for secular knowledge. Even though secular knowledge can describe beautiful and lofty ideas, nonetheless it does not have the ability to effect change on the inner essence of a person.

While each field of secular knowledge has a connection to that specific set of knowledge within a person, it does not have a connection to the rest of the forces of a person; nor does it relate to the inner essence of a person. The reason for this is because all matters of Kodesh are rooted in the Source of all life, in the Foundation of life that gives life to all of existence. The content of *Kodesh* has enough power to create infinite creatures, to sprout heaven and establish earth. Therefore, *Kodesh* has the power to imprint a new form into the soul of any person who immerses oneself in its words.

In contrast, *Chol*/Secular knowledge does not have this ability. The knowledge of *Chol* cannot revolutionize and create things anew on its own. Rather, *Chol* is focused on intellectually describing and showcasing what already exists in reality. It is therefore unable to transform the reader into a new creation. Secular knowledge does not have the ability to uproot within a person their essential negative traits and help them enter a new, pure, living reality, with an illumination of true life that can last forever. (SK 8:159, OK 1, p.1)

Holistic versus Disconnected

When it comes to how *Chol* comprehends life: the intellect acts on its own in the realm of knowledge; the imagination acts on its own in the realm of aesthetics; actions act on their own in the realm of practicality; and emotions act on their own in the realm of emotions. In stark contrast, when it comes to how *Kodesh* comprehends life: from the revealed content of prophecy and the holy spirit, each revelation is included in all other types of knowledges – actions, emotions, imagination, and intellect. All of these are connected in a holistic way. (MaR p. 401)

Transitioning Between *Kodesh* and *Chol*

Sometimes a person leaves the world of *Kodesh*/Religion and Spirituality and enters into the world of *Chol*/the Secular in a sudden and non-gradual way. This also happens in the opposite direction from *Chol* to *Kodesh*. The soul experiences something similar to what happens to the body and its senses when it goes from one extreme to the other – from darkness to light, from warmth to coldness. This causes suffering and sometimes even injury.

There are two ways of shielding oneself from such an injury. The first is to transition gradually from a higher *Kodesh* to a lower

Kodesh, little by little, until one reaches the *Chol* dimension. This is the path of the masses. However, there also exists a higher spiritual level: the elevation of *Chol* matters to the dimension of *Kodesh*. This is the path of the greatest *Tzadikim* (Righteous people) and the path that is longed for in the future. "On that day the words 'Kodesh to God' will be inscribed on the bells of the horses" (Zechariah 14:20). (SK 4:39, OK 2, p. 311)

Unintentionally Being Separated from Matters of *Kodesh*
Sometimes a *Tzadik* will be temporarily separated from pondering thoughts of *Kodesh*/Religious and Godly Matters. Nonetheless, this will actually give them more strength and power in matters of *Kodesh*. The reason for this is because when a person is separated from matters of *Kodesh*, they are able to increase their knowledge in *Chol*/Secular Matters. As a result, they will be able to transform this *Chol* knowledge into illuminating matters of *Kodesh*. Nonetheless, a person should not intentionally distance themselves from matters of *Kodesh*. Instead, this experience can be compared to the mitzvah of "*Shichicha*."[31] In such a situation, a pious person offers up a thanksgiving sacrifice. (SK 2:202)

New Combinations
The inner wisdom, deeper than all other depths, is the wisdom of *Kodesh*. It sustains everything and is not dependent on any other

---

31. Rav Kook is referring to the Torah law of "*Shichicha*," which literally means "forgetting." The Torah writes: "When you are haversting in your field and you forget a sheaf, do not go back to get it. Leave it for the stranger, the fatherless and the widow, so that God may bless you in all the work of your hands" (Devarim 24:19). In other words, one is obligated to leave for the poor sheaves of grain that they forgot in the field. Even though this person did the act of charity unintentionally, it is nonetheless considered a mitzvah since one helped the poor. Similarly, Rav Kook says that a person who was unintentionally separated from matters of *Kodesh*, will still get the benefits of all of the knowledge of Chol that they learned. In fact, Rav Kook says that they will eventually be able to use this *Chol* knowledge for a higher spiritual purpose.

type of wisdom. It is the higher river where paradise comes from. "The river that is blessed from its own riverbed" (Bechorot 55b). The reason for combining Torah and human wisdom is not in order to complete some deficiency.

Rather, it is for the sake of creating new combinations and revelations. When one combines the light of *Ruach HaKodesh*/the Holy Spirit, the inner dimension of Torah, together with human perception and wisdom, in both their full force and mutual respect – which is fitting for each one – this creates new souls in the world. It gives a new, fresh, and healthy color to life. From the depths of the abyss come great lights; to illuminate with a new light; with the light of the righteous, for all people on earth. (SK 1:888, OK 1, p. 63)

Perceiving *Chol* from the Perspective of *Kodesh*

One of the goals of revealing mystical Torah to the world is to perceive *Chol* from the perspective of *Kodesh*. Mysticism comes to help one recognize that in truth there is no such thing as absolute *Chol*. In fact, all the details of *Kodesh* are like *Chol* compared to the highest light of *Kodesh*, which is drawn from the source of infinity. Through understanding this principle, the *Chol* and *Kodesh* become closer together, and the universal oneness becomes manifested. The spirit of humanity develops and strengthens, and its actions become rooted in a higher life. (SK 8:86, OK 1, p. 143, MaR p. 399)

Kodesh and *Chol* on a National and Universal Level

Chol Cannot Rebuild the Nation without *Kodesh*

Our current national movement is *Cholonit Yoter Midai*/too secular. The nation's *Kodesh* voice is not heard. This is obvious and does not need further clarification. Wherever we turn we see matters of

Chol – secular thoughts, secular emotions, and secular literature. Where is the *Kodesh* content in our life? Is it really possible that it has disappeared and passed us by, wiped from existence and no longer? Could a person really think this who knows and is familiar with the greater world? Could a person really agree to this who has even a minimum knowledge of Jewish history?

The truth is that our strength of *Kodesh* is hidden, concealed in our individual and national soul. We are so focused on trying to protect our national existence and guard the nation from destruction and annihilation. Yet as a result, we have not paid attention to our current responsibility of creating and renewing our highest and most *Kodesh* insight....

To be sure, this is the way of the world: the force of *Chol* comes first. "Darkness comes before light," "the shell comes before the fruit." The leaders of *Chol* have come and taken the spotlight of life. In truth, they are preparing the groundwork for the leaders of *Kodesh* to communicate their vision, to reveal their inner morals, and to lift up their hands to do and act.

Who are the practical leaders of the national revival, if not the leaders of *Chol*? ... And who are the current leaders of sport and literature, if not the leaders of *Chol* who speak in the name of *Chol* in all values. In fact, even when they speak words of *Kodesh*, such words are not rooted in *Kodesh*, but rather in a type of *Kodesh* within *Chol*.

Zionism is a secular expression of something *Kodesh*. The Zionism and nationalism that are growing and expanding its fields in literature, the arts, and poetry, are nothing but Chol ideas. However, their source and life force is in the *Kodesh*. The reason for this is because the Jewish people is *Kodesh*; its land, language, essence, worth, hopes and dreams are all *Kadosh*. However, the Kodesh also has a dimension of life that expresses itself as *Chol*.

In truth, the *Chol* dimension of life was truly lacking and forgotten from us during the long destructive exile. Currently, the *Chol* dimension of life is returning to us gradually, little by little. However, can *Chol* revive our people all by itself? This would be a lie if we truly believed it; we would be deceiving ourselves if we agreed to such a reality. Not our Jewish inner world, nor the greater world of humanity would be able to accept us as an essentially secular entity. Instead, the secular form of the Jewish people must ultimately be revealed through the greater light of the *Kodesh*. (MaR pp. 415–416)

A True National Revolution

It will not be a true national revolution if it does not renew within us insights in prayer, insights in Torah, and insights in self-growth and an inner listening toward matters of faith. It will not be a complete national revolution if it does not penetrate the hearts of the masses that they are on a great spiritual journey, with longings for heavenly moments of *Kodesh*. Such spiritual longings are far away from the regular world and its inhabitants; such spiritual yearnings do not fit together with a regular way of living. (MaR p. 414)

Three Groups

A letter to the Agudat Yisrael/World Orthodox Union, Apri 18th, 1912

Let us discuss the land of Israel. We see three main forces, with each one building their own educational institutions.... The first is the ancient force, those people who have been living in *Yishuvanu HaKodesh*/our Holy City for a long time who are concentrated on their inner *Kedusha*. This group pushes away any innovations in whichever form they come. In its schools and Yeshivot, it forbids any foreign language – even the State language – as well as all *Limud Shel Chol*/Secular Studies, even the most necessary for practical living....

   The second force is relatively new and has come about as a result of the latest events in the land of Israel. It has become more recognizable since I began my work in Israel with the small strength that God has given me. This group says that it is *Chovoteinu HaKedosha*/our Holy Obligation to give strength to the spirit of God that has come upon our people; to raise up the flag of Torah and *mitzvot* with honor through acquiring the skills of our times. These skills strengthen those who have acquired them as well as earn respect in the eyes of those who see them. This group has focused itself on acquiring skills that prepare a person for the battle of life with a strong spirit.

To be clear, the main focus of the second group is to give honor to Torah, faith, *mitzvot*, and pure fear of God.... Only after this first priority of focusing on the holy Torah is there a second priority: to teach our children practical secular studies that are necessary for life. In addition, this group teaches our children a spirit of strength and good manners, as well as communicates to them in the *Sefat HaKedosha*/the Holy Language....

The third force is *Koach HaChiloni LeGamrei*/totally secular. This group shakes away anything *Kodesh*/Religious. It focuses its attention only toward the needs of the present moment – both individually and collectively. Based on this ideology, it has founded its institutions, schools, and educational philosophy. To be clear, the lack of attention toward *Kodesh* does not remain simply a matter of not obligating oneself in such matters. Rather, the greater the secular group grows and expands, the more it criticizes and destroys the powerful life of *Kodesh* and attempts to remove the light of God and the holiness of Torah from the masses in Israel.

On the other hand, it cannot be denied that despite all of this, the third group, the secular force, contains within it a strong connection to life, a powerful love toward the nation, and a clear and robust desire to build the country in a practical way in the land of Israel. This secular group desires to inspire the generation to reconnect themselves to their land and nation in the spirit of our national history. Therefore, despite the secular's dimension of alienation from the Jewish tradition, it does indeed contain a strong spark of

Kedusha, something that needs to be elevated and developed with hands of faith.

Just as these three forces have parallel educational institutions, so too each group has parallel institutions of employment, charity, and publishing houses....

In my opinion, the first thing that the Aguda needs to do is get in contact with the leaders of each of these three groups, whichever person has influence. This is in order to understand with clarity the situation and details of each group. To begin with, how to strengthen the older group, which is becoming weaker and weaker due to its inability to adapt to the outside order of life. Secondly, how to direct the second and relatively new group so that it will continually become stronger and stronger, as well as be a tower of strength for the first older group, by showing it affection and encouragement; to help it protect its unique spiritual qualities.

Lastly, the Aguda needs to help influence the third secular group; to minimize as much as possible the damages that it brings when it speaks in anger when turning away from anything religious and *Kodesh.* In general, the Aguda should be trying to awaken the spirit of *Kedushat Yisrael/*the Holiness of a Jew that is hidden inside all the hearts of the seed of Yaakov. This should be done in whatever way possible; in a careful and patient way; in different forms and styles dependent on the different situations.

To summarize, the honorable and holy Aguda needs to use its strengths to help all these groups; to support anyone who needs help; and to give physical and spiritual strength and benefit to anyone it can. (IR 2, pp. 79–80)

A True Example of Education in the Land of Israel
We need to try to publicize the values of the school *"Tachkemoni"* regarding its *Limudei Kodesh/*Religious Learning, Jewish studies, as well as its *Limudei Chol/*Secular Studies and all its various parts. This school can be a true example of education and Israeli culture in the land of Israel. (IR 2, p. 72)

I Do Not Recommend It

A letter to Rav Yaakov Leibowitz (author, educator, and father of Baruch Ben Yehuda, the Principal of the Gymnasium in Herzliya), December 4, 1910

I have already told you that the Gymnasium school over here is far removed from matters of religion. Therefore, I do not recommend it for any person who wants their children to be God-fearing, keeping Torah and *mitzvot*, like the rest of the religious Jews. On the other hand, there is a school called "Tachkemoni" in the holy city. They teach children worldly knowledge based on Torah, our holy religion, and fear of God. (IR 2, pp. 6–7)

The World Has Forgotten *Kodesh*

The world is suffering because it has forgotten *Kodesh*/Religion; and it will only stop suffering when it remembers what it has forgotten. When *Kodesh* returns and is remembered there will no longer be the attitude of *Kodesh*/Religion being the enemy of *Chol*/Secular; nor the attitude of *Kodesh* controlling and instrumentalizing *Chol*. Instead, when *Kodesh* finally returns, it will be a *Kodesh* full of freedom; a *Kodesh* that on the one hand has its own character that walks with confidence, while at the same time a *Kodesh* that does not cause damage to *Chol*. Eventually, *Kodesh* will no longer fight *Chol* but will instead yearn to refine and spiritually elevate it.

We are currently drowning in the swamp of *Chol*. We are in need of saving. Yes, we must be saved. This issue is relevant to the community, to the nation, and to the entire world. The light of *Kodesh* needs to express itself in its most illuminating form and repair all the damages of the world. However, a *Kodesh* that is totally disconnected from the health of *Chol* will never have this higher spiritual quality of refining and spiritually elevating *Chol*; of helping the world leave its darkness. This is because a *Kodesh* that is disconnected from *Chol* lacks the strength of practicality, which needs to be drawn from the lowest foundations of existence.

However, a *Kodesh* that penetrates all levels until it draws strength and life from the freshness of *Chol* – this is a higher and stronger *Kodesh* that contains the sap of life. This type of *Kodesh* will be able to rise up, awaken, live and give life. Our eyes are focused on this higher, fuller and more holistic type of *Kodesh*. (MaR p. 411)

Serving the Nation in a Holistic Way

Each Jew should know that as long as they are only dedicating themselves to the *Chol* dimensions of reviving the nation, then they are only serving the nation from one side. This person's service will not be complete and holistic until they also help and give support to elevating the revival of the *Kodesh* on a national level.

On the other hand, there is a Jew who is only building the nation through the *Kodesh* dimension. As long as this person isn't helping and giving support to the *Chol* dimensions of building the nation, then this diminishes their service to the *Kodesh* parts of the nation. In general, the more we spread this holistic consciousness, the more our national revolution will become complete and perfected. (MaR p. 43)

18

Peace and Unity

"All the events in this world are leading to one destination: to actu- alize the philosophy of unity and to overcome the philosophy of divi- sion." (SK 7:60)

SOMETIMES ONE COMES ACROSS ANOTHER PERSON WHOSE IDEOLO- gy is fundamentally opposed to one's own beliefs. For example, one person believes that keeping *Kashrut* and Shabbat is an obligation for all Jews, while another person thinks that these laws are outdat- ed and a Jew should be able to act however they please.

This is one of the central questions of Rav Kook's writings: How should one react when they come across another person who funda- mentally disagrees with one's core values? In response to this ques- tion, Rav Kook writes, "There are two main philosophies toward life: the philosophy of unity and the philosophy of division" (Ibid).

That is to say, there are some people who care mainly about achieving their own perspective on life. Such people are willing to do anything to reach their individual goals even if this means creating *Peirud*/Division, separation and war in the world. In contrast, Rav Kook encouraged his students to seek *Achdut*/Unity and *Shalom*/ Peace as the highest value in life. A person should be dedicated to finding a way to bring the world together even if they have opposing and contradictory beliefs.

In the beginning of this chapter, Rav Kook will encourage us to embrace a philosophy of *Achdut*/Unity and *Shalom*/Peace. He will then discuss the difficulties involved in being a person of unity, espe- cially when the other side disagrees with one's fundamental beliefs.

The Battle Between Unity and Separation

Two Philosophies

There are two philosophies toward life: the philosophy of unity and the philosophy of separation. The philosophy of unity perceives anything that is separate merely as a mistake of the senses, as a lack of enlightenment. But in the truth of reality, everything is one great unifying body. All the many separate parts are simply unique revelations, different limbs, and a spectrum of colors that make up one unified system.

The philosophy of unity looks upon everything and discovers the good qualities within all; the combination of all the details is the greatest possible good. In fact, it is better that the negative elements become revealed than to lack these different ways of expression. The more this philosophy of unity deepens and strengthens, the greater it will reveal its truth in all details of life; all emotions will be aligned with its philosophy. Everything will be experienced with a good feeling and this sense of goodness will increase – life will be unified. The more this philosophy of unity becomes rooted in society, the more it will bring real practical good to the world and life – eventually it will bring peace.

In stark contrast, the philosophy of separation perceives the world of division and separation as the true reality of life. The more things become drawn to its philosophy, the more its perception of life becomes true. The materialistic senses and all superficial thinking are strengthened through this philosophy of separation. It impacts life and results in an increase of darkness and evil.

There is no end to the profound battle between these two philosophies – on an external and internal level. In truth, all the events in this world are leading to one destination: to actualize the philosophy of unity and to overcome the philosophy of separation. The faith of divine unity comes from the soul. It contains all the treasure of life; all the inner wealth. Eternal happiness is found there. (SK 7:60, OK 2, pp. 456–7)

Leaders of Unity versus Leaders of Separation

The leaders of countries and all the intellectual experts of society are rooted in the philosophy of separation. They use the power of imagination to describe the world through the lens of separation. Unfortunately, the world is still not worthy of leaders who are rooted in the philosophy of unity. However, the essence of the light of the Mashiach... is built on the philosophy of unity. The more this attitude increases, the more it affects all the details and events in the world.

To be sure, it is necessary that the philosophy of unity be hidden from the world. For if people understood the unity of existence, that everything is really good in its essence in the context of unity, then the value of constant growth would be lost.... Indeed, the more the philosophy of unity is revealed, the less motivation there would be for clarifying and elevating each detail and transforming evil into good. Therefore, the very lack of awareness of the philosophy of unity is what causes its light to become deeper. It is the divisions and separations, the pain and tragedies that cause the greatest light to be revealed. Precisely the hiddenness of unity and the philosophy of separation enable the sparks of scattered holiness to be gathered up from the depths of darkness. (SK 7:61, OK 2, pp. 457–8)

Unity is More Spiritual

When the philosophy of separation strengthens and becomes more revealed than the philosophy of unity, materialism overpowers spirituality. The materialistic lusts of the body become the main values of life and the darkness of the world is very strong. However, when the philosophy of unity strengthens, then the spiritual desires and all sensitive yearnings increase. The world evolves and becomes enlightened. (SK 7:62, OK 2, p. 423)

Two Sounds in the World

There are two powerful voices heard in the world with great volume. Each voice requests its way of thinking with great precision. Each voice desires to build in its own way. The voice of harmony, the voice that requests from everything alignment, direction, and equality. This is the voice of peace, which rises higher than all the numerous voices of war that are heard in the world. In contrast, the voice of confusion thunders, a voice that roars out loud to strengthen each separate entity. This voice creates a life of rivalry so that each individual competes with each other. Each separate entity desires to stand out and swallow everyone else. Each separate element thunders, and the voice of war is heard in all the worlds.

However, amongst all the voices, there is a voice that stands out, a higher voice, the voice of harmony, the voice of unity, a voice that elevates and straightens. Amongst all the worlds comes such voice; toward all creatures; toward all spirit and soul; toward all body and flesh. These voices come to each individual in his or her own uniqueness; to each community in its unique way of community, and to all nations in its unique way of nationhood. There exists a type of soul who is centered, who contains within them the voice of harmony; who sense a holy fire burning within; who thirst for peace – these types of souls are the angels of peace in the world. (SK 5:120, OK 4 p. 493)

The Thought of Unity in One's Soul

Whoever feels the thought of unity near to their soul; whoever feels the vision of uniting all the worlds... grabbing their imagination and thoughts, this is a sign that they are rooted in the great visionaries of the world. The main spiritual focus of such visionaries is to unite all of existence, to bring about true and eternal peace. Such a person should not turn back due to any great obstacle. They should lift up their heart in the ways of God.

If sometimes it seems like one is pursuing fame and honor, one should do one's best to purify one's mind and be focused solely toward God. One should focus one's activities toward doing God's will; to reveal the light of God's oneness in all of the worlds. As a result, a higher spirit will descend upon this person; to purify their actions and plans as much as possible. (SK 2:16, OK 3, p. 325)

Disagreements and Contradictions

Learning from Many Lights
Regarding an individual, it is said, "A person who studies from only one rabbi does not receive blessings" (Avoda Zara 19a). This is even more true regarding general matters. Spiritual blessings only come about as a result of being influenced by the combination of all the greatest lights and teachers.

A person should not be discouraged if they see that leaders of one path will sometimes reject another path or even all other pathways. Indeed, this seems to be the way of gaining insight. A person stands in their own private realm and focuses inwardly; through rejecting outside matters, one guards one's own attitude. However, there is a space that includes all pathways, where all individual ideas pour into one great ocean of general ideas. "A river whose streams brings happiness to the city of God. The holy place where the Most High dwells" (Tehilim 46:5). (SK 7:16)

There is No Vision that isn't Complex
We do not have any vision that isn't complex. From our human perspective, we are not able to find anything that doesn't have a combination of internal and external elements, of higher and lower parts, of more essential principles and less essential principles. (KYK 2, Pinkas 1:10)

Do Not be Overwhelmed by Contradictions
Every world runs according to its own unique and essential order – both the physical world and the spiritual world. "One kingship does not come close to another kingship, even a little bit" (Yoma

38b). From this we can learn that a person should not panic or be overwhelmed by logical contradictions from different worlds. (SK 6:255)

Two Ways of Thinking

The regular way of thinking perceives each separate principle as contradictory. Yet it is precisely through such contradiction that the ideal world is built. Contradictions cause a person to make decisions; and by making these decisions a large amount of spiritual treasure is acquired. The spiritual world is then blessed with a great wealth.

However, there is a higher way of thinking, whereby peace is already envisioned. And it is precisely through the blessing of peace, tranquility, calmness, and pleasantness, that everything is blessed. When we stand in the valley of this higher vision, we are able to perceive the root of each separate principle. We can then see the way of peace inside of each principle; the common value in everything. (SK 8:40, OK 4, p. 496)

One Light Pushes Away Another Light

Sometimes good character traits and principles contradict each other when they are allowed to spread out inside of a person. It is because a person is unable to contain so many different lights that one light pushes away another light. We must look with compassion and respect toward people who are on the one hand blessed with the roots of good character traits, while on the other hand, struck by dark character traits that cloud their spirit....

If one character trait exists in all its fullness, then sometimes this fullness captures one's entire heart and all of the spiritual strength of one's soul. To be sure, concerning other traits and principles that a person has neglected and forgotten about, they will not cause a permanent damage to one's soul. It may in fact be that by this person's neglect of certain traits this will actually enhance their vessel so that it will contain an even greater blessing for the Jewish people and the entire world. (SK 8:78)

Detailed Ideas versus Visionary Ideas

Detailed ideas have the quality of clarification but they lack the quality of a greater vision and overall insight. As a consequence, details do not fill a person's soul with spiritual light. On the other hand, the more all-encompassing an idea is, the more it is filled with light and overall insight. Nevertheless, general ideas lack the quality of clarification and practical conclusions. However, when detailed ideas and general ideas become unified, both qualities come together. A person is then filled with detailed clarification as well as a higher insight. (SK 8:87)

The Connection Between Spirituality and Practicality

The depth of spiritual matters and the depth of practical matters are connected to each other. Each spiritual matter that we lack causes us to make mistakes in the depth of the practical matters of life and the world. And each practical matter that we become clearer about enables us to become more illuminated by the shining light of the depth of spirituality. Therefore, "It is good to hold on to this and also not let go of the other" (Kohelet 7:18). (KYK 1, Pinkas Yerushalayim 6)

Beauty is the Combination of Opposites

According to the ancient rabbis, the temple is called "the beauty of the world" (Zevachim 54b). Beauty is always found through the combination of opposites. Dirt is the opposite of beauty. The main purpose of beauty is to separate itself from dirt and to combine all the opposites into one higher spirit. (KYK 1, Acharon B'Boisk 18)

Opposition Produces a Third Unifying Force

When two forces oppose each other, a third force is produced as a result. Yet this third force does not cause the previous two forces to be lost. Instead, the original two forces continue to exist in all their strength. The third force accompanies them to enrich the world. This is a permanent principle regarding physicality, spirituality, and ethics. (YKY 1, *Eighty-One Pinkasot from Yaffo*, 1)

Different Energies

One type of wisdom does not contradict another type of wisdom; nor does one type of ethics contradict another type of ethics. One type of beauty does not contradict another type of beauty; nor does one type of truth contradict another type of truth. To be sure, everything is filled with contradictions as a result of how each characteristic is different from each other, with differing energies of illumination. Nonetheless, they do not inherently contradict each other. This can be compared to how skin covers the body. Only from this perspective are they opposed to each other. (SK 3:113)

Take the Deeper Value and not the Superficial

Sometimes when a person tries to receive and absorb from every idea, one misses out on the deeper value of the idea. A sophisticated person needs to learn how to receive from everything in a way that strengthens the inner holiness of one's life. One must learn how to acquire from everything only the good and deep value. In other words, a person must be careful not to absorb the negative values from everything; and that whatever spiritual value one absorbs, it should not be learned in a superficial way. Instead, a person should penetrate the inner depths of life, the truth of truths. One will then become unified with the greater good and it will become one's own river. "Let them be your own river, not to be shared with strangers" (Mishlei 5:7). (SK 6:54)

Rabbi Yehuda versus Rabbi Shimon

If Rabbi Yehuda said about Rome, "How good are the actions of this nation" (Shabbat 33a), all the more so we must search and receive the good from all actions and developments of the nations of the world. By doing this, a person becomes the "Head of Speaking in all places" (Shabbat 33a). In addition, one must combine the character trait of Rabbi Shimon Bar Yochai who criticized the damaged moral values of the nation, which impacts all of their actions. (KYK 1, Reshimot M'London 16)

The Way an Idea is Communicated

All good ideas can be argued against from a logical point of view. Nevertheless, if an idea causes some ethical goodness to come to the world, then it always has value. Any argument against an idea only comes about due to the specific way and style the idea is being communicated. Yet the inner goodness within an idea always remains.

From the perspective of absolute goodness, "there is no object that doesn't have its place" (Pirkei Avot 4:3). Everything is sustained through its inner quality of goodness. If there are ideas that are the cause of much foolishness, this is simply because we have associated with the external element of the idea. Nonetheless, a person who can see into the depths of something, will utilize the intrinsic goodness in every matter and perceive its divine goodness. Every idea contains a kindness that "fills the entire earth" (Yeshayahu 6:3), "in heaven above and on the earth below" (Devarim 4:39), in every action and thought. They are all acts of God the Creator. (KYK 2, Pinkas 3:17)

Opposition Helps to Create True Peace

Individual entities need to actualize their full potential in order to enrich the world. The masses include within it a mixture of many different individual entities. However, in order for each individual entity to shine its full light into the world, each separate part must be allowed to stand out and express its own uniqueness. Therefore, obstacles and opposition are necessary in order to pressure each individual to be something other than itself.

This is the spiritual principle of hatred that helps to build the world. It is the source of all the wars in life and society; it is the source of all the differences of opinions and faiths. As a result of this division, each unique individual entity is given its own space to develop by itself, so that other individuals, nations, theories, identities, opinions, and faiths, will not come to steal its uniqueness.

From this we can learn that the source of hatred is in fact love and peace. True love and peace come about as a result of aligning all fully actualized talents. After each individual entity actualizes its full potential separately, they will then be able to unify in creating a holistic, richer and fuller world. (SK 8:65, OK 4 p. 498)

Holistic Souls versus Specialist Souls

There are some people who include many branches of insight – many opinions, many character traits, many perspectives on Torah, and many types of work. Sometimes these inner branches will try to refute or deny each other due to the fact that all branches are trying to draw nourishment from one narrow source. Instead, they must rise up to a higher source of unity and oneness, where all branches can be included together, where one holistic insight can give nourishment to all of them.

To be sure, holistic people also need help from individuals who specialize in one specific field. These individuals are usually well known and famous since the masses give more attention to the light of an individual field than the greatness of holistic spiritual richness. Those souls who specialize in one specific field can have a great impact on the strength and holiness of unified souls. Indeed, holistic souls become enriched as a result of being connected with experts. Nonetheless, at the end of the day, holistic souls send back an even greater influence of light than they receive.

When an individual detail is influenced from a greater soul perspective, it becomes spiritually digested and transformed into something unified that encompasses everything. This all depends on the amount of unity and expansiveness of the general soul. (SK 2:219, OK 1 p. 50)

The Fear of Different Worlds

Worlds that are distant from each other tend to threaten each other. In every world that we stand in and are rooted in, there is a negativity and disapproval toward other worlds. This negativity turns into a crisis and fear rises up. Anxiety and hatred combine with insult and mockery. Eventually, all of this returns and impacts our own spirits.

The expansive spirit which thirsts for a great expansion, cannot constrict itself in one world. It must spread itself out to different worlds. At the beginning of one's footsteps, a person experiences fear and pain, deep bitterness and visions of panic.... However, this painful and crushing period will not last long. These sufferings will eventually purify, transform, and cleanse the spirit. These sufferings will deepen one's understanding, sharpen one's realm of desires, strengthen one's love of truth, and fill the soul with a spirit of strength. After this, a higher spirit will return and appear from the upper realms of understanding. (SK 6:184)

Differences versus Similarities

We must continuously walk down the path between the attribute of differences and the attribute of similarities. On the one hand, we need to understand people's opinions in a way whereby each side has its own unique spirit. On the other hand, we must focus on the value of similarity, whereby everything is included in one greater whole. (SK 1:24)

Creating Peace Within the Jewish People

Praying for the Whole Jewish People

A letter to Rabbi Noach Gottlieb (author of *Ohalei Shem* and secretary of Rav David Friedman of Karlin), June 6, 1913

It is clear that it is impossible to... face our enemy without the higher moral value of the "Whole Nation," the entire Jewish people. It is forbidden for us to separate and break apart. It is forbidden for us to say: "These belong to us and we are therefore worried about them. Those, however, do not belong to us."

It is true, at times when we immerse ourselves in the details, we will have to distinguish between each person and between each group. However, when we elevate ourselves to the essential value that includes everything, we are not permitted to distinguish between good people and bad people.

For the sake of God and the community, we must pray for the Avar'yanim/sinners as well. The hope in our heart needs to include everyone, the entire community, with all its different values. To be sure, I am not saying that we must agree with the attitudes of sinners. Nor must we invite them into our camp as followers and leaders. However, we must pray with them. That is to say, we must desire in our heart and soul a collective peace and salvation, in the most expansive form. (IR 2, pp. 171–172)

We Cannot Bear a Lack of Oneness
More than any other people and language, we cannot bear contradictions and a lack of oneness in the soul. Inside of us is the eternal ability for peace and unification – in their most idealistic forms. Therefore, all of our brokenness and scatteredness is only temporary. Ultimately, we will unite and be "one nation on earth" (Shmuel Two, 7:23). (SK 3:154, OK 1, p. 21)

I Am a Man of Peace
A letter to Rabbi Avigdor Rivlin (student of Rav Kook, *Talmid Chacham*, teacher, author, and emissary sent to the Diaspora to raise funds for Israel), May 5, 1908

Your spirit is different from mine. I can see this even in the style of your book. It is filled with battles from head to toe. To be sure, these are battles for the sake of God. Nonetheless, "I am a man of peace who pursues peace" (a paraphrase of Pirkei Avot 1:12). This is true in areas where most people would not even imagine finding peace. Nonetheless, this is my personality. In addition, I am from the seed of Aharon, who is promised the "covenant of peace" (Bamidbar 25:12, Malachi 2:5). (IR 1, p. 168)

Following One's Own Path Without Insulting Other Paths

A person who is drawn to Chassidut, divine connection, and higher spiritual wisdom, must know that it was for such things that they were created. Indeed, if they let go of this higher spiritual service – which only a select few are capable of – then who will fill this great deficiency?

Therefore, a person should "rejoice in one's portion" (Pirkei Avot 4:1). One should not degrade or perceive in a negative light other people's portion even though it may be very distant from one's own portion. Indeed, there is no doubt that such people possess many good and beneficial capabilities that are distant from one's own portion. In general, a person should continually be filled with joy in one's mind, with a good eye, respecting other people, loving everyone, and seeking the goodness and elevation of all. (SK 3:118, OK 3, p. 207)

No Group Has All the Truth

An open letter to the youth of the Holy Land who love Torah, 1905

I refuse to enter the disagreement between "the Zion Zionists" and the "Uganda Zionists."[32] It is certain that in both of these groups we can find honest people who truly love their nation and are not turning their back on the past. This is also true regarding people who oppose the Zionist movement in general. Indeed, it is a bad

---

32. When Rav Kook mentions the "Zion Zionists" and "Uganda Zionists" he is referring to an essential debate that occurred in the Sixth Zionist Congress in 1903. The "Uganda Zionists" refers to Jews who accepted the proposal of creating a Jewish homeland in Uganda as a temporary refuge for Jews in Russia in immediate danger. In contrast, the "Zion Zionists" refers to Jews who rejected this proposal and believed that the Jewish homeland could only be created in the ancient land of Israel.

sign for any group who thinks that only they have the source of life, all the wisdom and honesty, and everyone else is full of emptiness and bad character. (IR 1, p. 17)

Uniting the Gra and the Baal Shem Tov
A letter to Rabbi Pinchas HaCohen Lintup, January 21, 1910

The vision of wholeness means uniting all the good elements that come to us from different perspectives- from the ancient times all the way up until the current generation. This holy work includes removing the obstacles and creating bridges between all of the realms that separate us. I would love it if this work be cherished by all those who are immersed in the soul of Torah just as it is cherished by me.

Indeed, recent generations have found it beneficial to learn from both the teachings of the students of the Gra as well as from the teachings of the students of the Baal Shem Tov- which were so opposed in their own time period. Through a lot of hard work and skill we will create a holistic literature that unites these spiritual divisions. (IR 1, pp. 304–305)

Uniting the Rambam and the Ramban
There were two great leaders that rose up for the Jewish people to straighten out the path of Torah and faith – the Rambam and Ramban. Both were filled with the blessing of God in Torah and wisdom, crowned with greatness and holiness, with justice and honesty. They included inside of them all of the treasure of the life of the Jewish people and humanity.

The Rambam and Ramban express the two sides of listening to the soul. On the one hand, the cognitive side is filled with intellect and calculations, clarity and logic, which judges every value according to these categories. On the other hand, the mysterious and internal side is where the intuition of deep faith comes from. From this second attitude, all inner kabbalistic understanding and higher spiritual truth comes about and is absorbed from the secrets of faith.

Together the Rambam and Ramban build the house of Israel. From this one and from that one. Through both of their hands of faith they are able to weaken Amalek and establish a hand on the throne of God. (MoR, p. 419)

Pushing Away and Bringing Closer

A letter to Rabbi Berman (educator, author, and one of the leaders of Mizrachi), May 30, 1923

Believe me my precious friend, if I found communal leaders in the land of Israel who were immersed in the right hand of bringing people closer, then it may very well be that I would be immersed in the left hand of pushing people away. Indeed, this second trait is also needed in the holy work of leading a community. However, since I see that the trait of pushing people away is emphasized in an overly strong way, I therefore need to combine it with the right hand of bringing people closer. To be sure, this must also be done in a measured and careful way, with the help of God. And any person who knows me well, understands that I am not doing this for self-serving reasons, God forbid. (IR 4, p. 163)

Destructive Tolerance

A letter to Rabbi Dr. Moshe Seidel, January 29, 1914

Tolerance is the source of life. However, when is this true? When tolerance is rooted in the purity of wisdom and morality; when it is clarified through the clear awareness of the essence of the life of the nation and its history. However, when tolerance comes from a softness of the heart, a weakness in the spirit, then it acts like poison that kills and destroys....

We look and contemplate the inner worth of the Torah, which is the word of God to the Jewish people. It is the spirit and essence of the nation throughout its wonderous long life. We recognize and understand immediately that any tolerance that comes to hold back and block this powerful way of life... is similar to a type of tolerance whereby a person sees that their honorable house and family are being trampled and crushed, yet due to their weakness, overlooks and neglects it. (IR 3, p. 157)

The Spiritual Calling to Unify

All imperfections in the world – both physical and spiritual – come about because each side only comprehends one point of view of existence. In a person's eyes, their own attitude is praiseworthy while all other points of view are incomprehensible and must therefore be wiped away from the world. This general way of thinking continues to grow and influence individuals, groups, generations, and entire time periods. Indeed, anything that is outside of one's own individual world must be damaged and destroyed.

As a result, confusion and complications increase in the realm of opinions and beliefs, attitudes toward life, and communal matters. In fact, the individual person also suffers endless confusion inside of themselves. One emotion does not approach another emotion with the appropriate respect and affection; one thought pushes away another thought in an insulting and aggressive way. The ability to have a respectful conversation between the different feelings inside of oneself becomes impossible and the general feeling of beauty to restore one's soul decreases and fades away.

Indeed, the world in general and we specifically are suffering from so many flaws and imperfections. *Tzadikim* – those individuals who are able to unify matters of intellect and desire – are being called upon to repair, connect, and create peace in the world. They accomplish this through creating peace inside of their own souls; through embodying a greater and more holistic form of wisdom that sends out light and life to all places.

This is the ultimate goal of people who serve God with faithfulness; it is through such people that the spiritual secrets of the world increase. (SK 1:637, OK 1, pp. 120–121)

Combining Both Paths of Spirituality

19

Rav Kook's Individual and Collective Spirituality

"All the effort I do to purify myself, my thoughts, my character traits, and my feelings, will help to purify the entire world." (SK 2:78)

JUST AS WE EXPECT A DOCTOR TO NOT ONLY PREACH THE IMPORtance of health but also to apply this medical knowledge to their own body, so too, a rabbi must not only teach spiritual wisdom to his students but also apply this wisdom to his own soul. Indeed, one of the most powerful things about Rav Kook's writings is that he shares with his readers his own spiritual goals and struggles. In one piece, Rav Kook writes:

> I am constantly searching for that which is inside my soul. All types of external work distract my mind from this inner search. It causes me to search in vain in the corners of the earth for that which I can only find in the depths of the soul. (PR 2, p. 114)

Why did Rav Kook choose to share with his readers his spiritual goals and struggles; his ups and downs; his hopes and fears? It is impossible to know for sure. However, it seems that one of Rav Kook's educational goals was that we would recognize that he does not simply preach spiritual wisdom to the world, but is also actively involved in trying to apply this wisdom to his own life.

In this final chapter of writings, Rav Kook will describe to us by personal example how he strove to apply spiritual wisdom to himself. Rav Kook will be very honest with us; he will not lie about his struggles, nor will he hide from us his incredible spiritual longings and dreams. In general, Rav Kook will invite us into his individual and collective spiritual worlds.

Rav Kook's Search to Understand Himself

I Seek Freedom Therefore I am Free

If my body is weak, should my soul suffer from this? If a thousand times my body pains me, should my spirit become pained? Am I not full of freedom, searching for light and liberation? And if I seek freedom, I must already be free. In my entire being, I am a child of freedom. (SK 7:196)

I Am Unable to Speak Superficial Words

I am unable to speak superficial and unnecessary words due to how I feel in my soul. When the influences of people cause me to speak mindless words like most of the world does, I feel a protest from the depths of my soul. I need help knowing how to experience and express the movements of my soul in all of life, in action and in speech. (SK 6:53)

What is My Soul Searching For?

My soul experiences great suffering. What is it searching for? The logical mind cannot solve this secret. Instead, the solution will only be found by searching the depths of the soul and the root of its existence. (PR 2, p. 119)

Searching Inside My Soul

I am constantly searching for that which is inside my soul. All types of external work distract my mind from this inner search. It causes me to search in vain in the corners of the earth for that which I can only find in the depths of the soul. (PR 2, p. 114)

My Own Purification Will Help the World

All the effort I make to purify myself, my thoughts, my character traits, and my feelings, will help to purify the entire world. "Each person is obligated to say, 'The world was created for me'" (Sanhedrin 37a). (SK 2:78)

I Exaggerate but Do Not Lie

If I exaggerate when I speak, if I speak with embellishments, is this really lying? Am I not revealing the thoughts of my soul? Am I not uncovering the light of my spirit? The revealing of lights and the uncovering of the soul is an enormously significant creation. I am standing on the heights of "the remnant of Israel will do no wrong; they will tell no lies. A deceitful tongue will not be found in their mouths" (Tzefaniah 3:13). (SK 7:195)

I Cannot Focus on Only One Thing

It is very hard for me to be involved only in halacha or only in agada. So too, it is difficult for me to be involved always in the surface level of the Torah (*Niglah*) or always in the hidden level of the Torah (*Nistar*). Likewise, it is hard for me to only think about faith in a simple and pure way or only think about faith in a sophisticated and logical way. It is also difficult for me to be always on my own in solitude or always with friends and the community. All forces rule inside of me. (SK 3:233)

My Many Emotions

I am full of joy, full of greatness, full of lowliness, full of bitterness, full of pleasantness, full of pleasure, full of love, full of jealousy, full of anger, full of kindness, full of goodness to all. Happy is one who listens to me. Happy is one who gives me the inner worth that is fitting for my unique personality. This person will rise higher and higher. Higher than all shortage. This person will be sanctified and purified. God is with him. (SK 3:235)

I Need to Recognize My Inner Beauty

I need to push away any thoughts that bring down my spirit and hold back the soul's happiness and divine confidence. I should not be overwhelmed by the possible mistakes that might happen to a person like me more than other people. This is because most people are immersed mainly in the limitations of the senses and the material mind.

I need to recognize my inner beauty. By recognizing the special qualities inside of my soul, I will come to recognize the greatness of the Jewish people. This will lead to an expanded mindset regarding the greatness of God, which expands the world to a higher freedom. By forgiving myself of all mistakes, I will be able to transform the Jewish people's sins into merits. I will be able to find good qualities in all human beings and continually draw forth a higher kindness upon the Jewish people. (C, p. 164)

I Am My Greatest Enemy

I will not give up my unique path. Even if my enemies and those who oppose me are numerous. The truth is that more than all my enemies, I myself am my biggest opposition. My smallness is fighting against my greatness. (SK 7:192)

A Prayer of Humility to God

Master of all worlds, I pour out my words before You. Do not hold me back from encountering Your greatness. Is not true greatness humility? There is no end to this, just as there is no end to all character traits.

I am aware of my lowliness and nothingness. Nonetheless, do not hold back the strength needed to come close to You – the Light of life and the Source of good. There is no end to the greatness that my heart senses due to my being one of Your creations. If there are creations of Yours that I look down upon from above, who are imperfect in my eyes, it is only because of my foolishness. Only You, the Source of wisdom, know Your greatness, and with the power of this greatness, all of your creations are treasured. They are Your deeds. The great and wonderous God.

It is enough for me that I am considered one of the creations of Your hands; this truth covers over all my imperfections. I approach You my King with holy awe. Save me. Save me from all my sins.

Redeem me from all of my enemies. Please save me, please save me. Father of compassion and mercy on all creations. "From God comes deliverance. May Your blessing be on Your people" (Tehilim 3:9). (KYK 1, Pinkas Yerushalayim 18)

I Put Down my Harp, but Did Not Break It

I put down my harp, but did not break it. I continue to see hope. Hope shines from the corners of the East. I will continually return to the song that I stopped. Yes, my strength is broken and my nerves are in shock due to accumulated anger, darkened thoughts, and confused effort. But there is a healer who stands behind the wall, who yearns to enter the chambers of my soul. My broken strength will be healed and returned. My beloved song will return to joy. She will charm me with her eyes and sustain me with her beloved kisses. (KYK 1, Reshimot M'London, Poems)

Thirst for God

My soul yearns for a higher light, for the infinite light, for the light of the true God, for the God of life. The God of life, the life of all worlds. And this yearning consumes my physical and spiritual strength. I do not have the ability or proper experience to satisfy this great yearning. I am filled with yearning before the King of the world, who opens His hand and satisfies all those who need (a paraphrase of Tehilim 145:16). Please satisfy my desires; satisfy me in the light of Your beauty. Quench my thirst for Your light. Illuminate Your face and then we will be saved. (KYK 1, Pinkas Yerushalayim 1)

I Am Love Sick for God

Who can understand the depths of my suffering, who can comprehend it? I am imprisoned within many constraints and limitations. My soul yearns for expansive heights. My soul thirsts for God. The life of my spirit is the most exalted light. The joy of my life is faith in an expansive God without any obstacles of nature, logic, behavior, and ethics. Anything that is well-defined is secular in the eyes of the highest holiness- which is what I seek. I am lovesick. How difficult it is for me to study. How difficult it is for me to adapt myself to details. I love the oceans and heavenly realms – I long for them. "Open my eyes and I will see wondrous things from Your Torah" (Tehilim 119: 18). (SK 3:222)

My Main Purpose in Life

It is not by chance, but rather the essential nature of my soul, that I feel a deep pleasure and peace of mind when immersed in divine secrets in an all-expansive and free-spirited way. This is my main purpose. The worth of my other talents – whether practical or intellectual – are secondary to my essence. I need to find happiness inside of myself and not through social approval or any type of career. The more I understand my essence, and the more I permit myself to be original and stand on my own feet… the more my strengths will be developed and be a blessing for myself and the entire world. (SK 2:77)

Rav Kook's Relationship with *Mitzvot*

I Want to Experience Happiness During Halacha

I experience such happiness and inner peace when I am immersed in spiritual thinking and mystical thoughts. I need help knowing how to experience such happiness when I am doing practical *mitzvot*, prayer, and all Surface Layer Parts (*Niglah*) of the Torah. (SK 6:24)

I Need to Experience Spiritual Pleasure in Everything

I need to experience the spiritual pleasure of divine connection in everything I study, do, pray, and speak. The halachot will then be saturated with meaning, full of the pleasantness of the highest holiness. This clear awareness will help me understand, comprehend, and sense how all the complex parts of halacha lead to and come from the same source where all spiritual pleasures come from. (SK 6:105)

Honoring My Feelings and Thoughts

My heart will not fall into despair even if my thoughts are considered matters of the imagination. Indeed, when the imagination is directed toward holiness and morality, it can be something beneficial and even necessary. And regardless, can anyone really know if someone's thoughts are made up of nothingness?

What matters most is that each person develops their own soul's talents in a way of light, truth, and goodness. One must do this according to the insights of their root soul. Personally, I feel an inner leaning toward certain thoughts; they flow around inside of me continuously. I feel this strongest when I speak and influence others. For this reason, I know that this is my portion and inheritance. To be sure, I need to strengthen myself in other realms of the Torah, specifically regarding the laws of the Torah. Nonetheless, to go against my natural spirit, this is something that I cannot do, nor is it necessary. (SK 6:52)

Studying in a Free Way

My soul demands from me, after every study and research, after every contemplation and thought, to free myself from the spiritual chains that detailed thoughts imprison the soul. My soul demands from me to search in the world of freedom for the essential hidden insight found within all details studied and contemplated. (SK 8:171)

Rav Kook's Struggle with Writing

I Cannot Write in a Simple Language

I need to liberate myself from the chains of writing. Why is it that I cannot write the depths of my thoughts in a simple language, without complexity and extra embellishments, to say things just as they are, to express them in a structured way? This is indeed a mystery…. There are great obstacles that stand before all revelations of spirituality, which prevent them from appearing in all their greatness. While the world is not worthy of too much light, we must nevertheless fight against these obstacles. The depths of kindness will overcome everything, the dark clouds will disappear, the shade will pass, and God's glory and light will appear….

"Then I said, 'Here I am, I have come with a scroll that is written for me.' I desire to do Your will, my God; Your Torah is in my depths. I have proclaimed Your righteousness in the great assembly. Indeed, I will not hold back my lips, O God, You know this" (Tehilim 40:8–10). (SK 3:237)

My Soul Cries Out

My soul cries out because I do not allow the power of my thoughts to expand in all their fullness and goodness. This is a great cruelty, and in truth, all of humanity suffers from this. It does not elevate and expand itself higher and therefore sinks lower and lower into muddy waters. This is caused by two things: External fear… and the dirt of materialism….

But we need to overcome all of this. The expansive mind, the sensitive desires, and the strength of life need to be expressed in their most powerful and fullest form. (SK 6:98)

I am a Free Poet

My thoughts are more expansive than many oceans. I am not able to express them in a plain and structured language. It is not for my benefit that I must be a poet, a free poet. I simply am not able to be connected to the structured rules of writing and rhymes. I run away from simple structured writing due to its heaviness and limitations. In truth, I am not able to place myself in any form of restriction, things which are far more restrictive than the restriction of structured writing. I run away from all this. (C, p. 63)

Why Did I Become Confused?

Why did I become confused? I will never know. Why have my thoughts stopped flying? Who is blocking my thoughts from expressing themselves? Who is oppressing my soul inside of me? I walk around the city, in markets and streets, and I search for the one who hates my soul, who pressures my life, who enslaves my fresh and living spirit. I will destroy this thing, I will shatter it, in order to liberate my pure and powerful talents from its prison. By doing this I will bring life and redemption to the world. (C, pp. 45–46)

I Should Have Written Down My Thoughts

How many of my thoughts have been strangled over time because I didn't write anything down? To be sure, these thoughts definitely exist somewhere in the depths of the soul; they have not been totally lost from reality. Yet water needs to be continuously drawn and used for some benefit. Thoughts need to be watered and actualized. "Write down the vision and explain it on tablets" (Chavakuk 2:2). (C, p. 65)

Revealing the Depths of My Thoughts

Who is stopping me? Why do I not reveal and express all the thoughts and the hidden meditations of my soul through writing? Who is holding me back? Who is imprisoning these thoughts in a shell and not allowing them to be released to the world? Who is strangling all the beautiful life of the soul and not allowing it to reveal itself in all its glorious spectrum of colors?

My inner spiritual strengths cry out due to their great suffering. They feel as if they are prisoners sitting in a cell; these poor prisoners are complaining that they have been unfairly and unjustly imprisoned. Indeed, the court ruling is with them, honesty and righteousness is on their side. They are so close to forcefully breaking out, of tumbling down the walls of their prison cell, to go free in the world. They will sing at the top of their lungs great songs of holiness, happiness, something filled with the strength of life....

Oh, when – when will their redemption come? When – when will I speak and write all that touches my heart. I will speak and be quenched. My mouth will speak the praises of God. The mouth will say everything that the heart thinks. The pen will explain that which is hidden in the depths of an idea. From darkness will come light – light, light, light. "God is my light and my salvation; from who will I fear? God is the strength of my life; from who will I be afraid?" (Tehilim 27:1). (KYK 1, Pinkas Yerushalayim 2)

Explaining the Midrash is Not My Main Goal
From Rav Kook's introduction to his book *Midbar Shor*

I must be honest and inform you that most of these words could have been written in the form of a logical book, full of clear philosophy, without arranging them in the form of Midrash, centered around explaining the words of the ancient rabbis and verses from the Torah....

However, due to time constraints, I have not been able to organize my thoughts as my heart desires. As a result of being occupied with both religious and secular work, the words in this book are formulated in the same style that I originally thought and spoke them before various congregations. I initially communicated these words in the common style of a sermon, beginning with words of the ancient rabbis. Since I personally find it difficult to reformat the order and style, I have left it as it is, and this is the style written down in this book.

It seems that the reader would have benefited far greater from the ideas if they were not written in the style of constantly referring to Midrashim. Indeed, my main goal is that the reader will ponder the depths of these new ideas, and not be overly focused on whether or not the ideas fit with the specific language of the Midrash. Nevertheless, I hope that the deep spiritual seeker will understand how to navigate oneself and recognize the times when I have simply come to explain a Midrash – and there are some like this – and the times when my main goal is to communicate deep and logical wisdom, which is sourced in the ways of Torah and agada. (MS Intro)

The Limitations of the Modern Language

A letter to Rabbi Meir Bar-Ilan (Secretary of World Mizrachi, founder of the Hebrew newspaper *HaIvri*, and the son of the Natziv), December 16, 1910

I was very happy when I received the first edition of the newspaper *HaIvri*. Thank God, it is physically beautiful. As a first edition, there is nothing to complain about regarding its inner content. I personally have an inner desire to be involved with your important work – as much as I am able to.

I very much want to help fix any imperfections that exist. Indeed, at the present moment, we lack content that contains a deeper perspective of life. To be sure, we also lack content regarding general academic knowledge. Such knowledge will be covered by various experts, each in their own fields. Nonetheless, when it comes to elements of depth from a unique Jewish perspective, there is truly a great lack in our books. This is something I worry about a lot.

With my limited talents, I truly desire to fill this lacking as much as I can. However, it is important to realize that there is an essential contradiction between the modern style of writing and the content of the deepest Jewish ideas. I find it very difficult to combine these two values. I continuously feel that the more I try to concentrate on writing in a modern style, the more I damage the depth of the idea. And so, I am *navoch*, perplexed by how I should act.

I have already thought about the possibility of sending my unedited journals to a publisher, and with their own wisdom, they can edit and change it to fit the current style of writing as much as possible. My friend, if you agree with this idea, then I imagine my contribution to the newspaper will be easier and more consistent for me. I await your important answer, and sign off this letter with the blessing "Rise up and succeed" (Melachim One, 22:15), "God's right hand is lifted up" (Tehilim 118:16). (IR 2, p.7)

You Changed My Original Words
A letter to Rabbi Meir Bar-Ilan, March 11, 1911

Regarding the fact that you have changed the title of my essay. I say to you, my friend, with an open mouth: Well done. The truth is that I myself never gave the essay that title. Rather, it was my son who copied and edited the essay from my journals.

I have found only a few small changes of my words. In my opinion, certain ideas would be more accurately expressed if the words were left as they were originally written. For example, the original words "That which illuminates all the darkness of a person," is preferred to "That which elevates above everything." In particular, I disagree with the removal of the verse *VeHaya Emunot*, which summarizes the entire idea of the essay. Nonetheless, the general essay is true to the original spirit of my words. (IR 2, p. 12)

Publishing a Collection of My Writings
A letter to Rabbi Dr. Moshe Seidel, January 29, 1914

I am pleased with your suggestion to publish my writings as a special collection. Indeed, how wonderful would it be if someone would find the strength to undertake this project. That is to say, to publish and prepare my writings with the help of God; a collection of everything that has been printed up until now as well as a large portion of my notes and other writings. This project would include additional notes, editing, and perhaps even small explanations and introductions.

In addition, my work on *Ein Yaakov* (a spiritual commentary on Agada) needs time for the mind to expand. This is also true of other important projects that my mind is focused on at the moment, such as a book on general spiritual ideas; a book of principles and introductions for the ideas of the Torah – both practical and in-depth. The same is true regarding other ideas of mine that I need to actualize. If only I had the proper financing so that I would be able to free myself from the work of the *Rabbanut*, and instead dedicate my time to the work of spirituality and writing – to fulfill all my deepest desires.

But will this dream ever come about? Only God knows. It is my prayer that God will help my request come true whereby this righteous deed will be done by righteous people. (IR 2, p. 264)

People Who Criticize My Writings
A letter to Rav Kook's parents, 1920

Do not pay attention to people who criticize my book *Orot*. This is simply the way of people who are not used to in-depth study of spiritual and philosophical matters; it is the way of people who get upset at any explanation or insight that seems new. The truth is that the foundations of my ideas are ancient and sourced in religious sources, and people far greater and more righteous than me in previous generations have suffered similar criticisms.

In my opinion, it is enough that spiritually aligned souls with an authentic fear of heaven comprehend what I write. Such people will benefit from these writings, which I believe will have a collective and spiritual benefit to publish from time to time. There is no need to explain and show the sources for my writings. In general, sources do not really explain my thoughts. Rather, they become self-evident after much contemplation and deep sensitivity. The people who criticize my writings, or even those pure of heart who are not used to such ideas, will not accept what I wrote even when they are shown the religious sources of these writings.

I request from you, my precious and honorable parents, that you will not suffer from these matters. This is the obligation of the holy service of God, Whose signature is truth: to not fear any criticism and insult. (IR 4, p. 69)

Rav Kook's Love of All People

I Experience the Sufferings of the World

I experience inside of me the sufferings of the world and all its mistakes. I experience inside of me the world's depressing poverty, the prisoners of shortage who have despaired of any hope; those who are filled with bitter poison in the depths of their wounded hearts. I am a friend of the embittered soul; I suffer with the sufferings of their souls. (SK 3:236)

I Desire to Do Good to All Human Beings

My many imperfections will not hold me back from helping the world. I desire to do good; I desire to do good to all human beings. Indeed, what I truly desire is to want to be good in the purest way. My heart is filled with a holy fire of love and affection toward the Jewish people and the entire world – to elevate everything to its source of goodness. This desire of mine is a holy desire. I need to acknowledge its holiness. (C, p. 191)

Help Me Feel the Pain of the World

May my heart be open to comprehend the truth of the divine light; to pray for all of those who sigh and are depressed. Indeed, everything needs compassion – the world, the generation, the rejected souls, any form of pain and imperfection. May my eyes be illuminated to feel the pain of the world as well as the pain of the divine presence (*HaShechina*). (HA, p. 337)

I Feel all the Nation's Pain

A letter to Rabbi Pinchas HaCohen Lintup, January 29, 1909

I am a slave to the masses, to serve and to help God's people that have begun to put down its roots in our land of inheritance.... I am busy with a lot of practical work due to the nation's current transition into its new form… and I am standing in the midst of all of this.

I must thank God, Who has created this type of soul for me. My soul lives and feels all of the different groups within the nation and their various struggles – including all of their inner sufferings and pains. On the other hand, my soul also feels all the strength of the nation's life and faith. These matters come to me in a visceral way and I am forced to deal with them in action and deed. I suffer all the crises of the different groups within the nation as well as the intensity of their struggles. I feel compelled to listen to both their external and internal voice. (IR 1, p. 240)

I Do Not Need External Approval
A letter to Tzvi Hirsch Jaffe, October 26, 1910

I am very surprised that you my friend are upset at me because the secular people are praising me.… From their perspective, they see certain people who are trying to uproot settlements from their roots.… They see people who are trying to prevent these settlements from expanding and developing. And for the secular Jews, this value is their entire connection to Judaism.

I am the only one amongst the well-known rabbis who is trying to stand in the midst of the battle ground. I have relinquished my honor, status, and everything that is mine. All I care about is helping the settlements and anything that is involved in this issue. I do this without any agenda. And so, how could these secular people interpret this in anything but a positive way?

Regarding your question: Who is on my side? This includes all people who fear God, great *Talmidei Chachamim*, and those with an honest heart. All such people are outraged by the new controversy, and specifically regarding the disrespectful behavior.… Nonetheless, I have never asked for anyone's help. In my opinion, the need for external approval is an embarrassment and a desecration to the honor of truth. (IR 2, p.2)

Why Do You Judge Me Unfavorably?

A letter to the Ridvaz, Rabbi Yaakov David Wilovsky, June 29, 1913

I am amazed by what you wrote regarding how in your younger years you learned from me the trait of discipline, good character traits, and a fear of God. I do not know what you found in me back then to learn. Nonetheless, if because of your great humility you did manage to learn something from me when I was living in the Diaspora, how can you think that I am worse off now that God has gifted me with living in the Holy Land?

Indeed, why do you judge me unfavorably? My ways and actions are not for my own honor God forbid. Nor are they for any other external motivation in the world. Instead, I am motivated by a love for God, a love for the holy Torah, a love for the Jewish people and the Holy Land. "I have worn myself out groaning" (Yirmiyahu 45:3) until God inspired my soul and formed my heart to walk in purity in this holy path. A pathway of sanctifying the name of God, helping people love the Torah and those who follow it, helping to bring many people close to the Torah, to increase strength and courage, and to help settle people with God in His Holy Land. (IR 2, pp. 185–186)

My Main Intention

A letter to the Ridvaz, Rabbi Yaakov David Wilovsky, March 28, 1913

Regarding what you said about how people are saying that I am one of them (secular), God forbid. Was not Avraham Avinu promised that "All people of the earth will be blessed through you" (Bereishit 12:3)? And weren't the ancient prophets and Tzadikim praised by the nations of the world? Yet is this a flaw to their honor, God forbid?

Believe me, I do not have any intention of finding favor in their eyes, nor in the eyes of any person in the world. Rather, my main intention is for the sake of God. (IR 2, pp. 153–154)

Stories about Rav Kook

WHENEVER A PERSON IS SEARCHING FOR SPIRITUAL AND ETHICAL transformation, it is important not only to study "words of" great people but also "words about" such people. "Words of" great people include their insights and wisdom as expressed through their writings, commentaries, journals, and letters that give us direct guidance about how to live the ideal life. In contrast, "words about" great people include insights and wisdom as expressed through biographies, stories, and anecdotes about the way they lived their lives. These stories help us see how these great people attempted to embody and live up to these values in a real concrete way in their own day-to-day lives.

According to Rav Kook, when a person studies stories about a *Tzadik*, a *Geon*, or a great spiritual and ethical role model, it creates within them a type of holy jealousy that inspires within them a desire to imitate this person's good traits. In his book *Eder HaYakar*, Rav Kook writes:

> There are two main benefits to studying the life of a *Geon*/spiritually great person: a practical benefit and a spiritual benefit. The practical benefit is connected to the principle: "Jealousy of wise people increases wisdom" (Bava Batra 21a). When the reader sees the spiritual glory and inner beauty that this person has achieved, this will awaken within oneself an inner desire to try to follow in their ways. (EY, p.23)

In Rav Kook's eyes, if a person truly desires to go through an inner transformation, then it is not enough to study correct and insightful ideas; one must also study the lives of great people. Through studying the way they lived their lives, one becomes inspired to commit to a life of higher meaning. For example, when one reads stories about the way a *Tzadik* prays, studies Torah, or does acts of kindness, this awakens within a person the motivation to embody these values in their own life.

To be sure, one must not lie to themselves. Rav Kook says that sometimes a person will read a story about a *Tzadik* and find themselves unable to imitate this person's higher values and actions. Nonetheless, one should not therefore conclude that these stories are not helpful, relevant, or transformative for one's life. Instead, Rav Kook says that the very act of reading these stories affects a person – even if in a small and subtle way – and motivates one to choose a life centered around spiritual and ethical meaning.

> **And even if the reader does not succeed in imitating this great person completely, nonetheless it is not possible that the reader will not be moved even in a small way from their current place to a more elevated place. Such a person will be inspired to choose a life of righteousness and work toward attaining valuable spiritual goals, just as this great person dedicated their life toward. (Ibid.)**

Lastly, Rav Kook says that one of the greatest lessons that we can gain from reading stories and anecdotes of a *Tzadik*, of a great person, is that it humanizes them. We not only learn about their successes and spiritual achievements, but also about their struggles and obstacles; about how they persevered in times of darkness and refused to give up.

> **The practical benefits come about through describing some of this great person's behavior. For example, through telling stories about the unique ways they worked hard, descriptions of the**

obstacles that stood in the way to developing their greatness; and lastly, how they battled through these obstacles and overcame them. (Ibid.)

In Rav Kook's eyes, it is essential that a person study not only the spiritual and ethical achievements of a *Tzadik's* life, but also how they searched for a deeper meaning in moments of darkness and suffering.

> When they give meaning to their own sufferings, they give meaning to the world's suffering. The *Tzadik's* soul is the root of many souls. The *Tzadik* is their foundation. (SK 1:210)

Much of this book focuses on "words of Rav Kook," his spiritual wisdom and direct guidance for our lives. We have studied Rav Kook's words and wisdom about topics as diverse as the need for solitude, the meaning of *mitzvot*, dreams, death, love, connecting to the Jewish people, choosing peace over division, and so much more.

We now turn to the last section of the book, "Stories about Rav Kook." In this short but important part of the book, we will read small and insightful stories about Rav Kook that describe how he attempted to embody the spiritual wisdom he wrote about. These stories are collected from many books that include first-hand accounts from family members, friends, students, and contemporaries who saw how Rav Kook studied Torah, prayed, performed acts of kindness, and much more. In continuation of the two main themes of the book, these stories are split up into two parts. The first part includes stories about Rav Kook's individual spirituality while the second half is focused on Rav Kook's collective spirituality.

To use Rav Kook's own language, two important things happen to us when we study the life of Rav Kook. The first is that we develop a holy jealousy that awakens within us a desire to imitate his great values in our own lives. In addition, we are given a window into the human side of Rav Kook, how he faced his struggles and obstacles, and did not give up in moments of hardship and darkness.

A Debate Between Father and Mother

In Rav Kook's home, it was a known thing that when he was a young child there was a debate between his father and mother. His father – who was a student of the Volozhin Yeshiva – would say about the young Rav Kook: "He will be a great Torah scholar." His mother who was the daughter of Chasidim would say: "He will be a great Chassidik Rebbe."

During the six days of the week, Rav Kook's father's prophecy came true (through his intense Torah study), while on the holy Shabbat, it seems that the prayers of his mother during candle lighting affected Rav Kook. Indeed, during the third meal of Shabbat, Rav Kook revealed himself as a Chassidik Rebbe. (MoR, p. 21, told by Rav Moshe Tzvi Neria)

How Does It Feel to be in Yeshiva?

When Rav Kook finished studying at the Volozhin Yeshiva, the Rosh Yeshiva "The Natziv," asked him how he felt while learning in the Yeshiva. Rav Kook answered: "I felt like I was dwelling in the land of Israel." (BSH, p. 28)

Creating Rhymes in Hebrew and Aramaic

The students of the Volozhin Yeshiva would come to the Rosh Yeshiva HaNatziv's house for a meal on Purim. As is the custom of those who desire to increase joy on Purim, the students created rhymes about the Yeshiva. Rav Kook, however, was different in this regard from the other students. Rav Kook created rhymes not in Yiddish, but rather in Hebrew and Aramaic. During that time period, there were a few students in the Yeshiva who were known for being attracted to literature, and other students who had studied secular enlightenment books and had been negatively affected in matters of faith. Such students were amazed to hear Rav Kook's incredible control over words and language.

The Rosh Yeshiva HaNatziv turned to these students and remarked:

Look at the knowledge of this student (Rav Kook). He is not only great in Torah and awe of God; even when it comes to his abilities with words and language you do not reach his ankles. (SHR, p. 99, told by Rav Ephraim Teitelbaum)

A Special Love of Wearing *Tefillin*

Rav Kook acted with the character of *Chassidut*/piety even when he was in his youth. This trait did not go unnoticed by his father-in-law, the Aderet. In particular, this young nineteen-year-old's love of the mitzvah of *tefillin*, who was soon to become the Aderet's son-in-law, is what caused the following incident.

> On the eve of Purim, on the Shabbat before his wedding in Yeshivat Volozion, a beautiful gift arrived from Rav Kook's future father-in-law, the Aderet. The gift included three pairs of *tefillin*. A pair of Rashi *tefillin*, a pair of Rabeinu Tam *tefillin* – in their regular sizes. The third was a pair of mini Rashi *tefillin* so that a person could hide it on his arm and underneath his hat and wear it all day long. Indeed, this is what Rav Kook did from his youth until old age. He dressed in *tefillin* most of the day; immersed in the study of Torah as its spiritual glory was wrapped around his head with God's name written upon it. (SHR, p. 165)

Overworking Oneself

Rav Kook once said to me "You should know that I owe a lot to your grandparents and great-grandparents. I was a regular visitor in their house. They looked after me like they would look after a son. When I studied in the city of Smargun I became sick due to working myself too hard. The doctors said that I was at risk of doing serious damage to my health and that I needed an urgent increase in nutrition. Your grandmother, Rivka, would cook for me chicken soup and send it to my residence. She would also send me cream and butter until I recovered and became healthy again, thank God." (SHR, p. 77, told by Rav Chayim Korlinski)

Davening Shaas

During Rav Kook's time as the rabbi of Zeimel, he was focused on doing big reviews of Shaas time after time in a continuous and fast way. Rav Kook called this style of learning "Davening the Gemara" (learning Gemara in a fast way similar to prayer that is fluent in one's mouth). One time Rav Kook pushed himself and finished all the Jerusalem Talmud in depth over six months. However, as a result of pushing himself so much, he became sick and needed to spend time in bed to recover. (BSH, pp. 28–29)

Knew all of Shaas by Memory

Rav Kook knew all of Shaas by memory. A person could feel this. (LHR p. 212, told by Rav Yitzchak Hutner)

Whatever Topic We Would Speak About

We are considered *Gedolim*/Great Sages until we reach the doorstep of Rav Kook. Whenever I would begin speaking with Rav Kook about a certain *Sugiya*/religious topic, it always seemed to me as if he had just now been holding a Gemara and closed it before I entered the room. In every section of the Torah – in Shaas and the Rambam – everything was so clear and fresh for Rav Kook. Whatever topic we would speak about, it always seemed as if he was just now reading about that topic in a book. (BSR p. 234, told by Rav Isser Zalman Meltzer)

To Go Through All of Shaas Quickly

In the last year of his life, when Rav Kook became sick with the illness that would ultimately lead to his death, his back began to hurt and he became weaker and weaker each day. When Rav Kook knew the seriousness of the situation, he started to prepare for the long road ahead.... Rav Kook set up a *chavruta* in Gemara with one of the students from the Yeshiva. Rav Kook said to him: "I want to go through all of Shaas quickly." (BSH, p. 43)

Studying Kabbalah Amidst Tragedy

When the terrible tragedy happened and Rav Kook's wife died, this caused him to increase his study of the surface layer of the Torah (*Niglah*) as well as to deepen his study of the spiritual world (*Olam HaNistar*). In Rav Kook's first year of mourning, he studied a lot of the teachings of the Zohar as well as the writings of the Arizal. However, there was no one close by who could help Rav Kook clarify these difficult topics in the Torah. Therefore, Rav Kook asked permission from his congregation and then traveled for a month to the city of Shavel, where he studied with the Lion of the Great Mystics/ *Gedolei HaNistar*, the Geon and Kabbalist, Rabbi Shlomo Elyashiv, the author of *Leshem Shebo VeAchlama*. (SHR, pp. 142–143)

What did Rav Kook and Rav Shlomo Elyashiv Study Together?

Rav Kook traveled to the city of Shavel to study with Rav Shlomo Elyashiv. Rav Kook sat with him for an entire month and together they studied the writings of the Arizal, manuscripts of the Ramchal that were hidden in his house, and the writings of the Geon of Vilna. In addition, they studied the books and explanations of the Geon and Kabbalist Rav Yitzchak Issak Chaver, the rabbi of Sovlak. (SHR, pp. 148–149)

Studying Kabbalah in Jerusalem

This higher connection that Rav Kook developed with Rav Shlomo Elyashiv during the time in Shavel, also continued many years later. Rav Areye Levin said that when the Geon and *Tzadik* Rav Shlomo Elyashiv arrived at the end of his life to Jerusalem, there were times when Rav Kook would come to Rav Shlomo Elyashiv's house after midnight and for the next couple of hours they would study Kabbalah. (SHR, pp. 151–152)

Studying Agada and Midrash

One time Rav Kook said to me "I have studied Midrash in-depth just like one studies Gemara." During another time, Rav Kook added "In my youth I dedicated an hour and a half each day to the study of Agada." (SHR, p. 141, told by Rav Moshe Tzvi Neria)

The Books on Rav Kook's Table

In Rav Kook's small room on the window shelf was placed the entire Torah: a mini-sized version of the *Tanach*, *Shaas Bavli* and *Yerushalmi*, a small set of the *Zohar*, the *Rambam*, and the *Shulchan Aruch*.

On Shabbat, in the same small room, Rav Kook's table was crowned with three additional books: *Likutei Torah* by the Alter Rebbe, Rav Shneur Zalman of Liadi, *Sefat Emet* by the Rav Yehuda Leib Alter of Gur, and the *Kli Chemdah* by Rav Meir Dan Plotsky, the rabbi of Dvohrt of Polen. (MoR, p. 19)

I Also Do Not Understand What is Written in the Book

Reish Milin is a book Rav Kook wrote when he was living in London in 1917 about the kabbalistic meanings of the letters of the Alef Bet and its grammatical vows. Rav Kook once said that just having the book *Reish Milin* in one's house is a *Segulah*/spiritual protection even if one does not understand its meaning. On Purim 1935, five months before Rav Kook passed away, he gave a copy of *Reish Milin* as a gift to his student and famous Talmudic scholar Saul Lieberman. It is told that when Rav Kook gave Lieberman the book, Lieberman said "But I do not understand anything written here." Rav Kook replied, "I also do not understand what is written in the book. However, when I wrote the book, I understood everything." (https://blog.nli.org.il/sodot-sholem/)

How Rav Kook Would Write

When Rav Kook was living in London, I would often come and visit him in his home. Rav Kook would sit wrapped in his small *tefillin*, a gift from his father-in-law, the Aderet. Sometimes a flash of insight would take a hold of Rav Kook. He had a notebook of empty pages. Each time a thought would pour into specific words, he would write it down in his notebook. (SHR, p. 172, told by Rabbi Dr. Yeshayahu Meir Lerman)

Writing in Notebooks Late at Night

At the end of Simchat Torah, after a day of singing and festivities, many people had already left Rav Kook's house. We, the students of the Yeshiva, continued to celebrate until the late hours of the night. When we were about to leave, we entered Rav Kook's office to say goodbye and to our surprise, he was sitting at his table busy writing in his notebooks. (BSH p. 65)

The Uniqueness of Rav Kook's Writings

The famous Zionist poet Nachman Bialik once said "Anything small that I write, I need to erase, change, rewrite several times, and then polish off at the end. This is not true for Rav Kook. I personally know that Rav Kook does not edit his words. They are published just as they were written in the first draft. To be able to write in such a way on the first draft – only Rav Kook can do such a thing." (SHR, p. 250)

Crying Because I Cannot Write

Rav Kook was crying on his deathbed during the last days of his life. Rav Shmuel Kook asked Rav Kook, "Why are you crying? Is it because of the terrible pain you are experiencing?" Rav Kook answered, "I am not crying due to the pain I am feeling. Rather, I am crying because of all the thoughts and insights roaming around in my mind, and I don't have the ability to write them down." (SR p. 386, told by Rabbi Shmuel Kook, Rav Kook's brother)

Why Don't You Publish Your Writings?

One time, Rav Kook's student, Rav Moshe Tzvi Neria asked him why he doesn't try to publish his books. Rav Kook gave him two answers. He began to explain that when he was young, he also asked his rabbi, Rabbi Ravola of Dinaborg, why he doesn't try to publish his interpretations of the Torah (*Chidushei HaTorah*). Rabbi Ravola answered him, "I don't have any money to publish my writings. And to ask others to use their money to publish it for me, I haven't found a good enough justification."

The second answer was specifically connected to philosophical and spiritual books. "I know that in my writings there are things that today would be considered divine revelations. Therefore, if God inspires another person to publish my writings, I will accept, since this is a sign that my writings should be revealed. But to put in my own effort, this I cannot do." (SHR, pp. 359–360)

My Censors

When Rav Kook's book, *Orot HaKodesh* was about to be published, his students asked him what from inside the book should be published, and what should not be published. Rav Kook responded, "My opinion is that everything should be published, but you have to ask 'my censors.'" (SHR, p. 37)

I Wrote It This Way for a Reason

When people started working on editing and organizing the writings of Rav Kook, some suggested that Rav Kook's words needed to be fixed grammatically and the order of the words needed to be changed. But Rav Kook did not permit these changes. He said that right now he doesn't remember the reason why he wrote the words in this specific way. Nevertheless, in the moment he wrote it down there was definitely a reason why it had to be written precisely like this. (SHR, p. 379)

How Rav Kook Would Teach

Rav Kook's holy way was to teach for hours about many different topics without any preparation. His thoughts were very spiritual and the originality of his ideas was very deep. People who came to hear him speak didn't always understand the depth of his ideas. Sometimes a person listening to Rav Kook, who didn't fully understand what was being discussed, would ask him about something. Then Rav Kook would let go of the first idea he was discussing and begin talking for hours about the idea raised by the person. (SHR, p. 200)

Regular Mincha

One time Rav Isser Zalman Meltzer prayed *Mincha* in the same *Minyan* as Rav Kook. In the break between *Mincha* and *Maariv* they sat together and immediately began speaking words of Torah. These two old friends from the Volozhin Yeshiva renewed their friendship and there was a joy of Torah between them just as there was in their youth in the Volozhin Yeshiva run by the Geon HaNetziv.

On the way out, Rav Isser Zalman Meltzer began singing the praises of Rav Kook to a student and talking about Rav Kook's incredible knowledge of Torah and fear of God. In humility, Rav Isser Zalman Meltzer added: "If only I could pray Mincha on Erev Yom Kippur like Rav Kook prays Mincha on a regular day." (BSH, p. 109, told by Rav Yitzchak Epstein)

The Melodies of Chabad

The melodies of divine connection were always present on Rav Kook's lips each morning during the prayers of *Shacharit* in the lead-up to the *Shema*...

One could sense how Rav Kook had reached deep concentration of the heart, deep contemplation in the mind, and how Rav Kook was accepting the yoke of the kingship of heaven with complete oneness with all his body and soul.

The special melody Rav Kook would hum during morning prayers was filled with the spirit of Chabad *Nigunim*/melodies. It seems that the origin of these melodies came from Rav Kook's youth when he was surrounded by Chabad Chasidim led by Rabbi Yechezkel Yanover. These Chasidim would pray at length in the Chabad Kopust

Shtibel/Synagogue in Greiva built by Rav Kook's maternal grandfather. (BSH, p. 108)

Rav Kook's Excitement About Prayer

I loved seeing Rav Kook become spiritually elevated when he prayed. One time I came to visit him in Yaffo in the morning after the *Shacharit* prayer. When Rav Kook finished saying the prayer *Ein KeElokeinu,* he was filled with such excitement and began explaining to me the meaning of this prayer.

In Jerusalem, I saw Rav Kook write a lot about the meaning of the prayers of the *Siddur*. He would expand and explain each prayer at length. Rav Kook had a very special connection when he would pray at night the *Aravit* prayer. I loved looking at him. (BSH, p. 113, told by Rav Yosef Tzvi Rimon)

I Have Never Heard Someone Study Tanach Like That

One time I came to Rav Kook's house on Erev Shabbat to ask him for help regarding something urgent. When I came near his small room where he would normally study and write, I didn't knock on the door at first but rather put my ear to the door to see if he was in the middle of learning, since I didn't want to interrupt him.

I could hear a yearning voice filled with emotion. I stopped and listened. I realized that Rav Kook was studying a chapter of Tanach with a strong melody. He was repeating the verse with even stronger emphasis. Suddenly, Rav Kook's voice grew louder and he returned and read the same verse with even more emotion, as if the words of the prophet had been revealed to him for the first time. After this, Rav Kook proceeded to the next verse and the same thing happened again, as he continued to study.

I grew up in Jerusalem amongst great sages, people who feared God; *Tzadikim*, and *Chasidim.* I saw them all study and pray, but I have never heard someone study Tanach like this. This was not study but prayer, and it was not regular prayer but service of the heart. (BSH, p. 113, told by Rav Shlomo Zalman Zalaznik)

The Mountains of Israel

When Rav Kook returned to Israel from his visit to America, he commented about the greatness of the mountains. "It is true that in America I saw great and mighty mountains, the creations of God the Master of all lands. However, those mountains over there did not speak to us in the same way that these holy mountains speak to us here. These mountains speak to us in a clear language." (SHR pp. 254)

To Kiss Every Rock and Animal

Rav Kook was once asked to arbitrate a dispute in the colony of Rishon LeTzion. On the way there, he said to his escort, a relative of Rav Moshe Leib Shapiro: "I would be prepared to kiss every single rock in this Land. I would even kiss the donkey that we just passed." (*An Angel Among Men* p. 272)

Our Motherland Longs for Her Children to Return

Once Rav Kook was on his way to Tel Aviv with some escorts when their car developed engine trouble. Forced to pull over and stop for a while, all the passengers dispersed in different directions to find something to do to pass the time. Rav Kook also disappeared.

After a while, Rav Kook's escorts decided to search for him. They found him a short distance away, completely outstretched on the ground whispering the words "My Land! My Land! O'holy soil of the land of Israel." When Rav Kook rose to his feet, he said to the people who had gathered around him, "When else do I have an opportunity to speak with our Motherland who longs for her children to return to her borders?" (*An Angel Among Men* p. 273)

Saying the Words: "The Jewish People"

When Rav Kook would say the words "The Jewish people"/*Knesset Yisrael*, *Klal Yisrael*, his entire being would become excited. It was as if Rav Kook had placed his entire essence and longings of the soul into these words. (BSD p. 178, told by Rav Hutner)

Speaking Yiddish for the Sake of Peace

When Rav Kook would give a *Drasha*/Sermon in the Churbat Rav Yehuda HaChasid Synagogue in Jerusalem, he would usually speak in Yiddish. One time, Menachem Ussishkin[33] came to the synagogue in order to hear the *drasha* of Rav Kook. When Ussishkin heard that Rav Kook was speaking in Yiddish, he left immediately. When Rav Kook found out about this, he said, "We must be considerate of everyone, even with the older generation. There is no other way." (SHR, p. 221)

Picking Up the Phone on Shabbat

One time, Rav Kook was in the city of Tiveriah for Shabbat, in the Guberman Hotel. During *Seudat Shlishit* (the late afternoon meal on Shabbat) the telephone kept on ringing over and over again. But no one answered the phone. Rav Kook asked, "Why is no one answering

---

33. Menachem Ussishkin (1863–1941) served as Secretary of the First Zionist Congress, was the President of the Jewish National Fund, championed the revival of the Hebrew language, and was one of the founders of the Hebrew University.

the phone?" The people around him responded, "Isn't it Shabbat today?" Rav Kook said, "There are *Moshavim*/villages close by and there is no doctor or midwife there. Perhaps they need a midwife?"

They immediately answered the phone and found that this is exactly what had happened. There was someone calling from *Moshav Kinneret*/the village of Kinneret to say that there was a woman giving birth and that they desperately need a midwife. (SHR, p. 225)

Giving Away Books for Charity

One time a poor person entered the house of Rav Kook to ask him for money, but he didn't have any money on him. Rav Kook explained to the poor person that even though he didn't have any money to give, nevertheless Rav Kook insisted, "Choose any book from my library and sell it to get money." (SHR, p. 138)

Masters of Creating Disagreements

One time, Rabbi Shabtai Bornstein asked Rav Kook, "Why do you get angry at those who try to harm you? If indeed they are incorrect in their approach, don't you yourself always judge favorably all the Jewish people? And aren't these people also a part of the Jewish people?" Rav Kook replied in these exact words, "They are *Baalei Machloket*/masters of creating disagreements, and one should not judge favorably those who are masters of creating disagreements." (SHR, p. 324)

What Do They Want from Me?

During the seven days of Succot (*Chol HaMoed*) the religious zealots publicly embarrassed Rav Kook in the most terrible way. When Rav Chaim Kaminetzky came to visit Rav Kook and entered his Succah,

Rav Chaim saw Rav Kook walking back and forth saying, "Master of the world! What do they want from me?" (SHR p. 324)

Not Guilty Because They Don't Understand Me

Rabbi Leibkovitz was loyal to Rav Kook and would host him when he would take time to rest in the city of Rechovot. When Rabbi Leibkovitz read in the newspaper about how the religious zealots publicly embarrassed Rav Kook, he immediately traveled to Jerusalem in order to visit Rav Kook.

Rabbi Leibkovitz entered Rav Kook's home on Shabbat afternoon during Succot (*Chol HaMoed*). To his great fortune, Rabbi Leibkovitz found Rav Kook sitting alone in his Succah, and was therefore able to have a quality conversation with him. Rav Kook welcomed Rabbi Leibkovitz with warmth and asked him, "How are you doing?" Rav Kook could see that the face of his visitor was saddened. Rav Kook asked him, "Why are you so sad?" Rabbi Leibkovitz replied, "Because of how they embarrassed you." Rav Kook said, "I ask you not to speak about this issue at all. I forgive them completely. I have instructed my family and all my friends not to file any legal complaint."

Rav Kook then added, "They are correct since they don't understand me, nor do they understand any of my books or any of my ideas. Indeed, it is because they don't understand me that they are not guilty. If they understood me, they would not do such a thing." And so it was; no legal complaint was filed, just as Rav Kook instructed. (SHR, pp. 324–235)

Speaking the Right Language

One time Rav Kook gave the following metaphor. Let us say there is a person who speaks only French and does not understand any other language. If we rebuke such a person in all the languages of the world except French, it is obvious that we did not fulfill the mitzvah of rebuking a person since they did not understand our words.

In truth, what is the difference between the language of the mouth and the language of the mind? If the mind of the person we are rebuking does not understand the halachik explanations, it is obvious that we have not fulfilled the mitzvah of rebuke. Therefore, why are we so hateful toward such a person? There is no doubt that it is forbidden to hate such a person. (HA, p. 423)

Enjoying the Students' Questions

When Rav Yitzchak Hutner was younger, he was one of Rav Kook's closest students. Rav Hutner had great admiration for Rav Kook. At the same time, he would argue with Rav Kook and ask him questions regarding certain thoughts and opinions Rav Kook held. Not only did Rav Kook enjoy this, it caused him to love Rav Hutner even more. (SHR, p. 293)

Close to the Ways of Faith

Rav Kook was also well-versed in the spiritual world of non-Jewish philosophers. There was a period when his beloved student Rav Shimon Stzerelitz was living in Rav Kook's house. One time Rav Shimon was sitting at the table in the main room while studying the book of a well-known non-Jewish philosopher. As Rav Kook was passing by, all of a sudden, he stopped next to Rav Shimon and took a look at the book. Rav Kook said to his student, "That book is close to the ways of faith." (BSR p. 255)

Nullified in Sixty

Rav Kook once asked me to give him copies of my books. I replied that I had indeed thought about giving him one or two of them. He said, "I want all of your books, and you intended to give me only some of them?!" I replied, "Your desire is my honor."

A while later, he saw me and said, "I read your works." "All of them?" I asked. "All of them," he replied, "and I want to tell you something: The author of the *Pri Magadim* wrote a small work entitled *Mattan S'charan Shel Mitzvot* (Reward for Mitzvot), in which he writes: If a drop of forbidden food falls into sixty times its volume of permissible food, the forbidden drop is nullified in sixty (*batel be'shishim*). In that case, the permissible food gains from the forbidden one, for there are now sixty-one parts of permissible food (instead of just sixty).

The same is true of your works. Even if some forbidden food material 'falls' into your books, it is nullified in sixty and becomes permissible. Thus, the permissible material gains from the forbidden." (Told by Shai Agnon, *An Angel Among Men*, pp. 399–400)

The Spiritual Importance of Art

When I went up to Jerusalem and visited Rav Kook... the conversation quickly turned to the topic of art; and I – the professor of art – suddenly saw myself as a student sitting before his master, listening with admiration to his comprehensive knowledge.

When Rav Kook began talking about the place of art in universal culture, I thought to myself, "It is indeed fascinating that this great Torah scholar knows about such matters, but that must be part of his broad knowledge of general philosophy," of which I was already aware. However, when he went on to discuss – effusively – the art of painting, and even relating to great and famous painters and their artistic genres, I was completely amazed. When and how did he attain such wide-ranging proficiency and such subtle distinctions in this complex discipline? Suddenly, I realized that this great rabbi sees all; his poetic soul is open to the entire range of artistic expression.

During that broad conversation, Rav Kook had a special request for me: He asked me to devote more of my energies to painting the scenery of the land of Israel. "As an artist," he said, "you have an important mission. You must reveal the beauty, grace, and sanctity of our Holy Land. You must depict historical sites which, when seen, will inspire Jews to love the Land and yearn for its hills and valleys."

Rav Kook concluded with a blessing, "May the God Who gave wisdom to Betzalel and Oholiav for the purpose of building the *Mishkan*, continue to give wisdom to anyone whose artistic talents are devoted to the Jewish nation and its Land." (Told by Herman Struck, *An Angel Among Men*, pp. 410–411)

Labels

Rav Kook once told a group of students that he disagreed with using labels such as religious, *Chareidi*/Ultra-Orthodox, and *Aduk*/Pious. Instead, Rav Kook said that a person should simply use the term "a kosher Jew." (LHR, p. 167)

Saving Someone's Life on Shabbat

Rav Kook was once in a synagogue on Shabbat when a person suddenly burst in and told Rav Kook that this man's wife was dangerously sick and a certain doctor refused to treat her. Rav Kook left the synagogue immediately and traveled to the home of this doctor. Rav Kook asked him: "Why do you refuse to go and save this woman?" The doctor replied, "Today is Shabbat, the location is far away, and I do not have enough energy to walk there." Rav Kook replied, "Take a wagon and travel to the location." The doctor said to Rav Kook: "If I travel in a wagon, the religious zealots will stop me and rise up against me. I will only travel in the wagon if you Rav Kook will travel with me."

Rav Kook said "It is forbidden for me to travel on a wagon since I am not a doctor and therefore, I do not have Halachik permission. Only you have permission due to the law of *Pikuach Nefesh*/saving a person's life. Therefore, you should travel on the wagon and I will accompany you on foot next to the wagon. When the religious zealots see that a rabbi is walking behind the doctor, they will be quiet." And so it was. Rav Kook walked and accompanied this doctor for a few kilometers until they reached the home of the sick person. (HA, p. 236, told by Rabbi Shmuel Aharon Shezori)

Honoring Your Teacher

When Rav Shlomo Elyashiv (Rav Kook's main Kabbalistic teacher) made Aliyah to Israel and visited Rav Kook's house for the first time it was winter. Upon entering the house, Rav Kook saw that Rav Elyashiv didn't have any warm clothes. Rav Kook walked over to his cupboard, took out a coat, and put it on his visitor. "I present this to you as a gift," Rav Kook urged the surprised guest. From then until the end of his life, Rav Elyashiv used this coat. (HA, p. 190)

Declining an Honorary Degree

When Rav Kook visited America in 1924, one of the heads of an important university expressed their desire to bestow Rav Kook with an honorary degree. Nonetheless, Rav Kook declined their generous offer. To his close associates, Rav Kook said: "The title 'Rabbi' is sufficient for me; it was given to me by my teacher, rabbi, the Geon HaNatziv." (SHR, p. 104)

Healing Oneself of Anger

One time a person published a slanderous article against Rav Kook and then sent it to him through the mail. When Rav Kook read it, he was very pained and stayed in his room for three days not receiving any guests. A few days passed and this same slanderous person published an open letter telling people not to purchase products from the food company Tenuvah due to the laws of desecrating the Shabbat. As a result of this slanderous letter, the Supreme Court of Justice fined this person fifty Lira (the Turkish currency). The company of Tenuvah said that they would only forego the fine on condition that this person would bring a letter from Rav Kook saying that Rav Kook forgave him. When this Jew came to Rav Kook and requested the letter, Rav Kook agreed immediately.

After this person left Rav Kook's presence, Rav Kook explained to the people around him his general attitude. "The Rambam's opinion in *Hilchot Deot* is that the way to fulfill the mitzvah of 'walk in God's ways' is through following the middle path. However, if a person is weak in a certain character trait, they need to go to the opposite extreme to fix it."

Rav Kook continued, "Since I was pained so much by this person's slanderous articles against me, and I got frustrated and became angered, therefore the best way to heal myself is through going to the other extreme – to let it go and forgive them." (HA, pp. 261–262)

Tolerance Must Go Both Ways

One time a conversation took place at Rav Kook's table regarding his extreme tolerance toward his religious opponents who have caused him a lot of pain. Some of Rav Kook's supporters said that he forgives too much – forgoing his own honor and the honor of his Torah.

When Rav Kook overheard this discussion, he responded in a calm tone. "When I analyze my actions and look inside my heart, I too sometimes have the same thought. 'Perhaps my religious opponents are right? Maybe I am too tolerant toward the secular and treat those who have abandoned Torah and *mitzvot* with too much kindness?' As a result of such a thought, my conscience bothers me.

However, then I remember and recognize that I also don't hold a grudge against my religious opponents; and how I try to help them out any way I can; and how I feel a strong affection for everyone – even toward those who hurt and belittle me. This acts as a way of self-examination and proves to me that all of my actions are truly for the sake of heaven; and that all of my ways of tolerance are really sourced in a love for the Jewish people. Indeed, God has placed inside of my heart the consistent trait of loving all Jews. In addition, I have trained myself in the trait of judging all human beings favorably." (HA, p. 262)

Bringing People Closer to the Torah

During the *Masa HaMoshavot*,[34] Rav Kook and a group of rabbis arrived at Moshava Poriya, which is close to Tiveriyah. There was a group of workers who ate non-kosher food and cooked on Shabbat. Rav Kook approached them in the kitchen and spoke with them in a calm, pleasant, and joyful way until he started dancing with them. Then, Rav Kook invited Rav Yosef Chaim Sonnenfeld to dance with them as well.

Through dancing with them, Rav Kook succeeded in koshering their dishes, immersing their vessels in the mikvah, and even appointing a religious woman to be the cook of their kitchen. In addition, this group of workers decided to stop working on Shabbat. (HA, p. 47)

---

34. In 1913, Rav Kook organized a rabbinical trip, including rabbinic figures such as Rav Yosef Chaim Sonnenfeld, around Israel to secular kibbutzim and moshavim in order to bring them closer to the Torah. The rabbis traveled for approximately one month, visiting twenty-six Yishuvim.

Looking at Suffering from a Different Perspective

When Rav Kook's young 12-year-old daughter Esther Yael passed away, Rav Kook was filled with suffering and sadness. After the seven days of *Shiva* (mourning) passed, I tried to take Rav Kook's mind away from this suffering. I rented a wagon and traveled with him around Jerusalem. Suddenly I saw an Arab approaching us who was holding a bag of manure. I said to the wagon driver that we should travel around this man in order to prevent Rav Kook from smelling the disgusting smell of the manure. When Rav Kook realized what I was trying to do he stopped me and said "What is manure? Should we not focus on the flowers that will eventually grow out of it in the future? In addition, this manure will fertilize the Holy Land of Israel." (HΛ, p. 68, told by Rav Yisrael Porat)

Four Types of Love

Once I mentioned to Rav Kook the three spiritual principles of the Baal Shem Tov: love of God, love of Torah, and love of the Jewish people. Rav Kook responded "Now we need to add one more type of love. Love of God, love of Torah, love of the Jewish people, and love of the land of Israel." (HA, p. 81, told by Rav Hillel Zeitlin)

Some Matters Can Only Be Understood Later in Time

One time my father told Rav Kook how pained he was that there were religious people who did not understand the path of Rav Kook, and how they criticized many of his ideas and actions. Rav Kook calmed my father and said: "You cannot measure everything according to the current time and place. There are some matters where their truth can only be clarified later in time." Rav Kook added: "The more time that passes after my period, the more people will understand me and appreciate my ways. This is similar to what happened to the Rambam in his time period." (SHR, p. 257, told by Rav Yehuda Segal the son of Rav Shefatia Segal, a student of Rav Meir Simcha of Dvinsk)

Saved Me from Starvation

When World War 1 broke out, I met Rav Kook when he was stuck outside of Israel in Berlin on a city train. This was the first time we met and immediately we began discussing Torah matters.

Rav Kook did not neglect to inquire about my financial situation. At the time I was caught behind enemy's lines (Rav Weinberg was then the rabbi of Pilvishki in Latvia, which was a part of Russia). When Rav Kook became aware that I was in a difficult situation, he immediately turned to his wife and asked if they could give all of their money to help me.

I realized that this small amount of money was all that they had in their possession at the time. In addition, they themselves really needed this money since they were foreign citizens wandering in the storm of the war. I initially refused to accept their money. Nonetheless, Rav Kook refused to give up, urging and insisting. Rav Kook said to me "People already know who I am in the world. With God's help, I will not lack anything. However, the world is still not aware of who Rabbi Yechiel Yaakov Weinberg is. Therefore, you are more likely to suffer, God forbid." Eventually, I gave in and agreed to accept the money. Only later on did I realize that the generous heart of Rav Kook is what saved me from real starvation. (SHR, p. 162, told by Rabbi Yechiel Yaakov Weinberg, the Sidrei Aish)

Helping a *Shochet*

One night I was sitting in Rav Kook's home in Jerusalem. Suddenly, the front door opened and a young man entered and asked Rav Kook for a recommendation letter so that a certain Moshav would appoint him as the official *Shochet*/ritual slaughterer. Rav Kook stopped and inspected his character and saw that he was full of Torah and halacha. Immediately, Rav Kook wrote him a warm recommendation letter. When this young man stood up to leave, Rav Kook noticed that he was dressed in a ragged and torn coat. Suddenly, Rav Kook asked the young man to wait for a few minutes. Rav Kook walked quickly to another room in the house and a few minutes later returned with one of his own festive coats.

Then Rav Kook reached out to give the coat to this young *Shochet* and asked him to wear it. The young man, who seemed to be a modest person of low means, was taken aback and shocked. Nonetheless, Rav Kook calmed him down and said that he wasn't permitted to refuse the offer since the job in this Moshav could be negatively affected due to his current dress situation. Rav Kook calmly explained how the people in this Moshav... may hold back from giving him the job when they see him dressed in an undignified piece of clothing. Therefore, Rav Kook, reasoned, it would be better if he wore this beautiful, elegant, and new piece of clothing. The young man was persuaded by Rav Kook's logic and put on the coat immediately. Eventually, when he left the house, he was dressed in Rav Kook's own coat. It was truly incredible how Rav Kook encouraged and helped this modest *Talmid Chacham*/Torah Scholar, who until that night, he had never met. (SHR, p. 163, told by Dr. Binyamin Menasheh Levin)

The Seven Hakafot[35] of Unity

There is a special act Rav Kook did during his years in Zemeil on Simchat Torah that characterizes Rav Kook's trait of *Tzefiah L'yeshua*/anticipating salvation, settling the land of Israel, and redeeming it. One time on Simchat Torah, after *Shacharit* and *Hallel* had finished, the congregation was getting ready to start the *Hakafot*. Rav Kook stood up and asked the entire congregation to go outside of the synagogue. Rav Kook then began singing and dancing around the synagogue. Everyone circled the synagogue seven times, and at the end of the last lap Rav Kook led the congregation back into the Synagogue.

Then Rav Kook stood up on the *Bima* and announced: "Precious Jews, these *Hakafot*/circlings are a remembrance of how the ancient Jews conquered the city of Yericho. In a similar way, this is how we will conquer our land anew. However, only when we are united and connected as one will the walls fall down in front of us. Only then we will walk to Zion and our holy home Jerusalem with songs and eternal happiness." (SHR, pp. 199–200, told by Rav Moshe Tzvi Neria)

Relevant to All Types of People

Many people think that Rav Kook was a rabbi of great thoughts and deep emotions, whereas the simple people could not appreciate his light. Yet this is incorrect. Despite Rav Kook's brilliance and sophistication, he was accessible and understood by the simplest people – those who walked with purity and honesty. Indeed, as is the way of true greatness, Rav Kook's sophistication did not damage his natural simplicity. In fact, his sophistication helped him reach an even higher level of simplicity.

---

35. On the festival of Simchat Torah, the custom is to take the Torah scrolls out of the Ark and to do seven *hakafot*, literally "to encircle" the reader's platfrom and throughout the synagogue with great joy, singing, and dancing.

This truth was expressed during Rav Kook's third meal on Shabbat. At such meals, one could see not only those rare sophisticated individuals, but also the simple masses. Immediately after *Havdala*, one could tell how Rav Kook's ideas were received and how they had affected people.

The Chabad Chasid would stand up and proclaim: "Rav Kook's words were sourced in a chapter of Tanya and Likutei Torah!" In contrast, a Polish Chasid would answer back: "What are you talking about, it was Sefat Emet!"

In one of the corners a young immigrant professor from Germany would say enthusiastically: "Rav Kook's words were sourced in the Rambam's 'Guide for the Perplexed' dressed up in a spiritual language!" The calm and collected Lithuanian rabbi would lick his fingers from Rav Kook's precious Torah insights, while the *Lamdan* would take pleasure in the crumbs of Halacha that Rav Kook interspersed here and there.

However, beyond all of these different types of people stood a larger group of simple Jews who did not say anything, yet their facial expressions said it all. Their faces were illuminated from the sweet affection and pleasantness of God. Their hearts were filled to the brim as a result of Rav Kook's words of simplicity, love of God, love of the Jewish people, and love of the land of Israel- like a burning fire.

Rav Kook's ocean was filled with all these different rivers. Each person experienced the taste of their own world.

There is indeed something truly worthwhile to listening to the words of these people who personally heard and witnessed the conversations of Rav Kook. (MoR, pp. 21–22, told by Rav Moshe Tzvi Neria)

A Spiritual Letter to the Reader

DEAR READER,

I want to finish this book with a personal note to you. If you have gotten this far in the book, it means that you have already experienced the incredible spiritual wisdom of Rav Kook.

Indeed, I too am filled with awe and inspiration when I read through the pieces in this book. For the last six years, I have been translating and studying these pieces on my own, with friends, as well as teaching them to my students. I am always amazed by how I find myself uncovering more and more layers of meaning and relevancy in these pieces – for my own life and for the life of my students.

Just as a person can look at a piece of art several times and find deeper layers of meaning each time, so too, a person who goes through Rav Kook's writings over and over again will continue to uncover deeper layers of meaning. Indeed, when Rav Kook's son, Rav Tzvi Yehuda, sent the famous Zionist author Yosef Chaim Brenner a copy of Rav Kook's book *Ikvei HaTzon*, he gave him the following piece of advice:

> I am sending you the book *Ikvei HaTzon*. First of all, I want to request from you not simply to read this book, but rather to study it carefully – in-depth and with a serious mind. Superficial reading destroys a lot of the inner meaning when it comes to

words of deep wisdom. It is my belief that if you study this book repeatedly again and again you will gain new insights – and even new perspectives on life." (BSR p. 244)

This, therefore, is my spiritual challenge to you, the reader. If you have been inspired by the pieces in this book; if you have been touched by the words of wisdom of Rav Kook, then go back to the beginning of the book and go through it again. Yet this time, don't just read the words of Rav Kook, study them. Go through these pieces with a friend (chavruta), in a study group (chabura), or discuss them with one's family at a Shabbat meal. You will uncover new insights the second and third time. Indeed, according to Pirkei Avot, this is the ideal way to study Torah.

> Turn it over again and again, for it is all inside. Look into it and become gray and old. Do not move away from it, for you have no better portion than it. (Avot 5:22)

Rav Kook's Writings Help to Balance You

Allow me to make one final comment about studying the spiritual wisdom of Rav Kook. Sometimes a person will get lost in the first half of this book, in Rav Kook's writings about the search for individual spiritual meaning. The pull toward inward depth is very attractive since it helps a person get to know oneself and one's deepest fears and desires. It is therefore important from time to time to push oneself outwards in order to reach the second half of the book, the search for collective spirituality. There is a large world out there that needs love and kindness, patience, and forgiveness. A person must learn to connect oneself to the Jewish people, its ancient land and language, as well as seek the betterment of the entire world.

On the other hand, there are times when a person becomes so involved in looking after one's family, friends, and the greater community that one forgets oneself and one's own individual world. Since there is so much darkness and struggles in the world, it is tempting to spend all the hours of one's day in the second half of the book, faced outwardly toward collective spirituality, focused on giving kindness and help to society, the Jewish people, the land of Israel, and removing evil from the greater world. It is therefore important that a person push oneself to return to the first half of the book, to the world of individual spirituality. Indeed, if a person is so passionate about giving kindness to the world, one must also pay attention to one's individual self and inner world.

This, therefore, is one of the ways to study this book – to use the first half of the book to balance the second half of the book. Each side must be given time and attention. To be sure, a person cannot do everything at once. There are times when a person must focus on individual spirituality, and there are other times when collective spirituality must be allowed to influence and shape one's life. As Rav Kook writes:

> There is a type of *Tzadik*/Righteous Person who shouldn't leave the spiritual feelings of one's heart. Such a person doesn't need to look outside of one's private realm. However, there is another type of *Tzadik* who is involved with all the different aspects of the world. Such a person looks at heaven as well as earth, from the beginning of the world until the end. (SK 1:306)

According to Rav Kook, one of the main principles of spirituality is that there is no one correct path for all people. Each soul is different and therefore each person must decide what they will spend their days on earth doing. Nonetheless, the ultimate goal is to embrace both of these worlds; to hold onto a paradoxical way of thinking whereby one is dedicated to one's own individual spirituality as well as collective spirituality.

> And then there sometimes exists a great *Tzadik* who includes both of these values. At times this person doesn't look outside of one's private realm, while at other times, one's eyes look at everything. "Lift up your eyes and see, to the north and south, to the east and west (Bereishit 13:14)." (Ibid.)

Acknowledgments

I WOULD LIKE TO THANK ALL OF MY STUDENTS OVER THE PAST YEARS who have challenged me to clarify Rav Kook's words and helped remind me why his words have so much to teach us. In particular, a special mention goes out to a Chabura of students at Yeshivat Torah V'Avodah in 2023 as well as Macy Kisilinsky and Marc Shandler who were the first people to truly study this book with me. I would like to thank Rabbi Dr. Yoel Bin-Nun, Dr. Baruch Kahana, and Rabbi David Aaron, the three main teachers who introduced me to the many faces of Rav Kook. In particular, it was Rabbi Bin-Nun's doctoral thesis, "The Double Source of Human Inspiration and Authority in the Philosophy of Rav Kook," that opened my eyes to the sophisticated outlook needed to fully understand the wisdom of Rav Kook. I wish to thank Rabbi Levi Morrow, Rabbi Zach Truboff, Rabbi Moshe Nachmani, Rabbi Ari Shvat, and Rabbi Dr. Yehudah Mirsky for many insightful emails and conversations that have helped clarify certain topics about Rav Kook.

Thank you to my brother Jacob Schwartz for investing so much of his time in creating an aesthetically engaging front cover. Thank you to Urim Publishing House in general, and Tzvi Mauer and Pearl Friedman in particular, for their professionalism and generosity. I wish to thank my wonderful parents for their endless support and encouragement in everything I do. To my three children, Tzofia Leah, Yael Hadar, and Levi Shmuel, it is my prayer to God that you will study Rav Kook's writings together one day.

And finally, I want to thank God for leading me to Rav Kook, a role model who has truly changed my life, by teaching me to care for my soul, my people, and the entire world.

About the Author

RABBI ARI ZE'EV SCHWARTZ IS THE author of *The Spiritual Revolution of Rav Kook: The Writings of a Jewish Mystic* published in 2018 through Gefen publishing house. In addition, he has written several other books on the meaning of Shabbat, Prayer, and the Parasha.

Rabbi Schwartz is originally from Sydney, Australia, and studied at the University of New South Wales majoring in music and film before coming to Jerusalem, where he studied for eight years in several Yeshivot in Jerusalem.

Rabbi Schwartz received his rabbinical ordination at the Shehebar Sephardic Center in Jerusalem under Rabbi Yaakov Peretz, and studied Talmud and Jewish Philosophy at Herzog Academic College.

Rabbi Schwartz served as the head rabbi of Bnei Akiva's Hachshara program for three and a half years. From 2017–2020 he cofounded and was the dean of the Society of Independent Spirituality, an English-speaking learning center in Jerusalem that combined Jewish spirituality and Zionism. Currently, Rabbi Schwartz teaches at several Yeshivot and Midrashot in Jerusalem.